LEARNING WITH TRADE UNIONS

Contemporary Employment Relations

Series Editor: Gregor Gall
*Professor of Industrial Relations and Director of the Centre for Research
in Employment Studies, University of Hertfordshire, Hatfield, UK*

The aim of this series is to publish monographs and edited volumes on all aspects of contemporary employment relations including human resource management, employee branding, shared services, employment regulation, the political economy of employment, and industrial relations. Topics such as mergers, corporate governance and the EU – in the context of their affect upon employment relations – also fall within the scope of the series. Aimed primarily at an academic readership this series provides a global forum for the study of employment relations.

Other Titles in the Series

Labour Relations in Central Europe
Edited by Jochen Tholen
ISBN 978-0-7546-7093-3

Child Labour in South Asia
Edited by Gamini Herath and Kishor Sharma
ISBN 978-0-7546-7004-9

Trade Unions and Workplace Democracy in Africa
Gérard Kester
ISBN 978-0-7546-4997-7

Human Resource Management in Russia
Edited by Michel E. Domsch and Tatjana Lidokhover
ISBN 978-0-7546-4876-5

Changing Working Life and the Appeal of the Extreme Right
Edited by Jörg Flecker
ISBN 978-0-7546-4915-1

Employment Contracts and Well-Being Among European Workers
Edited by Nele De Cuyper, Kerstin Isaksson and Hans De Witte
ISBN 978-0-7546-4575-7

Learning with Trade Unions
A Contemporary Agenda in Employment Relations

Edited by

STEVE SHELLEY and MOIRA CALVELEY
University of Hertfordshire Business School, UK

Routledge
Taylor & Francis Group

LONDON AND NEW YORK

First published 2007 by Ashgate Publishing

2 Park Square, Milton Park, Abingdon, Oxon OX14 4RN
711 Third Avenue, New York, NY 10017, USA

Routledge is an imprint of the Taylor & Francis Group, an informa business

First issued in paperback 2016

British Library Cataloguing in Publication Data
Learning with Trade Unions: a contemporary agenda in
    employment relations. – (Contemporary employment relations
    series)
    1. Labor unions and education – Great Britain 2. Labor
    unions – Great Britain 3. Employees – Training of – Great
    Britain 4. Industrial relations – Great Britain
    I. Shelley, Steve II. Calveley, Moira
    331.8'8'0941

Library of Congress Cataloging-in-Publication Data
Learning with trade unions : a contemporary agenda in employment relations / edited by
Steve Shelley and Moira Calveley.
    p. cm. -- (Contemporary employment relations)
    Includes bibliographical references and index.
    ISBN 978-0-7546-4974-8
    1. Labor unions and education--Great Britain. 2. Employees--Training of--Great Britain. 3.
Working class--Education (Continuing education)--Great Britain. 4. Educational equaliza-
tion--Great Britain. 5. Industrial relations--Study and teaching--Great Britain. I. Shelley,
Steve. II. Calveley, Moira.

    HD6664.L427 2008
    331.25'920941--dc22

                                                                                    2007030996

    ISBN 13: 978-0-7546-4974-8 (hbk)
    ISBN 13: 978-1-138-26274-4 (pbk)

Contents

Section I: Union Learning: Setting The Scene

Section II: Union Learning: Actions and Outcomes

Section III: Union Learning and Union Renewal

Section IV: Developing a Future Agenda

List of Figures and Tables

Figures

Tables

Notes on Contributors

Moira Calveley is a Senior Research Fellow at the Centre for Research in Employment Studies, Business School, University of Hertfordshire. She has researched and published on trade union activism and employment relations in the public sector.

Keith Forrester is Senior Lecturer in Industrial Studies in the School of Education at the University of Leeds. He has a background in adult education and has worked educationally with British and European trade unions for many years. His research interests include differing conceptions and practices of learning in work and everyday life and the implications of these practices for contested policy agendas. His publications reflect these research concerns.

Gill Kirton is Senior Lecturer in Employment Relations, Centre for Research in Equality and Diversity, School of Business and Management, Queen Mary, University of London. Gill has published widely in the areas of gender, equality and diversity and trade unionism, including articles in Work, Employment and Society, British Journal of Industrial Relations, Industrial Relations Journal, Gender, Work and Organization; one single-authored and two co-authored books – *The Making of Women Trade Unionists* (2006), Ashgate; *The Dynamics of Managing Diversity* (with Anne-marie Greene) (2nd edition, 2005), Butterworth Heinemann; *Women, Employment and Organizations* (with Judith Glover) (2006), Routledge.

Caroline Lloyd is Senior Lecturer and Research Fellow at the ESRC centre on Skills, Knowledge and Organisational Performance (SKOPE), based at Cardiff University, School of Social Sciences. Her research focuses on the relationship between product markets, labour markets, work organisation and skills. She has written widely on the political economy of skill and the possibilities of developing a high skills economy in the UK. Her current work focuses on cross-country comparisons of the institutional and regulatory influences on the nature and extent of low wage work. She is co-editor of the forthcoming book *Low Wage Work in the UK.*

Anne McBride is a Senior Lecturer in Employment Studies, Manchester Business School, The University of Manchester. Anne's main research interests are workforce modernisation in the NHS, gender relations at work and trade union democracy. She is the author of *Gender Democracy in Trade Unions*, and is currently looking at the relationship between mergers and gender equity. Research within the NHS has focused on local responses (of employers, employees and trade unions) to Government policies and initiatives on workforce developments and skill mix changes.

Stephen Mustchin has worked as a Research Assistant at Manchester School of Management, UMIST, and latterly at Manchester Business School. His main research interests are contemporary industrial relations, public sector employment relations, healthcare policy and learning and skills policy. He is currently working on ESRC funded research on union involvement in learning at Manchester Business School.

Jonathan Payne is a Senior Research Fellow with the ESRC centre on Skills, Knowledge and Organisational Performance (SKOPE), and is based at Cardiff University School of Social Sciences. His research interests include the political economy of skill, UK education and training policy, the links between skills and productivity, Scandinavian approaches to workplace development and lifelong learning policy in Norway. He is currently jointly editing a SKOPE book on UK education and training policy in comparative perspective.

Liz Rees is the Trades Union Congress's (TUC) Trade Union Education Manager within *Unionlearn*, responsible for the TUC's extensive programme of training for workplace representatives and union professionals. She manages TUC Education including strategy, relations with external partners and bodies, course and curriculum development, the accreditation of the programme, tutor training and the building and maintaining of partnerships within the UK's network of further education colleges. Formerly a National Officer with a major civil service union with responsibility for national pay bargaining, she began her trade union career as an employee of the National Graphical Association (now Amicus), following a successful campaign to gain union recognition at her workplace.

Steve Shelley is Principal Lecturer in the Centre for Research in Employment Studies, University of Hertfordshire Business School. Steve has brought his interests in training and skills into the industrial relations arena with several publications and conference papers on the subject of union learning over the last five years. Other research interests and publications are in the field of leadership and management in public services. He is also an activist within his own trade union.

John Stirling is head of the Division of Sociology and Criminology at Northumbria University. He has been actively engaged in trade union education since 1979 and has worked delivering programmes with the TUC in England, the European Trade Union College, the AFL-CIO in the USA and the Sierra Leone Labour Congress. He has written and published trade union teaching materials for use in the UK and internationally has published widely on trade unions. He runs training programmes with European Works Councillors and has edited a book (with Ian Fitzgerald, Routledge 2004) on the subject which reflects his current research interests.

Mark Stuart is Professor of Human Resource Management and Employment Relations at Leeds University Business School and Director of the Centre for Employment Relations, Innovation and Change. He has researched and published widely on the role of trade unions in relation to the training and learning agenda, both in the UK and overseas. He has published research in this area in, amongst others, the *British Journal of Industrial Relations*, *Industrial Relations Journal* and the *European Journal of Industrial Relations* and is the co-editor of Trade Unions and Training: Issues and International Perspectives (2004). His work has been funded by the Trade Union Congress and numerous individual unions. He is an Associate Fellow of the ESRC Research Centre on Skills, Knowledge and Organisational Performance (Skope).

Emma Wallis is Research Fellow in the Work and Employment Relations Division at Leeds University Business School. Her research interests include workplace learning; factors that raise individual demand for learning and the difference this makes; restructuring in the coal industry and trade union renewal. Her work has been published in the *British Journal of Industrial Relations* and *Work, Employment and Society*.

David Wray is a Senior Lecturer, and Director of the Work and Employment Research Centre in the Sociology and Criminology Division of the University of Northumbria. In the last few years he has undertaken a number of research projects and evaluations of workplace learning, particularly in relation to trade union learning centres. These projects have included research into both the role, and educational needs, of Union Learning Representatives. He has also researched and published in the areas of post-industrial mining communities; social partnership in the workplace; and workforce drug testing.

List of Abbreviations

ACAS	Advisory, Conciliation and Arbitration Service
ACCI	Australian Chamber of Commerce and Industry
ACTU	Australian Council of Trade Unions
AEU	Australian Education Union
AFL-CIO	American Federation of Labor and Congress of Industrial Organizations
AIG	Australian Industries Group
ALI	Adult Learning Inspectorate
ASLEF	Associated Society of Locomotive Engineers and Firemen
ATL	Association of Teachers and Lecturers
AWA	Australian Workplace Agreement
BDA	Bundesvereinigung Deutscher Arbeitgeberverbände (German Employers' Association)
CEA	Council for Education Advance
CGPME	Confédération Générale des Petites et Moyennes Enterprises
CIPD	Chartered Institute of Personnel and Development
CIR	Commission on Industrial Relations
CLC	Central Labour College
CNC	Central Negotiating Committee
COHSE	Confederation of Health Service Employees
CWP	Changing Workforce Programme
CWU	Communication Workers' Union
DBG	Deutscher Gewerkschaftsbund (German Trade Union Federation)
DfEE	Department for Education and Employment
DfES	Department for Education and Skills
DfID	Department for International Development
DIHK	Deutscher Industrie- und Handelskammertag (Association of German Chambers of Industry and Commerce)
ECDL	European Computer Driving Licence
EPA	Employment Protection Act
ESOL	English for Speakers of Other Languages
ETPs	Employer Training Pilots
EUIRD	European Union and International Relations Department
FBI	Federation of British Industry
FE	Further Education
FEFC	Further Education Funding Council
FTO	Full Time Officer
GMB	General Municipal and Boilermakers' Union

GMP	Glass, Molders, Pottery, Plastics & Allied Workers International
GPMU	Graphical, Paper and Media Union
HSWA	Health and Safety at Work Act
IAG	Information, Advice and Guidance
ICT	Information Communication Technology
IFWEA	International Federation of Workers' Education Associations
ILEC	Institute of Labour Education and Culture (Japan)
ILO	International Labour Organisation
IRRA	Industrial Relations Reform Act (Australia)
IT	Information Technology
ITBs	Industrial Training Boards
JFC	Joint Functional Council
JLF	Joint Learning Forum
JTUC	Japan Trade Union Confederation
KSF	Knowledge and Skills Framework
LDA	London Development Agency
LDP	Liberal Democratic Party (Japan)
LEC	Local Enterprise Council
LFA	Learning for All
LLP	Local Learning Partnership
LSC	Learning and Skills Council
LSG	Learning Steering Group
MEDEF	Mouvement des Enterprises de France
MSC	Manpower Services Commission
NCLC	National Council of Labour Colleges
NEC	National Education Centre
NHS	National Health Service
NHSU	National Health Service University
NIACE	National Institute of Adult Continuing Education
NOCN	National Open College Network
NSTOs	Non-Statutory Training Organisations
NUT	National Union of Teachers
NVQ	National Vocational Qualification
OECD	Organisation for Economic Co-operation and Development
PAT	Professional Association of Teachers
PCS	Public and Commercial Services Union
QCA	Qualification and Curriculum Authority
QCF	Qualification Credit Framework
RCN	Royal College of Nursing
REO	Regional Education Officer
RMT	National Union of Rail, Maritime and Transport Workers
RUL	Rail Unions Learning
SERTUC	South East Regional Trades Union Congress
SfL	Skills for Life
SMEs	Small and Medium-sized Enterprises

SOP	Standard Operating Procedure
SSCs	Sector Skills Councils
TEC	Training and Enterprise Council
TGWU	Transport and General Workers Union
TSSA	Transport Salaried Staffs Association
TUC	Trades Union Congress
TUTA	Trade Union Training Authority
UCATT	Union of Construction, Allied Trades and Technicians
UEO	Union Education Officer
UfI	University for Industry
ULF	Union Learning Fund
ULR	Union Learning Representative
USDAW	Union of Shop, Distributive and Allied Workers
VET	Vocational Education and Training
WEA	Workers' Educational Association
WELL	Workplace English Language and Literacy
WERS	Workplace Employment Relations Survey
WETUC	Workers' Education Trade Union Committee
YTS	Youth Training Scheme

Foreword

Brendan Barber

Unions have always been active in the world of education and skills, both through the delivery of their own education and training programmes, which develop the next generation of activists and officials, and through influencing governments and employers on behalf of their members. The launch of Unionlearn in 2006 signals a step change in unions' commitment to this agenda, and that is one reason why this book is so timely. It provides a valuable assessment of the opportunities and challenges facing Unionlearn, and those working with education and skills through trade unions more generally.

More and more union members are recognising that their employability and career progression are dependent on having transferable skills. In addition high skills levels lead to better productivity and better wage returns. And lifelong learning also reduces social inequality. All key issues for unions.

In the league table of the top 30 developed economies, the UK still lies eleventh in high skills, it is twentieth in intermediate skills and seventeenth in essential skills. This means that we have a mountain to climb. To reach the top employers are crucial. For without employer commitment, real progress is impossible, but a powerful partnership approach, and strong union representation is the key to success.

Without question, Unionlearn is the single most important development in trade unionism in a generation. It can act as a catalyst for a trade union resurgence in the years ahead. This will show that we are fully attuned to the challenges posed by globalisation and labour market change. And it proves we are in step with the aspirations of today's workers.

Brendan Barber
TUC General Secretary
May 2007

SECTION I

UNION LEARNING: SETTING THE SCENE

Chapter 1

Introduction

Steve Shelley and Moira Calveley

Rationale and Aims of the Book

This book has been written at an important time in the development of trade unions' roles in learning activities and in employment relations more widely. The last few years in the UK have seen new opportunities for unions to become involved in education, training and particularly 'learning' activities as part of the government's learning and skills policy. At the same time, trade unions have had to cope with a declining membership and reduced influence, which has led to a keen interest in a variety of strategies for union renewal. Three issues for examination are therefore, firstly, the nature of the learning itself, its variety of forms and purposes, and the outcomes for individuals involved in learning activities. Secondly, the role of union learning in public policy and political economy of skill; in overcoming disadvantage in qualifications and access to training; in linking to national competitiveness and economic growth; and the learning and skills policies of government and agencies. Thirdly, around the relationship between the learning and union renewal agendas and the role that learning plays for trade unions and the trade union movement as a whole. Paramount in this, as will be seen, is consideration of the distinctiveness and sustainability of trade union learning activities and links to the power of unions to influence employment relations at workplace and national level.

The book brings together chapters that between them explore the range of union learning activities across the terms of 'learning', 'education', 'training' and other descriptors for this field of work. It is only relatively recently that the term 'learning' has been used in government and union policy circles in the UK, although the terms education and training have been synonymous with trade union activity for more than a century in the UK and are similarly long-lived in other countries. Historically, as Moira Calveley shows in Chapter 2, unions have been actively involved with worker education, campaigning on employment practices and education policy to enable access to education, and providing their own education programmes through, for example, Ruskin College, the National Council of Labour Colleges and the Workers' Education Trade Union Committee. Although 'neutral' definitions suggest that education is 'to develop the knowledge, skills, moral values and understanding required in all aspects of life' (Reid *et al.* 2004, 2), trade union education can be delivered in a specific context for a specific agenda. In varying ways, such education was seen as a way out of poverty and had a political and class based agenda of liberation and equality. On the former, education was seen as a way for individual workers to obtain economic advancement and a share of the profits of capitalism. On the latter, workers' education was intended to bring about societal change, although whether this was through radical change and teaching on an explicitly political agenda or whether through more incremental change based on less partial liberal humanist education, has long been a point of controversy. Nevertheless, as Chapter 2 shows, the class based and collective nature of this education was distinctively for and by the trade union movement. There were also strong elements of financial independence and sustainability, with much, but not all, funding from union sources, albeit that a decline of such education is partly linked to reduced trade union income during the mid twentieth century.

In addition to these education activities, trade unions have also run their own training programmes for activists, developing their workplace representatives with the necessary skills for effective workplace bargaining and representation and also including knowledge of contemporary workplace 'issues' and of union context, labour history, economics and politics. This training came much more to the fore in the second half of the twentieth century, with the formation of the Trades Union Congress (TUC) Training College in 1957 and then using legislation such as health and safety and equal opportunities as a basis for training in the 1970s and 1980s, with the need to organise in the face of union decline in the 1990s a more recent cause. As Liz Rees shows in Chapter 13, this training of activists is high on unions' and TUC agendas, clearly with a union and collective oriented purpose and is funded from within the union movement albeit not without some recent external scrutiny. In 'traditional' terms, the general terminology used by those working in and researching this field, is of trade union 'education', that encompasses education and training of representatives.

A third area of trade union involvement has been in workplace vocational education and training, in providing knowledge and skills required in job training for employees to perform their work. Historically such involvement was limited to particular crafts and occupations and to restrictive practices such as recruitment and the 'closed shop', and was for the economic benefit of individuals and to strengthen the bargaining power of the specific unionised group of members. Albeit rather exclusive in nature, such arrangements were clearly distinctive in favour of the workers involved. Union involvement became more formalised with their inclusion in tri-partite Industry Training Boards at sector level, and at national institutional level with the Manpower Services Commission of the 1970s. However, both sources of power dwindled during the 1980s and 1990s, as institutional structures were disbanded and traditional occupations closed down.

Finally, in the last decade trade unions in the UK have been increasingly involved in an agenda of 'learning', the terminology of which appears to be replacing the former nomenclature of education and training. This is particularly following the election of the 'new' Labour government in 1997. Current policy context is witnessed in government documents 'The Learning Age' (DfEE 1998), incorporating a vision of 'lifelong learning' in a 'learning society', this being reinforced further with the establishment of the Learning and Skills Council in 2001 resulting from the Learning and Skills Act (2000) and, most recently, the Leitch Review of Skills in 2006 (Leitch Review 2006). As the Leitch Review makes clear, the UK has skills shortcomings, including a large proportion of the workforce unskilled and low skilled, does not compare well with other countries in terms of productivity, and has social problems of disadvantage and relative poverty. In this set of policies all 'learning' is deemed inherently 'good' to the benefit of all, individuals, economy and society, enabling economic growth and greater social inclusion and advantage. This is in a generally voluntarist non-interventionist government approach to training, with, as Caroline Lloyd and Jonathan Payne observe in Chapter 4, a prevailing low skill emphasis in the UK economy, with minimal training efforts by many employers.

In this context unions have increasingly re-established their involvement in this policy arena. There is trade union representation in the Learning and Skills Council, edging slightly towards the tripartite models of countries such as Germany. In 1998 the government established the Union Learning Fund (ULF), funding the development of Union Learning Representatives (ULRs), union-run learning centres and other union learning initiatives in the workplace. Although this, to some extent, may be viewed as an attempt by the 'new' Labour government to mollify the trade unions (they had already announced that they were not going to reverse the restrictive trade union policies introduced by their Conservative predecessors), an explicit rationale for this has been empirical correlations between training incidence and union recognition and the access to hard-to-reach learners that trade unions are thought to have (CIPD 2004). Thus there is now a substantial amount of public funding for learning channeled through trade unions and, in addition, a partial reinforcing of trade union rights in the statutory recognition for paid time-off for union learning activities given to ULRs under the 2002 Employment Relations Act. In line with these policy moves, trade unions and the TUC have established their own organisations as support to the government's learning and skills agenda. To support ULRs and their role in the workplace, the TUC Learning Services was established in 1998 to train ULRs and provide them with advice on moving the training agenda forward. The TUC's Unionlearn, originally set up as the Union Academy in 2005 and renamed in 2006, is now responsible for both the traditional education and the emerging learning activities (see Chapter 13 particularly), exemplifing the use of 'learning' as the over-arching terminology for the field of activity.

There is undoubtedly a positive enthusiasm for learning, and one which has been reified in government policy and management practice as well as trade union circles over the last decade or more, suggesting that all learning is good. However, there are also critiques which question this, particularly in the context of examining who makes judgements about what is 'good' and how this is measured. Prevailing understandings tend to be neutral in tone, so that learning is 'any experience or event whose outcome (whether or not intended) develops or changes peoples' knowledge, skills, values or behaviour' (Harrison 2000, 2).

However, in examining what he terms the cultist character of 'learnerism', Holmes (2004) exposes weaknesses in this prevailing mainstream policy context, warning that the learning process can result in outcomes that are detrimental as well as positive. Further, the emphasis on the learner, who is no longer a passive recipient of what others have decided should be learnt and how it should be learnt, but who may be actively engaged in and manage their own learning, free to determine for themselves what and how they should learn, is also open to critique. The current learning context is predicated on the basis of normative understandings of what are correct learning outcomes, all too often, as the likes of Karabel and Halsey (1977) and Ainley (1999) have stated before, based on existing occupational and societal structures. Pressures for learners to conform with normative standards, behaviours and to reproduce identities and social practices, may mean, as Holmes (2004) asserts, that the current learning paradigm is oppressive rather than emancipatory in nature.

Nevertheless, it would seem that trade unions now have 'workplace learning' much more at the forefront of their agendas. Unions and the TUC play an active role in promoting the Government's strategy of 'lifelong learning' the aim of which is to create a 'learning society' seeking to link vocational education with learning for career and personal development. This increasing role in the learning agenda requires examination and critique not only in terms of the meanings of the learning for the individuals involved, but also in terms of the contribution that trade unions make to national economic and social improvement through participation in learning and skills policy.

This examination also sets the scene for analysis of the role and orientations of trade unions in employment relations more broadly, getting to the heart of what the trade union movement is about – the purpose of trade unions and their independence, and their role in the employment relationship between employer and employee and between capital and labour. Thus whilst trade unions represent workers' opposition to employer and state authority, they are, recognise Spencer and Frankel (2002, 169):

> at best, contradictory social formations [for they also] negotiate the terms of workers' compliance to that authority. However, they are still important organisations of working people, and represent the potential for democratic challenge at work and in society ... even if this challenge is to be understood as a relatively weak countervailing power to that of capital, a power that can only moderately influence terms and conditions.

This may be all the more so in the contemporary situation of declining union membership. In the UK, between 1979 and 2006 the number of trade unions declined from 453 to 186 and union membership fell from 13.3 million to 6.5 million (Certification Officer 2006), with declines also experienced in other comparator countries (see Chapter 3), under the influence of legislative changes, management practices and occupational changes.

In this context, trade unions have adopted a number of strategies in their need for renewal and resilience (Stirling 2005). These include those that might be seen as passive, reactive and accommodating, which may be based on an accommodative/ adaptive form of 'business unionism' (Salaman 2000), or on a view of members as consumers in which unions provide a service to their members. Other strategies may be based on a re-assertion of the importance of activism and organising of a more oppositional or militant nature; indeed Kelly (1998) asserts that militancy rather than moderation is more likely to win concessions from employers and ensure union survival by appealing to members.

Understanding the role of and approaches to learning in union organisation and renewal is thus of key significance. Analysis of the nature and outcomes of union learning in terms of servicing and organising (Hope *et al.* 2003) are considered throughout this book. Such an investigation also provides a means of analysing the relationship between union learning and the bargaining agenda and to explore and critique contemporary 'partnership' approaches to industrial relations.

In this respect, it is particularly useful to compare the more 'traditional' trade union 'education' activities with the more recent field of 'learning'. Education may be seen as central to trade unions' organising agendas and at the heart of political and ideological stances. It also has a history of delivery that is often distinctive to the union movement. It is thus insightful to consider the extent to which these characteristics shape the broader contemporary union learning agenda too, thus enabling a greater understanding of the ways in which trade union learning is distinctive from learning provided by other organisations. This distinctiveness may be through sources of funding, determination of curriculum, the learners themselves and through the collective and worker-based nature of the learning delivery and the dynamics involved in pedagogy; also defined by the sustainability of unions' learning provision in terms, for example, of funding sources and organisation.

Such a distinctiveness is explored throughout this volume, and may be important, for example, in bringing new benefits to individuals and in enabling fresh economic and societal advances at national level. It may also be important in appealing to union members and in union renewal and organisation, in influencing trade unions' power and enabling independence of unions' agendas both at state level and at workplace level. An associated issue for exploration is the extent to which unions' learning activities are integrated with other bargaining and representational activities (or are separate from these).

In summary, the more recent union involvement in 'learning' gives rise to the questions explored throughout this book, about the nature of learning that individuals gain from such experiences, about the unions' contribution to skill levels at national level, and about the outcomes for union organisation. As stated at the outset, such an analysis is particularly well timed, given the heightened emphasis on union learning by unions themselves in seeking to 'mainstream' learning as a core activity, and the role of unions in government learning and skills policy in the UK. Prompted by this context, the book aims to provide an historical, international and contemporary understanding of the range of learning that is enabled by trade unions, and the agendas around that learning, against which contemporary initiatives can be judged.

The nature of union distinctiveness and independence in learning in the contemporary employment relations scene is at the heart of the critical analysis included in this volume. It is necessary to explore the extent to which the union learning initiatives of the last decade have been symptomatic of unions' need to 'buy in' to state and government curriculum and funding structures, and to structures that reinforce a global employer agenda which individualises responsibility for being employable. Given the constraints facing the union movements in the UK and elsewhere, in terms of legislation and membership density, it may be difficult not to view such a 'buy in', if it may be deemed that, as an indicator of unions' desperation to survive and regenerate, at the expense of independence from state and employers. As previously indicated, and explored further particularly in Chapter 2, the extent of trade unions' independence from state and employer structures has been the subject of debate since the founding of the union movement. Nevertheless, an acceptance of what may be deemed to be more traditional aims and outcomes of union education, distinctively emphasising class and collectivism, enables the book to explore the extent to which current union learning can embody these characteristics and the efforts made to perpetuate such emphases within contemporary initiatives.

Whilst it is clear that there can be outcomes from such an analysis for trade unionists, the insights presented here will also be important for government and policy and also for those involved in the management of work organisations, particularly in human resources and training departments. It is anticipated that the book will make a contribution to debates about public policy on learning and skills. In this respect it will enable analysis of government policy in the field, the relationship with employers' strategies towards training and skill; and the outcomes and benefits to learners themselves.

A key feature of the collection is the way it draws upon a variety of subject areas, including industrial relations, training, skills and education, as well as seeking to incorporate more recent areas of interest in Information Technology-based distance learning, geography and community. As such, it provides comment on employment relations at workplace and institutional levels. Contributing chapters are of a variety of styles (research-based, illustrative case studies and broader theoretical chapters) and the overall aim is to include a range of methodologies and a blend of perspectives so incorporating critical analysis with practitioner outcomes.

The Structure of the Book

This volume is organised into four sections, each containing a number of chapters. Section one sets the scene for union learning, historically, internationally, and in terms of political-economic analysis. Section two focuses on the nature and outcomes of various union learning initiatives whilst section three explores outcomes of involvement in learning for unions' organisation and renewal. Finally, section four seeks to develop a future agenda for union learning.

The remainder of this first section continues to set the scene for understanding union learning. In Chapter 2, Moira Calveley provides a historical background of trade union involvement in learning, education and training in the UK over the last hundred years, and sets out important issues against which to compare contemporary activities, notably those already raised on the matter of ownership, independence and outcomes of union learning. In Chapter 3, Calveley provides more context with her comparative international review of the ways in which trade unions are involved in training, education and learning activities in other countries. A variety of countries are included, with a focus on other developed economies. Such a comparison with economies which have differing institutional arrangements, approaches towards regulation and social partnership models, enables better understanding of the scope and potential for trade union involvement in learning.

As the earlier passages of this introductory chapter discuss, the unions' role in and contribution to the national learning skills agenda is of major importance. In Chapter 4 Caroline Lloyd and Jonathan Payne examine whether unions can make a difference in tackling the UK skills problem. The chapter assesses British trade unions' contribution to the development of a high skills economy/society in the

UK, their potential role in developing a more inclusive and relatively egalitarian society, and highlights the challenges that unions currently confront in this area. In understanding UK government's policy towards skills it argues that the country suffers from weak employer demand for high skills, rooted in the UK's distinctive political economy and wider institutional structures. It asks whether unions can engage government and employers in measures aimed at raising the demand for and utilisation of skill in the workplace. Not only does this chapter examine the key issue of learning and skills in its own right, it also provides further context for other sections of this volume, as it explains how unions have the opportunity to extend their involvement in 'learning', with potential advantage not only for national economy and society, but for individuals and for trade union renewal.

Section two of the book includes chapters that focus primarily on documenting and interpreting the nature of the learning provided through trade union involvement, and attempts to understand the outcomes of the learning for the learners involved. Thus, in Chapter 5, Anne McBride and Stephen Mustchin provide an example of union involvement in developing skills in the UK health service. Their historically contextualised qualitative case study approach highlights the opportunities and limitations this involvement provides for learners, through analysis of the Knowledge and Skills Framework (KSF) learning and development initiative and the integration of skills into career progression through the Skills Escalator initiative. However, McBride and Mustchin's work also raises significant questions about the role and purpose of trade unions in the learning context, questions that are considered further by chapters in section three of this volume. In particular, they examine some of the tensions inherent in union-employer partnership arrangements.

By contrast, in Chapter 6 David Wray provides insights into three very different union learning projects which illustrate the potential to work with 'hard to reach' learners in situations both in and outside of the workplace. The first case study focuses on a group of school kitchen staff, working very short shift patterns and who are geographically dispersed across a local authority area. The second case study examines a project that failed, following repeated attempts to deliver an ESOL (English for Speakers of Other Languages) course to female Asian employees working at a food preparation plant. In both of these two cases, the learners are hard to reach as a result of the structural conditions of their employment. However, the third case illustrates union involvement in a learning project for residents of a womens' refuge, a group of individuals not in employment but excluded from learning through the individual conditions of their lives. All three case studies demonstrate the challenges such initiatives face, the commitment of those involved, and the achievements of the individual learners who are re-engaging with the educational process.

In Chapters 7 and 8, both Steve Shelley and Keith Forrester instigate further analysis of union learning, derived from an awareness of current mainstream interpretations of union learning that tend to emphasise a human capital rationale. There is an awareness in both chapters that historical, class and other societally-located frameworks, together with other theoretical perspectives such as those drawn from adult education, have the potential to provide alternative interpretations of union learning.

In Chapter 7 Steve Shelley seeks to interpret the usefulness and distinctiveness of outcomes from union learning initiatives through consideration of subjects learnt and taking account of learning environment, methods, contexts and purposes of the learning in the wider work and social environment of the learner. Interpretations of what may be 'useful' learning are sought firstly in the context of the prevailing mainstream understandings of learning in current UK learning and skills policy and the neo-liberal approach to the work environment. The meanings of learning are then discussed by drawing upon liberal humanist, vocational and radical interpretations. This enables further examination of the multiplicity of purpose and the assumed unproblematic unitarist nature of learning, taking into account consideration of the individual and social context of the learning, the nature of work opportunities, learning diagnosis and development, and the economic contexts and political agendas that may influence the purposes of the learning. The chapter enables understanding of learning outcomes both within and outside mainstream policy orientations, and of what has been and what might be, thus opening up opportunities for the potential of union learning that might otherwise be by-passed.

Whilst Shelley draws on numerous examples of union learning, in Chapter 8 Keith Forrester uses the discussion with one union learner as the start point to extend the application of other theoretical frameworks to understand union learning. The chapter reviews approaches to understanding and discussing trade union learning and education, with a strong but not exclusive use of debates and discussions from the adult education field. It argues that understandings of union learning historically have been dominated by institutional, curriculum and evaluative frameworks, without sufficiently addressing the richness of worker knowledge production and without challenging the dominant discourse of human capital formulations. It suggests that situating worker learning within a framework shaped by activity theory has the advantage of returning concrete and 'lived' work and labour concerns to the centre of conceptions and practices of work learning in general, and to understanding union learning in particular.

Section three begins with Mark Stuart and Emma Wallis exploring how union engagement in learning at the workplace connects with, and evolves in relation to, broader and typically more established structures of workplace industrial relations in the UK. Trade union learning agreements may be seen as representing an agenda of mutual concern for employers, trade unions and their members, established as examples of management-union partnership with clear lines of demarcation between their operation and the more 'distributive' bargaining agenda. Drawing on two detailed case studies of union-management learning agreements, the chapter shows the emerging dynamics between management and unions over the control of the learning agenda, assesses the scope for unions to situate learning within the broader bargaining agenda and the potential gains that may or may not accrue for trade unions from such involvement.

In Chapter 10, Gill Kirton explores gendered aspects of trade union learning through analysis of participants in women-only trade union schools. The chapter considers the organising agenda and outcomes for unions in terms of activists and their empowerment. It also examines the implications of the involvement in the learning for the women learners themselves through individual and collective understandings of empowerment. It finds that for some women their involvement translates as developing individual autonomy and taking greater control of their own lives. But it also finds that the majority of women involved develop a greater sense of collective empowerment, with trade union participation being the vehicle through which influence over gendered social conditions can be achieved. The chapter's focus on womens' involvement in trade union education and its longitudinal research methodology, suggest important lessons for the extension of such practices into the wider union learning agenda and for researching the outcomes of the broader subject in future.

In Chapter 11, Steve Shelley presents a case study of a union learning centre, enabling discussion and critical examination of a complex set of multiple partnerships with a variety of stakeholders in the learning and skills agenda. The notable forms of partnership identified here are multi-union, partnership between trade unions and employers, partnership between education and training providers and partnership with the community. Partnerships such as these would appear to have considerable potential, both in terms of furthering the learning and skills agenda, but also as a way of engendering union renewal. Whilst there is some optimism that cases like this demonstrate 'capacity-building' for unions, particularly through multi-union partnerships and through community links, the cessation of the project and its replacement by another bid that de-emphasises both these partnership forms, illustrates the difficulties involved in building infrastructure over a long term. The precarious nature of funding reveals the difficulty for unions' own partnerships, the need to further strengthen partnerships with mainstream education and training providers, and the dangers of defaulting to an employer-union partnership that is more heavily influenced by employers.

Moving into section four, the volume seeks to develop a future agenda for those working in and researching the broad field of union learning. It does this firstly through John Stirling's chapter which examines the major challenge to trade union education programmes of internationalism and the role of these programmes to be at the centre of supporting workers in responding to global change. Acknowledging that local labour is shaped and controlled by global capital requires workers and their unions to understand and deal with the shaping process and to build solidarities that stretch beyond the local. It is argued that trade union education can play a key role here. Drawing widely on evidence from trade union education in the UK, Europe, the USA and Africa, the chapter analyses the ability of such programmes to re-introduce the political into education, the pedagogical issues around learner or tutor-centred delivery, the relationship between education and action, and the issues involved in delivering programmes to multinational groups. The chapter also enables understanding of the possibilities and limitations of internationalised approaches that may be relevant in unions' learning as well as education role.

Chapter 13 is written by Liz Rees, TUC National Education Manager, and outlines the new developments in union learning in the UK, through the eyes of the TUC. This includes a review of developments including the use of e-learning and distance learning, information technology, interaction between union learning for employees who are union members and the wider community. In particular, TUC policy is outlined, and there is discussion of the role of Unionlearn and the potential that this new organisation has to bring together and make mainstream both TUC education and learning activities.

Finally, the concluding chapter brings together analysis of the various agendas and outcomes of the learning, recognising a likely symbiotic relationship between outcomes for individual learners and outcomes for the union movement as a whole, providing a critique, highlighting lessons to be learnt for new developments and outlining a future agenda for those involved in related policy, practice and research.

References

Ainley, P. (1999), *Learning Policy. Towards the Certified Society.* (London: Macmillan).

Certification Officer (2006) Annual Reports. <http://www.certoffice.org>

CIPD (2004), *Trade Union Learning Representatives: The Change Agenda.* (London: Chartered Institute of Personnel and Development).

DfEE – Department for Education and Employment (1998), *The Learning Age: a Renaissance for a New Britain.* (London: HMSO).

Harrison, R. (2000), *Employee Development*, 2nd Edition. (London: Chartered Institute of Personnel and Development).

Holmes, L. (2004), 'Challenging the Learning Turn in Education and Training', *Journal of European Industrial Training* 28:8/9, 625–638.

Hope, R., Stirling, J., Wray, D., Calveley, M., Healy, G. and Shelley, S. (2003), 'Servicing, Organising or Community Unionism? The role of Union Learning Representatives'. Paper presented at the British Universities Industrial Relations Association (BUIRA) conference, University of Leeds, 3rd–5th July 2003.

Karabel, J. and Halsey, A. (eds.) (1977), *Power and Ideology in Education.* (Oxford: Oxford University Press).

Kelly, J. (1998), *Rethinking Industrial Relations. Mobilization, Collectivism and Long Waves.* (London: Routledge).

Leitch (2006), *Prosperity for all in the Global Economy – World Class Skills. The Leitch Review of Skills.* (London: Her Majesty's Stationery Office).

Reid, M., Barrington, H. and Brown, M. (2004), *Human Resource Development: Beyond Training Interventions*, 7th Edition. (London: Chartered Institute of Personnel and Development).

Salaman, M. (2000), *Industrial Relations. Theory and Practice,* 4th Edition. (Harlow: Financial Times Prentice Hall).

Spencer, B. (ed.) (2002), *Unions and Learning in a Global Economy. International and Comparative Perspectives.* (Toronto: Thompson Educational Publishing).

Spencer, B. and Frankel, N. (2002), 'Unions and Learning in a Global Economy', in Spencer, B. (ed.).

Stirling, J. (2005), 'There's a New World Somewhere: The Rediscovery of Trade Unionism', *Capital and Class*, 87, 43–64.

Chapter 2

An Historical Overview of
Trade Union Involvement in
Education and Learning in the UK

Moira Calveley

Introduction

This chapter will provide an historical overview of trade union involvement in
education and workplace learning. It does not claim, nor attempt, to be an exhaustive
account as neither time nor space would allow for this. A general understanding of
the historical context is both relevant and important, however, in order to highlight
issues and discussion points, reference points against which to analyse contemporary
union learning activities and to enable the understanding of outcomes for the
individual and the workers' movement as a whole, together with the relationship
with employers and institutions. In particular, the past rationale for and agendas
behind trade union involvement and the variety of forms of this involvement are key
to an understanding of the present.

'Educate, agitate, organise' has long been a battle-cry of trade unionists. In the early
days of the organised labour movement, when education for people from the working
class was rare, trade union leaders saw education as a means of enlightenment with
regards to capitalist oppression and social inequality. It was argued that only through
education would workers desire a change in society, thus allowing them a better
standard of working life; here the strategy of trade unions was to educate in order to
organise. As we shall see in this chapter, the trade union movement has, throughout
the decades, continued to pursue the drive for equality in the provision of education.
Unions have consistently fought for the right to influence educational policy, whilst at
the same time promoting the development of a skilled labour force.

This book is about the role that trade unions play with regards to education and
learning in the contemporary workplace. What this chapter demonstrates, however, is
that although the Union Learning Fund (ULF) and Union Learning Representatives
(ULRs) are fairly recent, union involvement in education and learning is not. As
such, it presents the historical setting for the current context.

The first section of this chapter considers the role of trade unions in national
education. It begins by looking at the forces behind the early trade unionists and
their drive and commitment to getting a fair and equitable education system for
all. It goes on to consider the involvement of the Trades Union Congress (TUC)
and union activists in the development of educational policy before looking at their

struggle for adult education. The chapter briefly considers the development of the Workers' Educational Association, Ruskin College and the Central Labour College. The second section of the chapter moves on to consider the involvement of trade unions in workplace learning and development prior to the establishment of Union Learning Representatives before finally providing a short historical overview of the training and learning of trade union representatives.

The Early Days

Trade unions have a complex history of involvement with both the provision of national education in the United Kingdom and workplace learning and training. Such involvement, which dates back to the late 1800s, stems from the desire of the early trade union leaders to educate working class people from underprivileged and deprived backgrounds. This desire developed from a number of different reasons. To begin with, many of these early pioneers were themselves victims of child labour, long hours and labour exploitation and were thus denied the opportunity of schooling and education afforded to the 'higher classes'. For example, Keir Hardie, the founder of the Scottish Labour Party in 1888 (the first Labour Party in Great Britain) was working as a messenger boy at the age of seven and at the age of ten, working a ten hour day in the mines (Stewart 1925). Will Thorne who founded the Gasworkers' Union in 1889, was similarly outrageously exploited when at the age of six he worked a twelve hour day spinning twine (Thorne 1989). Due to such long hours and the financial situation of their families, formal schooling for many working class children was, in the mid-1880s, an impossibility. Not only was the socialism of the early trade unionists borne of exploitation and deprivation as children, so was their conviction that schooling and education helped provide a means of moving forward for the UK's working classes.

In addition, it was the belief of these early trade union activists that education would enlighten the working classes to the miscarriage of justice acted out by the ruling classes. Therefore, not only was it important to educate the workers for their own good, as in providing a means of moving out of poverty, it was also seen as a way of enjoining them to the socialist political cause. Once more literate, clearly working class people would have a greater understanding of the importance to them of socialism and in becoming active socialists. Education was seen as both liberator and equaliser and was the right of all, regardless of class or occupation.

One of the visions for a more widely educated workforce was the shortening of the working day and this went hand-in-hand with the socialist policies advocated by the 'new unionism' which developed in the last decades of the 1800s. Much criticism was levelled at the 'old' unionists who, it was argued, failed to strive for better social conditions for working people (Thorne 1989). Among the 'new unionists' were Tom Mann, a member of the Amalgamated Engineers, Keir Hardie and Will Thorne. Mann and Thorne were particular advocates of the eight-hour day and the latter was successful in obtaining this for the Gasworkers in 1889 (Thorne 1989). Mann had himself benefited from a reduction of working hours in 1871 with the introduction of the nine-hour day in the engineering factory where he was apprentice (Torr

1956). Using his time effectively he attended evening classes three times a week and later attributed the furthering of his education to the trade union movement. His own educational achievements later influenced him to become leader of the 'Eight Hour' movement which aimed to make the eight-hour working day law; he called for 'Leisure to think, to learn, to acquire knowledge, to enjoy, to develop; in short, *leisure to live*' (Torr 1956, 38) [author's original emphasis]. In his campaign for the eight hour day (which he took to his first Trades Union Congress in 1890) Mann was heavily critical of the 'old unionists' who, he argued, were so focussed on protecting wages from falling that they ignored the wider social responsibilities of their roles (Torr 1956). Such attacks were partially responsible for fuelling a spilt between the 'old' and 'new' unionists.

Although having the backing of many leading socialists and trade unionists of the time, the petition for eight-hour day legislation was not uniformly supported. In fact whilst the Miners Federation of Great Britain defended the call for legislation, the Northumberland and Durham Miners who had already gained an agreement to a seven hour day and saw eight hour legislation as a threat to this, vigorously opposed it, thus causing debate at Trades Union Congresses during the latter end of the 1880s (Pelling 1992). Interestingly, the campaign was not always supported by the TUC executive and in 1887 Broadhurst, the then secretary, subjected Keir Hardie 'to ridicule and abuse' (Simon 1965, 42) for moving a motion in support of eight hour legislation. Nonetheless, following constant and increasing pressure, the eight-hour day policy was eventually taken up by the TUC in 1890 albeit that it was not until after the First World War that the unions won their battle. Even so, as Simon argues 'this pressure to reduce working hours is of key significance in the history of education' (1965, 41). It is also significant in that it established education at the forefront of TUC and trade unions' agendas. Later chapters in this book will identify how unions are still campaigning for more time for workers to participate in training and education whilst also pushing for this to become an accepted collective bargaining issue.

Influencing National Policy Making

Trade unions and the TUC have also, historically, been actively involved in lobbying Parliament with regards to educational policymaking. In the late 1860s unionists such as Robert Applegarth, the General Secretary of the Amalgamated Society of Carpenters and Joiners, were active members of the pressure group the National Education League which campaigned for compulsory free school education. During this time, the TUC was also vociferous in promoting free and accessible education for children of the working classes. Although the 1870 Elementary Education Act went someway to realising this, making education more accessible to working class children, it had its limitations as compulsory attendance was at the discretion of local school education boards (therefore not eliminating child labour) and free places were offered only to the poorest of children (Simon 1965). Despite its limitations, the TUC viewed the act as a success and hence removed education from the forefront of its agenda for more than a decade.

It was in the mid-1880s that the TUC again lobbied the government with regard to free education for all children and TUC conference resolutions were passed reflecting this aim in 1886 and 1887. In 1891 the Free Education Act was passed which provided 'fee' money to elementary schools. Nonetheless, free education was still not fully available (Simon 1965) as many elementary schools still charged fees.

The issue of child labour and thus the impossibility of working class children receiving a good standard of education was also a concern of trade unionists. From the mid-1890s the Gasworkers' Union took a series of motions to the TUC conference calling for the raising of the age for entry into employment, causing disagreement with the unions representing textile workers. It was not until 1899 that the government raised the employment age to 12, with the exception of agricultural work where children could be employed from age 11. Unions and the TUC continued to campaign for the raising of the school leaving age and the abolition of the much abused half-time system (which allowed employment of children on a half-time basis) throughout the early 1900s (Simon 1965).

The 'new unionists' were at the forefront of the drive for education for the working classes and it was Will Thorne in 1895 who pushed forward a TUC conference resolution calling for a 'remodelling of the education system' (Simon 1965, 201). This marked the start of the TUC fight for free education up to the age of sixteen, making secondary education 'within the reach of all' (Simon 1965, 202), a fight that continued for many decades to come, featuring continually on TUC Conference agendas.

Due to some extent to the administrations of the trade unions and other socialist bodies, the working classes were becoming more aware of the imbalance in the provision of education between themselves and those who had greater wealth. Simon tells how by 1914 'of every 1,000 pupils in the 10–11 age group in elementary schools only fifty-six found their way into secondary schools; the odds against such children gaining a free secondary education had been reduced but still stood at 40 to 1' (1965, 273). No small wonder then that the parents of these children looked to their trade unions and ultimately the TUC to voice their views for them.

Of course, there was also an economic rationale to the TUC's involvement in that they saw education as a way of improving the wage earning ability, and accordingly the wage levels, of workers who would thus have greater access to higher skilled and therefore better paid work. Perhaps not unsurprisingly, the involvement in education by trade unionists was resisted and resented by many employers. The Federation of British Industry (FBI), for example, believed that extending education would produce 'a large class of persons whose education is unsuitable for the employment which they eventually enter' (quoted in Lawson and Silver 1973, 394), indicating employer reluctance to create jobs above a basic level of skill and low wage.

In an attempt to balance the wishes of both the TUC and the FBI, the 1918 Education Act was introduced. This Act made education compulsory up to the age of 14 (thus abolishing the half-time system and as a consequence child labour) and also established a system of part-time continuation schools which allowed for children not in full time education to continue studying on a part-time basis until the age of 16. It was not seen as a qualified success by the TUC who continued to campaign for equality in education – compulsory, free secondary education for all.

The TUC consequently became established as a prominent pressure group committed to influencing educational policy which they felt could not be left in the hands of government ministers who had, historically, failed working class children. In 1942 it published a memorandum 'Education after the War' (Simon 1991) calling for what they viewed as the most important issue in education at that time, the raising of the school leaving age to sixteen (Taylor 2000). Around this time the TUC along with the National Union of Teachers (NUT) joined forces with the Workers' Educational Association (WEA, see below) and the Co-operative Union, forming the Council for Education Advance (CEA), an organisation committed to lobbying for educational change, including raising the school leaving age and creating a single, national and free system of education (Simon 1991). Their 'battle cry' was for 'immediate legislation to provide equality of educational opportunity for all children, irrespective of their social or economic condition' (Simon 1991, 67). The CEA campaigned vociferously and made continuous comment on all suggestions by the Government for educational reform, including an attack on delaying the implementation of the 'Educational Reconstruction' White Paper published in 1943 (Simon, 1991) which in itself had fallen 'far short of the TUC's proposals' (Taylor 2000, 94).

The raising of the school leaving age was finally achieved with the 1944 Education Act which raised it to 15 (although this was postponed for two years) with a qualification that it would be raised to 16 at a later date. This Act, which was viewed by some as a 'massive redefinition' of education (Musgrave 1968, 102) provided for free secondary education for all. It removed 'elementary' from schools, replacing it with three progressive stages of primary, secondary and further education. Somewhat more controversially, it legitimised the tri-partite system of secondary education which led to the establishment of 'grammar' schools for the children who were capable of abstract thought, 'technical' schools for those adept at technology and finally 'modern' schools which would cater for the remainder of pupils (the vast majority) (Simon 1991). This went against the ideas of the trade unions and TUC who viewed 'equality of opportunity' as all school children being given the same standard of education. Nevertheless, the Labour Government stood up for the tripartite system of schooling proclaiming that the new 'modern' schools were for working-class children 'whose future employment will not demand any measure of technical skill or knowledge' (Benn and Chitty 1997, 5). The Labour Party (as opposed to the Government) distanced themselves from this view, as did the unions and the TUC. There followed a prolonged drive for comprehensive schools which carried on throughout the decades. In 1964 the election manifesto of the Labour Party included a promise to abolish selection for secondary education, thus introducing comprehensive schooling. Although they acted on this promise, they allowed Local Authorities discretion over the introduction of comprehensive schools, resulting in a piece-meal approach to educational change. The debate surrounding selection for secondary education continues to this day.

More recently, the TUC, along with the teacher unions, have been vociferous in their condemnation of the introduction and format of school league tables, the 'naming and shaming' of schools at the 'bottom' end of these tables and the 'marketisation' of education in general.

Teacher Unions

A history on trade union involvement in the provision of national education would not be complete without brief mention of the teaching unions, of which there are currently six (including two for Headteachers) and which demonstrate a high propensity to unionise (Calveley 2005). Teacher unions are distinctive in that unlike most other unions whose main objectives are the welfare and working conditions of their members, the teacher unions promote quality and standards in education and (with the exception of the Professional Association of Teachers (PAT)) are willing to take industrial action to protect and maintain these. These teachers unionise in order to have a collective voice in UK educational policy.

The National Union of Teachers is the largest and oldest of the teacher unions, established as the National Union of Elementary Teachers in 1870; it is viewed as the most politically 'left-wing' (McIllroy 2000, 36) of the teacher unions. From its inception, one of the principal objectives of the NUT was the improvement of education for working class children. Writing at the beginning of the last century, Webb gives full voice to this concern, arguing that 'the activities of the NUT, taken as a whole, have had a beneficial effect on the great community of working-class children' and that 'in more ways than one the N.U.T. has identified itself with the needs of the wage-earning class family' (1915, 11). The NUT also later objected to the creation of secondary schools under the 1902 Education Act as they believed this would hinder the education of working class children. Thus, the NUT has gained (and maintained) a reputation for promoting social equality in the provision of education for working class children. Alongside this, it is renowned for its efforts (and successes) in influencing educational policy making (Calveley 2005) which it continues to do to the present day.

Adult Education

Not only have trade unions historically taken an interest in school-level education, they have also been actively involved in adult education which was viewed as a path to social freedom from the dominating capitalist class. Indeed, in the late 1860s Applegarth claims that his union's (the Amalgamated Society of Carpenters and Joiners) technical education classes were 'probably the first instance in the industrial history of the country, of a Trade Union undertaking to provide a plan for the education if its members' (quoted in Lawson and Silver 1973, 294). When, in the 1870s Cambridge University introduced a series of lectures delivered to workers across the UK (known as the University Extension Programme) local unions became actively involved in promoting them. The mineworkers on Tyneside were strong supporters of the programme, sometimes walking many miles to join in classes which only faltered following a prolonged strike that left the workers without the funds to support them.

Although the individual unions were involved in educating their members, it was not until the turn of the century that the TUC became actively involved in a coordinated manner as we shall see below.

Workers' Educational Association (WEA)

Founded in 1903 by Albert Mansbridge, an office clerk, the WEA was established to support the educational needs of working men and women and has played a prominent role in the higher education of working class people ever since. Mansbridge took a liberal-humanist approach to education, believing simply that education was good for its own sake. The aim of the WEA was not to educate workers to move out of their class but to educate them so that they would be able to influence other working class people. Mansbridge's non-confrontational approach allowed him to gain the confidence of Oxford University and the Church of England, both of whom endorsed the WEA's vision of promoting the University Extension Programme to working class people. Nonetheless, his approach was at odds with the more radical slant to trade union education taken by some sections of the labour movement, as we shall see below.

Although technically independent of the trade union movement at its inception, individual unions and the TUC soon became involved with the WEA, engaging with its socialist ideology and gaining representation on its Advisory Committee. Despite this, Pelling infers that the TUC and its Parliamentary Committee should have done more to support the movement in its early days, arguing that these bodies did not consider the work of the WEA 'as deserving of any considerable effort on their part to raise financial support' (1992:137). Nonetheless, union involvement was hardened in 1919 by the founding of the Workers' Education Trade Union Committee (WETUC) in conjunction with the Iron and Steel Trade Union Confederation. The aim of WETUC was to strengthen and support the WEA's education work with the trade unions. Union members were encouraged to attend educational activities including summer schools and week-end or day schools. These activities were often partly or wholly financed by the union.

That there was a market for the programmes supported by the WEA is evident in the uptake of its courses. By the start of the Second World War they attracted around 60,000 students and then by 1947–8 more than 100,000 (Lawson & Silver 1973). The WEA were fulfilling a need of many working class people who were unable to afford the further education offered by the State.

The WEA, in conjunction with universities, established evening classes which proved to be very successful. They were also the main protagonists in establishing Keele University, the first campus university built in the 1940s. Aiming to cater for the population of Staffordshire, the university set out to educate socialist workers and due to the left-wing orientation of its teaching staff, became known locally as 'the Kremlin on the hill' (BBC 2006). Over sixty years later, the TUC still supports programmes at the university.

The WEA claims to now be 'the UK's largest voluntary provider of adult education'; it is a registered charity which also receives government funding through the Learning and Skills Council (WEA 2007). Close connections continue between the WEA, trade unions and the TUC as they work in partnership to develop workplace learning. The TUC provide bursaries to delegates attending the joint WEA/International Labour Organisation School in Geneva.

Ruskin College and the 'Oxford Report'

Ruskin College was founded in 1899 in Oxford, close to but independent of the University, by two Americans, Walter Vrooman and Charles Beard. When these philanthropists withdrew their support in 1902, the college turned to the trade unions for the majority of their financial support and this support grew over the years; trade union leaders were among the governing body. Ruskin College was unique in that its two-year courses were aimed specifically at mature and experienced working class men. It was during this period that there was a growth in Marxist politics in the UK and this ideology (to the consternation of some members of the teaching faculty) resonated throughout Ruskin College with new radical educational agendas overshadowing the more liberal humanist approach. As a result, within ten years of its establishment the 'student body' of Ruskin was 'frankly socialist in colour, predominantly Marxist in outlook, and a thorn in the side of the university' (Simon 1965, 311). By this time, Oxford University had already made attempts to bring Ruskin within their domain; however, the students resented this threat to their independence (Holford 1993). In 1908 the principle of the college, Dennis Hird, and many of the students called for a Marxist emphasis in the teaching syllabus (Pelling 1992). This did not go down well with the neighbouring University and hostilities broke out between the two institutions.

   This has to be put into the context of the general view by trade unionists, voiced regularly by the TUC, that university education was elitist and tended to exclude the working classes who could not afford to attend. The Oxbridge universities were particularly under attack. It was within this environment that 'Oxford and Working Class Education' was published in 1908 by a joint committee of WEA members and university representatives. Known as the Oxford Report, this publication tackled the question of university education for working class people, acknowledging that 'workpeople will not be content with any substitute for University education, however excellent, which assumes they will be unable to enter the Universities themselves' (Simon 1965, 313).

   Ironically, like Hardie, Thorne and Mann, those early trade unionists and social reformers who believed that education was the way forward for the working people, so too did the authors of the Oxford Report. In contrast, however, the former believed that education would enlighten the working classes with regard to their exploitation by the capitalist employers whilst the latter thought it prudent to ensure that the working classes were educated so that their leaders 'should obtain the knowledge necessary to enable them to show foresight in their choice of political means' (Simon 1965, 314), in other words, once educated they would denounce socialist politics.

   Suggesting that the University Extension Programme (discussed above) should be seen as a preparation for university education rather than a substitution for it, the Oxford Report recommended the extension of tutorial classes across the country to allow students the chance to study for Oxford University Diplomas. Whilst recognising that discussion of Marxist economic theory be included in the curriculum so as not to alienate working class students by 'an unconscious class bias' (Simon 1965, 316) the Report made clear that rather than be a Labour college for working class students, Ruskin should become a college preparing students for university education. The outcome of the Report was not welcomed by either the Principal or most of the students, many of the latter being sponsored by some of the more militant trade unions. The feeling amongst them was that the University was attempting to subsume the College with the aim of providing a non-partisan approach to education whilst the education they desired was one which would prepare them for fighting the labour cause.

The Oxford Report was published just a year after the TUC had made an official appeal for financial support for Ruskin from unions, many of whom were already sponsoring scholarships for their members to the college. Thus, the students (and Principal) felt that they had the full backing of the whole of the Labour movement, and with this in mind, rejected all moves towards making Ruskin part of the Oxford establishment. The situation, however, brought to light tensions between different opinions within the trade union movement itself when the trade unionists on the College Board stood by the Oxford Report to which they had contributed. The result was a determined effort by students to spread their view throughout the trade union movement that the Oxford Report represented a threat to the nature of Ruskin College as a Labour college and that this move would undermine the principles of education for the working class. To this end, with the support of some ex-Ruskin students, the 'Plebs League' was formed and a journal the 'Plebs Magazine' launched. This was widely circulated to trade unions and became a cornerstone in the League's fight for independence from Oxford University.

Following the dismissal of Hird as Principal of the College in March 1909, the students went on a week-long strike in his defence claiming 'the Principal stood for Principle' (Simon 1965, 322). Receiving massive coverage in the press, the League took steps to ensure that their standpoint was understood by trade unions and the Labour movement as a whole and campaigned for a new Labour College which would educate the working class from a Marxist standpoint; thus the Central Labour College (CLC) was born, originally sited in Oxford but moving to London in 1911.

The Plebs League and Central Labour College

The Plebs League followed in the footsteps of the early trade union educational reformists in that they viewed working class education as a way forward in the fight against capitalist oppression. They were political by nature and working towards the overthrow of capital. Supporters and students of the CLC were founding members of industrial unions which were developing at the time, for example, the National Union of Railwaymen, established in 1913 (Simon 1965). The curriculum at the Central Labour College was based around educating future leaders and activists within the Labour Movement as was put forward to the Parliamentary Committee of the TUC:

> It aims not so much at culture or at individual advantages, but at the knowledge necessary for the improvement of the whole of the working class. It seeks to equip the Trade Unionist with the weapon of knowledge in the chief sphere of his [sic.] life's activities (Plebs 1914, 2).

In this address the League praised the support of the South Wales Miners' Federation (to which a number of the League's members belonged (Pelling 1992)) but called for greater support from 'the whole Trade Union movement' (Plebs 1914, 4). Their message prompted some unions, such as the Amalgamated Society of Railway Servants, to transfer their funded scholarships from Ruskin to the Central Labour College (Simon 1965). Other unions followed suite, particularly the mining unions. It was, however, a difficult struggle to gain recognition from the TUC, particularly as initially the TUC were committed to Ruskin College. It was not until the TUC Executive Committee had been challenged at conference as to their neutrality between Ruskin and the CLC, and only after this led to an inquiry by them into the CLC (Griggs 1983), that the TUC officially endorsed the college as having 'the same claims upon our regard as Ruskin College' (Simon 1965, 331).

The League established education classes throughout the country with un-paid ex-college members delivering them. The South Wales miners in particular joined up in numbers, engaging with the Marxist viewpoint promoted by the teaching. This led the Times newspaper to suggest that the striking miners in 1916 were motivated by the advanced educational standing they had, this due to the work of the CLC (Simon 1965). Indeed, the views of the Welsh miners were undoubtedly influenced by the CLC and at the time of the strike the Secretary of the Miners' Federation, A.J. Cook, was himself an ex-CLC student who took classes in the area (Simon 1965). The interest of the mining community in the League's educational classes spread across the UK.

As we saw earlier, the Plebs League was, from its inception, in confrontation with Ruskin College, however, they also took issue with the WEA whom they viewed as being of a capitalist nature. The two were competing both for students and trade union funding and this added fuel to their hostilities. Whereas the CLC was funded by the workers for the workers, the WEA accepted funds from all areas of society and grants from Government. In 1920 the League published a vitriolic '21st Birthday Greeting' to the WEA in which they attacked WEA (lack of) ideology and methods of fund-raising whilst emphasising the virtue of their own:

> You exist to extend the benefits of university culture to the working man that you patronise. We show our readers that your education, and all education that is not based on the central fact of the class struggle, is false history and false economics. You hold out your hands for donations from employers; our funds come exclusively from the workers' own voluntary contributions. You claim to be above party, and your organisation would collapse without its present plentiful subsidies from a capitalist state. Our education is directly intended to aid the workers in their emancipation from an outworn social tyranny, and we should esteem it a disgrace to become a dependent part of the instrument of that tyranny (WEA 2006b).

The rivalry strengthened with the WEA arguing that the CLC indoctrinated rather than educated their students. Competition between the two intensified, especially with regards to trade union funding. In 1921, not long after the establishment of WETUC, the League set up the National Council of Labour Colleges (NCLC) to bring national coordination to its activities. There was huge expansion of the League in the early 1920s and this led to intense competition with the WEA, especially as the NCLC was looking to provide educational classes for trade unions and thus aiming to poach both funding and students from the WEA.

The TUC stepped in to try and alleviate the intense rivalry by producing a co-operative plan for trade union education which involved both organisations. The League wanted to ensure that their ideological standpoint was not watered down and following much discussion it was agreed that the aim of the organisations involved should be:

> To provide working class education in order to enable the workers to develop their capacities and equip them for the Trade Union, Labour and Co-operative activities generally, in the work of securing social and industrial emancipation (WEA 2006b).

However, following Government pressure whereby they threatened to withdraw their funding of the WEA this coalition failed.

The Plebs League remained active for a number of years until there was a movement towards Communist political beliefs during the early 1920s and the CLC finally closed in 1929. The NCLC, however, continued to expand, being fully supported by trade unions. It finally closed in 1964 when both it and WETUC were taken under the control of the TUC. At that time, the NCLC claimed 'an affiliated or associated membership of organisations with over 35 million members in Britain and overseas' (WEA 2006b).

From the above, we can see that the TUC and individual trade unions have taken active roles in the promotion of education both at the school level and for adults. The next section will consider the extent to which trade unions have, or have not, engaged with learning and training at the workplace level.

Trade Union Involvement in Workplace Learning and Training

With minor exceptions as discussed below, the UK government has generally taken a non-interventionist, voluntarist approach to training, giving the training of the workforce over to the employers. As is also seen below, until the establishment of the Union Learning Fund in 1998, trade unions have taken little interest in the vocational education and training of their members (as opposed to the training of their representatives also discussed further below). Indeed, 'they have shown little interest in workplace skill formation strategies' (Forrester 2001, 319). This is surprising given that, as Rainbird points out 'for the labour movement training ought to be central to a policy promoting the interests of labour' (1990, 4).

During the 1950s it became evident that the UK was lacking behind in workplace skills as compared to their European counterparts (Lindley 1983) and the government began looking at developing a national training policy. The lack and poor quality of industrial training, combined with skills shortages, were seen as major contributing factors to the slow growth of British industry. Training by firms was minimum and often of poor standard. Those organisations who did train their employees stood to have them 'poached' by others who found this less costly than introducing their own training schemes. Although an Industrial Training Council was established in 1958 to oversee areas of training such as apprenticeships, this had no regulatory powers and little impact. At this time, both management and the TUC were reluctant to have government intervention in training. For example, the craft unions feared that extensive training outside of the apprenticeship system would provide substitute labour and the possible dilution of the skills of their members. They wanted to protect this 'closed' system which allowed them to negotiate a 'skilled labour' wage premium under collective bargaining agreements. On the other hand, management also wanted to maintain the length of apprenticeships for young people as this was a form of cheap labour.

By the early 1960s, it was evident that action needed to be taken to combat the growing unskilled workforce. In 1962 the Conservative government produced a White Paper 'Industrial Training: Government Proposals', the main thrust of which was:

i) to enable decisions on the scale of training to be better related to economic needs and technological developments;

ii) to improve the overall quality of industrial training and to establish minimum standards;

iii) to enable the cost to be more fairly spread (quoted in Lindley 1983, 341–2).

The Paper was enacted as the Industrial Training Act (ITA) in 1964 by a Labour government.

A significant element of the Act was the establishment of the tripartite Industrial Training Boards (ITBs), bringing industry and trade unions together in the drive to eradicate the lack of industry training and skills in the UK. The ITBs were empowered to operate a training levy scheme which was imposed upon firms, with grants being given back to those who established good training practice. By the early 1970s, there were twenty-seven ITBs covering around 15 million workers (Lindley 1983). Despite their tripartite nature, the ITBs cannot be viewed as an unqualified success being seen by many as overly bureaucratic. They were criticised by a number of bodies, including some educationalists and economists (Lindley 1983). Both industry and trade unions were reluctant to change training systems already in place particularly, for the reasons stated above, the apprenticeship system. Keep and Rainbird also point out that the general unions, unlike the craft unions, lacked established training policies and therefore 'did not use their rights to representation on ITBs and the MSC structures as effectively as they could have done' (2003, 410).

In 1973 the Employment and Training Act established the Manpower Services Commission (MSC) which would oversee the activities of the ITBs. Despite widespread criticism, the Boards were to survive into the early 1980s when the 'new right' Conservative government began its assault on trade unions; this impacted on tripartite bodies, including the ITBs. Most of the ITBs were abolished and replaced by Non-Statutory Training Organisations (NSTOs) and later Industry Training Organisations (ITOs), both of which were voluntary and trade unions were included in their membership only by invitation from employers. The government reverted to the pre-1960s hands-off, voluntarist approach to training.

Although trade union involvement at the national level was somewhat diminished, they still played an important role in some of the government's training initiatives, such as the Youth Training Scheme (YTS). However, in 1987 government policy with regard to the MSC changed, reducing union representation and increasing employer representation (Crouch 1995). The TUC subsequently boycotted the MSC in a protest against the government's Employment Training scheme, a move which Taylor (2000) describes as contributing to their own demise as members of tripartite bodies. Shortly after this, the Government abolished the MSC, replacing it with the government controlled Training Agency which later gave way to Training and Enterprise Councils (TECs), or Local Enterprise Councils (LECs) as they were known in Scotland. In 2001, the TECs were replaced by the Learning and Skills Council (LSC) which has both employer and trade union representation.

Despite the positive legislation of 1964 and 1973, unions have until recently had limited influence on training policy at a national level. Prior to the 1960s, this was due to lack of interest and a focus on collective bargaining for wages and conditions. During the tri-partite period starting in the late 1960s and continuing throughout the 1970s, they took what may best be described as an apathetic interest in training. The main focus of the unions was pay and conditions of workers. The 1980s saw a positive move by the Conservative government to exclude unions from any training policy intervention. During this time, the government began to change the apprenticeship system which they perceived as being the domain of the craft unions and which they viewed with suspicion (Gospel 1998).

Nonetheless, it might be argued that, paradoxically, as government hostility towards unions increased the latter became more proactive with regards to employee training. As union power with regards to collective bargaining declined, training became part of the negotiating agenda. In the early 1990s, as the focus of trade unions shifted towards offering services to their members, the TUC began to campaign for worker training rights and workplace training committees. In conjunction with TECs they launched a 'Bargaining for Skills' project which was aimed at promoting union involvement in workplace training. At the same time, 'partnership deals' were beginning to appear in the workplace which promoted a more conciliatory approach between management and trade unions, focussing on common agendas such as training. Arguably, therefore, without the overtly hostile stance of the Conservative government throughout the 1980s and early 1990s, the trade unions would not have engaged with workplace learning and training as a bargaining issue. Indeed, the training agenda can perhaps be seen as going some way towards providing unions with a new impetus and râison d'etre for their very existence. Certainly, as Heyes and Stuart identify, unions see involvement in training as both 'a path to membership renewal and as a way of maintaining employer acceptance at the workplace' (1998, 459).

Following the election of 'new' Labour in 1997, and as will be fully discussed elsewhere in the book, trade unions were given a positive role in workplace training and learning. The government established the Union Learning Fund in 1998 to fund the development of Union Learning Representatives (ULRs) in the workplace. Although this, to some extent, may be viewed as an attempt by the new government to mollify the trade unions (they had already announced that they were not going to reverse the restrictive trade union policies introduced by their Conservative predecessors), ULRs have been whole-heartedly embraced by the TUC and trade unions. ULRs were given statutory recognition in the 2002 Employment Relations Act which introduced paid time-off for union learning activities. To support ULRs and their role in the workplace, the TUC Learning Services was established in 1998 to train ULRs and provide them with advice on moving the training agenda forward. The TUC holds an annual Union Learning Conference.

Trade unions now have 'workplace learning' at the forefront of their agendas. Along with the TUC, they promote a strategy of 'lifelong learning' the aim of which is to create a 'learning society' seeking to link vocational education with learning for career and personal development. Unions and the TUC play an active role in the government's 'University for Industry' and its 'learndirect' learning initiative.

Training and Development of Trade Union Representatives

In addition to the broader educational activities so far discussed, trade unions have consistently trained and developed their workplace representatives in the necessary skills for effective workplace bargaining and representation. This is perhaps not surprising when we consider that the main focus of trade unions since their incorporation has been pay and working conditions of their members. Although the early trade unionists (see above) saw education as a way of encouraging socialism, trade unions have generally concentrated on trying to re-align the 'asymmetrical balance of power' (Blyton and Turnbull 1994, 31) in the workplace.

As Spencer suggests trade unions see the main (but not exclusive) purpose of union education as preparing and training 'union lay members to play an active role in the union' (2002, 17) whilst other purposes include educating activists to have an understanding of union policy and of the changing employment law. Spencer also identifies the use of labour education to develop the union consciousness of members and provide them with organising experience. All in all then, this education is generally union focussed rather than a personal development experience. Training trade unionists to be activists is high on unions' and TUC agendas, clearly with a union and collective focus.

Spencer divides union education into three categories (although not mutually exclusive), the primary of these being what he describes as 'tools' courses which provide training for shop stewards in grievance handling, health and safety etc. Next, he suggests, are 'issues' courses which focus on harassment, racism etc, whilst the third category of union courses he labels 'labour studies', seeking 'to examine the union context, labour history, economics and politics' (2002, 18).

Certainly the 'tools' courses, and probably 'labour studies', would have formed part of those offered when the training for shop stewards and workplace representatives was formalised and given 'a big boost' (Unionlearn 2006, 6) in 1957 with the formation of the TUC Training College.

Prior to the opening of the College and in conjunction with the work of the NCLC and WETUC, the TUC in the immediate post-war years ran a series of training courses for activists which were not, apparently, seen as a resounding success (Holford 1993). However, once the content of the training became 'more topic or problem-oriented' (Holford 1993, 59) demand grew whilst at the same time individual unions began providing training for their own activists and hence, arguably, duplicating costs. During this period there was not (indeed there never had been) any coherent TUC training strategy; the need for a centralised Training College became clear, as did the need for a centralised training policy. It was apparent that the days of NCLC and WETUC as separate institutions were numbered. Interestingly, it was in the same year that the tri-partite ITBs were established (see above), 1964, that the two separate colleges were disbanded. Also at this time the TUC established a national education department (Miller and Stirling 1992) as a means of co-ordinating trade union training.

This was an interesting period for trade union education in the UK as it coincided with a more corporatist approach to employment relations advocated by the Labour government of the time. Both the union leaders and the government were promoting a more conciliatory industrial relations climate. At this time, the shop steward organisation was also growing and their role was taking on greater industrial relations significance at the local workplace level (Terry 1983). Following the recommendations of the Donovan Commission in 1968, the training of shop stewards came to the forefront of the TUC training policy whose aim became to 'construct a coherent and properly-resourced system of union education which could compete with the facilities on offer to management and in other fields of industrial training' (Holford 1993, 81). There developed a 'British pragmatism' (McBride and Miller 2000, 309) to the provision of training for trade union activists.

Attempts were made at this time to encourage government investment in the development of educational institutions which would provide independent training provision for trade unionists. When, however, in 1972 the Commission on Industrial Relations (CIR) suggested that there should be joint management/union industrial relations training which would attract funding from the ITBs, the TUC vehemently opposed it (Holford 1993). The imperative of maintaining the independent status of the education and training of trade union activists was strongly advocated.

We then see the impact of legislation on the provision of trade union education and training. Firstly, the Health and Safety at Work Act (HSWA) (1974) provided for the appointment of trade union Safety Representatives in unionised workplaces which *de facto* increased the demand for training in this area, and secondly, the 1975 Employment Protection Act (EPA) which not only gave workplace union representatives the right to paid time off for trade union education, it also introduced an element of government funding towards union education. For trade union training, a major outcome of the EPA was the establishment 'of a framework of courses to be financed through public funding and located largely within local authority further education colleges' (Miller and Stirling 1992, 15). Thus, the result of both these pieces of legislation was a major expansion in trade union training (Miller and Stirling 1992).

In the past, as discussed above, there had been reluctance on the part of trade unions to seek government funding for trade union training. However, due to the Social Contract agreements in the mid 1970s, and the (at least rhetorical) greater role that trade unions were playing in formulating national policy they now felt more assured in seeking public money (Holford 1993). Perhaps not unsurprisingly, funding from the public purse was 'progressively' withdrawn (McBride and Miller

2000, 312) by the anti trade union Conservative administration elected in 1979 and finally ceased in 1996. Education courses hosted by public colleges are now financed by the Further Education Funding Council (FEFC) and other training by the TUC itself (McBride and Miller 2000).

Provision for trade union education has, nevertheless, continued and in 1984 the TUC established their National Education Centre as a focal point for training trade union personnel. This was followed by the development of the TUC Education Service and the launching of 'Unionlearn' in 2006 (see Chapter 13 for a full discussion of this). In 1998, faced with difficult member recruitment challenges, the TUC developed an 'Organising Academy'. The Academy offers training courses, based around member recruitment, for both new and experienced organisers.

In addition to the role the TUC has played in training and developing trade union activists, individual unions have also, consistently, provided their own training. Although individual unions have tended in the past to focus on 'tools' courses (Spencer 2002) providing their activists with the necessary skills to undertake their roles, more recently with the burgeoning employment legislation they would also be ensuring that their representatives are fully aware of 'issues' (Spencer 2002) such as discrimination. In these times of low trade union membership levels there is also more focus placed on the organising and recruitment side of representatives' roles. As managers of 'human resources' are developing their knowledge and skills through undertaking MA and MBA university degree courses, so too are union full-time officials; seen as 'the labour movement's professionals' (Nesbit 2002, 50) these officials both need and desire to be as well educated as their management counterparts.

Conclusion

The involvement of the TUC and its constituent trade unions in the education of working class people and the training of the UK workforce has been irregular, patchy and often contradictory.

Unions have been criticised by some as viewing education as 'one of the frills available to the curious and ambitious' (Lane 1974, 260). Lane puts forward two reasons for this as given to him by union leaders and which are contrary to what we know of the opinions of the early trade union leaders seeking education reform. The first is that the leaders themselves resisted it because they did not want to engage with 'the theorist and academic' who would 'cause them unnecessary work'. The second, suggests that the leaders do not want to 'politicise' the members as this may cause them to question decisions; 'they would be afraid that they might create opponents to themselves' (Lane 1974, 260). This latter point is interesting in that it emulates the opinions, albeit in a different context, of the nineteenth and early twentieth century 'ruling classes' who thought that educating the working classes would create challenges to their methods of management; whilst uneducated, the working class could be kept in its place. It is also in stark contrast to the views of the early pioneers of trade union education such as Tom Mann who welcomed the wider challenge that educated workers would bring not only to the capitalist classes but to trade union leaders themselves.

Throughout the twentieth century and particularly following the Second World War, the TUC and trade unions have become increasingly involved in the promotion of a good education system available to all children, regardless of class status. They have used their collective power to lobby governments and education ministers on issues such as raising the school leaving age and comprehensive education.

Trade unions and the TUC have also involved themselves with the provision of post-16 education, starting with the promotion of evening classes to mine workers and later providing funding for scholarships and bursaries to Ruskin College and other institutions.

In 1997 the context for trade unions with regard to workplace learning dramatically changed. 'New' Labour provided scope for trade unions to influence policy decisions with regard to workplace learning and training and following many years on the sidelines, the TUC and unions were brought in out of the cold (Forrester and Payne 2000, 154). As we shall see throughout the rest of this book, trade unions in the UK now have workplace learning at the forefront of their bargaining agenda.

Whist historically not engaging to any degree with the vocational education of workers trade unions, in conjunction with the TUC, have consistently provided training for their workplace representatives. In the fight against management exploitation, unions have sought to arm their front-line negotiators with the necessary skills to enable them to win their battles.

References

Bain, G. S. (ed.). (1983), *Industrial Relations In Britain.* (Blackwell: Oxford and Cambridge).

BBC (2006), 'The Idea of a University', BBC Radio 4. Broadcast 24th August.

Benn, C. and Chitty, C. (1997), *Thirty Years On: Is Comprehensive Education Alive and Well or Struggling to Survive?* (Penguin: London).

Calveley, M. (2005), *Teaching in Britain Today: Working in the Relegation Zone.* (Humming Earth: Glasgow).

Crouch, C. (1995), 'The State: Economic Management and Incomes Policy', in Edwards (ed.).

Edwards, P.(ed.). (2003), *Industrial Relations Theory and Practice in Britain*, 2nd Edition. (Blackwell: Oxford and Cambridge).

Forrester, K. & Payne, J. (2000), 'Trade Union Modernisation and Lifelong Learning', *Research in Post-Compulsory Education* 5:2, 153–171.

Forrester, K, P. (2001), 'Modernised Learning: An Emerging Lifelong Agenda by British Trade Unions?', *Journal of Workplace Learning* 13:7/8, 318–325.

Gospel, H. (1998), 'The Revival of Apprenticeship Training in Britain?' *British Journal of Industrial Relations* 36:3, 435–457.

Griggs, C. (1983), *The Trade Union Congress & the Struggle for Education 1868–1925.* (Falmer Press: Lewes).

Holford, J. (1993), *Union Education in Britain: A TUC Activity.* (Department of Adult Education: University of Nottingham).

Heyes, J. and Stewart, M. (1998), 'Bargaining for Skills: Trade Unions and Training at the Workplace', *British Journal of Industrial Relations* 36:3, 459–468.

Keep, E. and Rainbird, H. (2003), 'Training', in Edwards (ed.).

Lawson, J. and Silver, H. (1973), *A Social History of Education in England*. (Methuen & Co Ltd: London).

Lindley, R. M. (1983), 'Active Manpower Policy', in Bain (ed.).

Miller, D. and Stirling, J. (1992), 'Evaluating Trade Union Education', *The Industrial Tutor* 5:5, 15–23.

Musgrave, P.W. (1968), *Society and Education in England since 1800*. (Methuen & Co.: London).

Nesbit, T. (2002), 'Education for Labour's Professionals: Britain, Canada and the USA', in Spencer (ed.).

Pelling, H. (1992) *A History of British Trade Unionism*. 5th Edition. (Penguin: London).

Plebs Magazine (1914), *The Central Labour College Policy and Work.* Issued by the College Board to the Representatives of the Parliamentary Committee at an Inquiry, authorised by the Trades Union Congress of 1913, held at the College on July 27th, 1914. September issue. (CLC: London).

Rainbird, H. (1990), *Training Matters: Union Perspectives on Industrial Restructuring and Training*. (Basil Blackwell: Oxford).

Simon, B. (1965), *Education and the Labour Movement 1870–1920.* Studies in the History of Education. (Lawrence & Wishart: London).

——, (1991), *Education and the Social Order*. Studies in the History of Education. (Lawrence & Wishart: London).

Spencer, B. (ed.). (2002), *Unions and Learning in a Global Economy: International and Comparative Perspectives*. (Thompson Education: Toronto).

Stewart, W. (1925), *Keir Hardie: A Biography.* (Independent Labour Party Publication Department: London).

Taylor, R. (2000), *The TUC: From the General Strike to New Unionism*. (Palgrave: London).

Terry, M. (1983), 'Shop Steward Development and Management Strategies', in Bain (ed.).

Thorne, W (1989), *My Life's Battles*. New Edition. (Lawrence and Wishart: London).

Unionlearn (2006), *Changing Lives Through Learning: A Guide to Unionlearn* (TUC Unionlearn: London).

WEA (2006a). *21st Birthday greeting from Plebs to its sister organisation – the WEA (1924)*. <http://www.wea-yn.org.uk/About/century/birthdaygreetings.asp>

——, (2006b), *A Short Account of the Rivalry between the Plebs League and the WEA, or Why was our Sister Organisation so Mean?,* <http://www.wea.org.uk/aboutus/index.htm>

——, (2007), 'About the WEA'. <http://www.wea.org.uk/aboutus/index.htm>

Webb, S. M. (1915), 'Special Supplement on English Teachers and their Professional Organisation', *The New Statesman* (London).

Chapter 3

Trade Union Learning in the International Context

Moira Calveley

Introduction

Chapter 2 demonstrated how and why trade unions in the United Kingdom are not only concerned with the training and development of their activists, but how they become involved in national vocational education and training and in workplace learning. This chapter considers such involvement of trade unions from a comparative international perspective. The chapter draws upon secondary data[1] and focuses on five countries: Australia, France, Germany, Japan and the United States of America. Such comparative analysis allows us to not only have a greater awareness of what is happening in one environment it also allows us to compare and contrast approaches in other nations in order to assess the possible strengths and weaknesses of these systems. International comparison is always important as it helps contextualise the policies and practices of one's own country within the wider global economy.

In order to have any depth of understanding of the role that trade unions have in education, training and learning, it is important to firstly put this in the employment relations context of the country in which they operate. The extent to which trade unions are able to influence policy making at the national level, and the extent to which they are accepted in the workplace will shape the policies and practices they develop. We need to consider the nature of the relationship between trade unions, management and government and the degree to which the government employs an interventionist approach to the employment relations system and to the skills development of the country's workforce. The purposes and interests of each of these actors have to be taken into account, along with their differing interests and the power relations between them. We also need to consider the range and depth of interactions between employers, trade unions and governments with respect to training, education and skills development.

The chapter is broken down into sections covering individual countries alphabetically. Each section provides an overview of the employment relations system of that country and considers the relative power of trade unions within the system. It then goes on to discuss the role that trade unions play in the national vocational education and training system of the country whilst also considering their role in workplace learning and skills development and how they develop their

---

1   The chapter draws widely upon internet sources.

union activists. The sections which follow do not intend, nor attempt, to provide an extensive overview of either the employment relations systems of the country nor the involvement of trade unions in education, learning and training; they provide an overview upon which we are able to draw in order to locate union learning within an international context[2].

The chapter begins by briefly considering the global involvement of workers' organisations at an international level in the union learning context.

Trade Union and Workers' Education

As we saw in Chapter 2, the importance of workers' organisations in the provision of workplace learning and training is not new and we see this in an international context through the International Labour Organization (ILO). Established in 1919 as a tri-partite body bringing together governments, employers and workers across the world, the overarching aim of the ILO is 'to improve social protection and conditions of life and work throughout the world' (Kartaş-Özkan 2005, 35). To this end, it established the Workers' Education Programme in 1956 (ILO 1988), the main objective of which is 'to assist in the strengthening and development of workers' organisations' by, amongst other things, providing assistance in various aspects of trade union training, development and provision. The ILO established its vocational International Training Centre in Turin in 1964. The centre promotes social justice, human rights and labour standards across the world.

Another important labour institution which works for workers' education is that of the International Federation of Workers' Education Associations (IFWEA), founded in 1945 as a result of an agreement by the Workers' Education Association (WEA – see Chapter 2) in the UK to support workers' education in war-torn countries. The organisation unites national and international trade unions and workers' education organisations that are 'engaged in the provision of adult education opportunities for workers and the communities in which they live throughout the world' (IFWEA 2007). The main aim of this organisation is to educate workers in order that they have a greater understanding and awareness of 'democratic life and civil society' (IFWEA 2007).

Both these organisations provide important continuing support for trade union organisations' involvement in worker education across the world. Nonetheless, whilst they are able to promote social justice and equality and attempt to influence national governments with regard to education and skills policy making, what they are not able to do is engage with education and learning at the workplace level. Nor are they in a position to impose sanctions on either governments or employers who neglect the education and training of workers. This is where the collective strength of the workers, through their trade unions, is apposite. The extent to which trade unions have the ability to influence government and employer policies and practices in individual countries will be considered in the rest of the chapter.

---

2   For a more in-depth coverage of comparative employment relations see Bamber *et al.* (2004); likewise for labour education from an international perspective see Spencer (2002) and for the training of trade unionists in Europe see Bridgford and Stirling (2000).

Australia

Australia operates a dual system of government founded upon the Australian Constitution of 1901. A federal system of government was established which distributed power between the National Government and the six independent states. Under Section 51(35) of the Constitution, the Federal Parliament was given limited power to make laws with respect to 'conciliation and arbitration for the prevention and settlement of industrial disputes extending beyond the limits of any one state' (Parliament of New South Wales 2005) leaving the individual states with the primary responsibility for the regulation of employment relations. Thus, since 1904 and the passing of the Conciliation and Arbitration Act, Australia has practised a dual system of employment relations with power in this area greatly devolved to independent state level. The 1904 Act centralised state-level collective bargaining and established compulsory conciliation and arbitration, forcing employers to recognise trade unions and hence encouraging the establishment of employer organisations.

Although both employers and trade unions accepted this system of employment relations, the federal government has been less happy with it (Lansbury and Wailes 2004). Since the late 1980s the Australian government have intervened in employment relations practices although not always to the extent they would have liked; it is only recently that there has been a successful attempt to bring employment relations powers under the control of the federal government (see below). The 1904 Conciliation and Arbitration Act was finally replaced in 1988 with the Industrial Relations Act which was followed by the Industrial Relations Reform Act (IRRA) in 1993. This latter piece of legislation, introduced by a Labour government, focussed on the individual rather than the collective rights of the employee, starting a move towards the marginalisation of trade unions who were naturally aggrieved at this, more so perhaps because they had, prior to the Government's election in 1983, supported them by entering into an Incomes and Prices Accord (the 'Accord') with them. The 1993 Act also began to shift the employment relations powers towards the federal government.

In 1996, in a similar vein to what happened in the UK in the 1980s, the incoming Liberal/National coalition conservative government took a stance against trade unions. In their first term of office they replaced the IRRA with the Workplace Relations Act which focussed on enterprise based employment relations, emphasising a move away from collective bargaining whilst at the same time weakening worker rights. Aimed at further weakening the trade union movement the Act gave employers and employees the right to engage in individual Australian Workplace Agreements (AWAs) which allowed for the opting out of collective agreements. These agreements have, as expected, been strongly criticised by trade unions who argue that workers have no choice but to sign them (ACTU 2006a). These initial attempts at widespread change to the employment relations system were, however, frustrated by the Labour controlled state governments who were mostly keen to keep employment relations powers under their control.

When the coalition party was re-elected in 2004 (for a fourth term in office) it also took control of the Senate, the upper house of the Australian system of government. This was particularly important with regards to employment relations legislation as it was the Labour Senators who had blocked previous moves to bring control of employment relations regulation under the Federal Parliament. In 2006 the WorkChoices Act was passed, finally taking such control away from the states and investing it in the Federal government. The aim of WorkChoices is to promote a 'flexible labour market' and a unified national employment relations system (Australian Government 2007) but it is again heavily criticised by trade unions who argue that it encourages exploitation in the workplace.

Partly due to the dual system of employment relations with individual states each historically having its own independence in employment relations matters, there are a number of employers' organisations in Australia. The largest of these is now the Australian Chamber of Commerce and Industry (ACCI) followed by the Australian Industries Group (AIG). According to Lansbury and Wailes (2004), employer groups are less united than the trade unions and the fact that they now offer membership services puts them into competition with each other.

Although there was a rapid growth in trade union membership early in the twentieth century with around half of the workforce unionised by 1921 (Lansbury and Wailes, 2004), as in most countries, trade union membership in Australia has dramatically declined. In 1995 around 33 per cent of workers were unionised; by 2005 this had dropped to 22.4 per cent (ABS 2006). The main union confederation under which unions unite is the Australian Council of Trade Unions (ACTU).

Due to the nature of the Australian employment relations system there has historically been little scope for collective bargaining at the enterprise level and hence workplace union organisation tends to be weak (Lansbury and Wailes 2004). Trade union power was already diluted prior to the recent change to more decentralised bargaining.

Clearly, the Australian trade unions are far from being recognised as 'social partners' with both government and employers attempting to marginalise them at every chance. This does not bode well for their involvement in national skills development or workplace learning and training. What is evident in the next section is how a change in government, combined with a change in employment relations practices, can have an effect on the role trade unions play in these areas.

Australian Workplace Learning and Training

Like many developed countries, Australia is seen to be facing a skills deficit, being identified in an OECD (Organisation for Economic Co-operation and Development) report as 'one of the countries with large numbers of citizens at the lowest level of literacy' (OECD 2000, 15). This is despite efforts over the past two decades to tackle such literacy deficits. In 1991 for example, the Workplace English Language and Literacy (WELL) training scheme was launched and government funding was provided to organisations who were implementing literacy and numeracy training programmes. The scheme is still ongoing.

The role of trade unions in workplace learning is patchy. In the early days of the WELL project, for example, they were involved in the tri-partite management of these schemes, however, their representation on consultative committees has dwindled more recently (Holland and Castleton 2002). Recent lack of trade union representation in the area of vocational education and training is a situation which some trade union activists lay at the door of the poor strategies of their union leaders (Brown 2006), discussed further below. As Brown describes, such marginalisation was not always the case.

Between 1983 and 1996 (the era of a Labour Government) the Australian union movement was heavily involved in promoting the reform of the country's vocational training system; indeed, they were seen as providing 'the inspiration for the new system' (Brown 2006, 491) which was closely aligned to the centralised collective bargaining system. Working alongside the government training institutions, the aim of the unions was to link the acquisition of skills and qualifications to award classifications (Brown 2006) and hence pay; thus, skills development became part of the collective bargaining agenda and training reform underpinned the 'Accord'. Participation in vocational education and training strategy was a new direction for the trade unions who had previously been more concerned with training their own workplace activists and union officers. Such involvement was, however, seen by trade union activists as fundamental to 'entrenching unions' position in society [and] in overcoming declining trade union membership' (Brown 2006, 494). Trade unionists embraced their roles on tri-partite training bodies, became 'prominent as promoters and leaders of reform' and 'the training reform agenda became one of the foundations of the agreement between Labour and the ACTU' (Brown 2006, 494).

Nonetheless, by the early 1990s the trade unions were to lose their influence on the national training reform agenda. Brown (2006) identifies the devolvement of collective bargaining and training reform to the enterprise level as a significant factor in this. Decentralised training initiatives allowed management to separate awards from training thus taking the training agenda out of the collective bargaining arena and back under their control. Trade union input was accordingly reduced. At the same time there was also a concerted effort by the employer organisations to 'reclaim' the training initiative from the trade unions; this was subsequently supported by the incoming anti trade union Conservative government in 1993 who initiated a series of policies to deregulate the training system whilst marginalising ACTU and trade union input.

In Brown's (2006) paper, trade unionists argue strongly that once training and wage awards were separated then their role in setting the training agenda was diminished; they felt that union leaders should not have agreed to enterprise level training as workers were no longer being trained for the industry in which they worked and their transferable skills were being undermined by enterprise specific skills.

The turn of the new century saw the Australian government still concerned about their competitive position in the world-wide trading markets, viewing skills shortages as a major problem. Consequently they proceeded to fund 'skills-ecosystem' projects throughout the country. These projects, which are supported by trade unions, are industry or region focussed and bring together a number of factors (e.g. business environment, extent of capital investment, education and training) in order to improve work and skills in Australia (see Buchanen *et al.* 2001; Buchanen 2006).

In 2006 the Australian Government announced an AUS$837m five-year investment plan entitled 'Skills for the Future'. Aimed primarily at workers in their late twenties and early thirties, the scheme includes government paid training vouchers and wage subsidies for those taking up an apprenticeship. The Australian Education Union (AEU), whilst recognising the government's admission for a need in skills investment, have criticised the 'voucher' programme upon which the package is based, arguing that more general investment is needed in further education (AEU 2006) whilst other unions have suggested that the level of funding is not enough.

Perhaps still stinging from being sidelined in the development of the national vocational training system, ACTU has been vociferous in its criticism of the Liberal-National coalition government for the perceived under-investment in Australia's Technical and Further Education (TAFE) colleges, whilst also blaming them for countrywide skills shortages. It must be remembered, however, that apart from their somewhat short-lived foray into developing and promoting changes to the vocational training system, historically neither ACTU nor the individual trade unions throughout Australia have paid much notice to workplace learning and training (Holland and Castleton 2002). On the other hand, the training and educating of trade unionists to organise and carry out their duties in the workplace is taken very seriously.

ACTU heavily promotes union representative specific training and has an Education and Campaign Centre which offers 'formal education and training to members and officials of affiliated unions' (ACTU 2006b). Although in 1996 (early in its first term of office) the Liberal-national government abolished the Trade Union Training Authority (TUTA) which had been established under the Trade Union Training Act (1975), this was soon replaced by the ACTU funded 'New TUTA' (Trade Union Training Australia).

Clearly, Australian trade unions endeavoured to become a leading light in the Australian training reform agenda of the 1980s and 1990s. Having made some headway with this whilst there was a Labour government they were, however, quickly sidelined once a Conservative administration was in place. Not only were the new government more hostile to trade unions than their left-wing predecessors, they also felt that skills and education were the domain of government and management.

It would seem that the lack of focus on workplace learning and training by Australian trade unions is a result of the centralised system of collective bargaining with which they developed. Having been fully integrated into the system the union movement was caught lacking when bargaining was devolved to enterprise level. It might be argued that the local activists were not quite prepared for local bargaining. Thus, more recently union learning has focussed on organising mechanisms and providing representatives with the skills for local bargaining. As Holland and Castleton suggest, Australian trade unions have 'perhaps missed critical opportunities to have significant input into *how* workplace-based basic skills should be formulated and delivered' (2002, 93, their emphasis).

It must be noted that although the unions saw the training reform agenda as a way of improving workers working lives, they also saw involvement in this in a pragmatic light at a time when trade union membership was declining. They may feel that their failure to secure input was indeed an opportunity lost. In a country where trade union membership has fallen dramatically over the past two decades, learning and training may begin to figure strongly on the workplace bargaining agenda.

France

The government in France take a highly interventionist approach to employment relations reflecting 'the traditional reluctance of unions and employers to use voluntary collective agreements' (Goetschy and Jobert, 2004, 186). Although viewed as 'social partners', there is a distinctive lack of recognition between what are often viewed as revolutionary socialist trade unionists and paternalistic or reactionary employers (Goetschy and Jobert 2004; EIRO 2007a). Hence, there is government involvement in employment matters. Employment relations issues are enshrined in law with legislation covering areas such as worker representation and collective bargaining. The content of the legislation can sway from employer centred to worker centred depending on the political leanings of the government introducing it at the time.

Most employers (three out of every four) are members of an employer organisation with the majority uniting under the umbrella of the Mouvement des Enterprises de France (MEDEF); smaller and medium sized employers tend to join the CGPME (Confédération Générale des Petites et Moyennes Enterprises) (EIRO 2007a).

Organisations in France are legally bound to have worker representation in the workplace. This is done in three ways: firstly, through Works Councils which have consultation and information rights; secondly through (non-union) worker representatives who pursue individual grievances; and thirdly through formal trade union representatives (Hollinshead and Leat 1995). The first two categories are elected by the workers from the workforce, the latter clearly coming from the trade unions represented in the workplace. These channels of dialogue with workers are commonly recognised as 'social partners' with managers in workplace employment relations.

Although dating back to the mid 1800s, the trade union movement in France is fragmented and unions are now formed around political and religious ideologies rather than craft or industry as in the earlier days of their existence. Despite union density being traditionally low (for example, it was around 23 per cent in the mid 1970s when UK density was around 50 per cent) membership has declined even more over recent years, being about 8 per cent in 2004 (EIRO 2007a). Similar to most countries, there is a higher union density in larger companies and in state owned enterprises. Unlike the UK which has one main trade union confederation (the TUC) there are five main trade union confederations in France. These are ideologically divided which not only makes consensus on issues extremely difficult it also means that they are competing for members within individual workplaces. These confederations all have 'representative' status which gives them various rights including the right to negotiate (EIRO 2007a). Due to their ideological stance French trade unions tend to focus on wider social and economic issues rather than local issues at the enterprise level. Combined with fragmentation, this makes their presence at workplace level relatively weak (although Works Council representatives are often also union members (Goetschy and Jobert 2004)).

Collective bargaining in France has historically taken place at industry level (Hollinshead and Leat 1995). Although apparently well intentioned, the strong pro-worker legislation introduced by the 1982 Auroux Reforms did little to strengthen the trade unions (Gumbrell-McCormick and Hyman 2006). In an attempt to protect the non-unionised workers and to give more voice to employees the Reforms introduced compulsory annual pay negotiations between employers and employee representatives at the workplace level and extended all collective bargaining agreements to cover non-union members. Neither of these practices was particularly helpful to the unions as it meant that negotiations would not only take place regardless of trade union presence in the workplace, but workers did not have to be union members to benefit from the outcome. The introduction of the 35 hour working week under the Aubry law in 1998 and the corresponding bargaining over this has introduced more scope for enterprise level bargaining. Nonetheless, industry level bargaining remains mainly the case (Goetschy and Jobert 2004).

In 2004, the 'Fillon' law was passed to enforce major changes to the collective bargaining machinery; where in the past industry or sectoral level agreements could only be changed at enterprise level if this was beneficial of the employee, the new law allows deviation from these agreements at local level (EIRO 2004a). The new law also incorporated a 'majority' clause whereby agreements had to be endorsed by the union with the majority of members (previously one union could agree for all). Trade unions being weakly represented at enterprise level were strongly opposed to these changes, however, the first round of collective agreements following the implementation of the new law showed little change (Eurofound 2005).

Despite being fragmented and having weak local representation, trade unions in France are viewed very much as a social partner. In this respect it could be assumed that they would play an important role in national skills development and this would fit with their general aim of influencing the wider social policies of the country. At, the workplace level the unions have, historically, tended to avoid local issues and hence would not, therefore, become involved in negotiating or bargaining over workplace learning and training. Nonetheless, the next section will show how a change in national employment relations practice can impinge on employment practices in the workplace.

French Workplace Learning and Training

Training and development in France is characterised firstly by 'the influence of the school-based model' and secondly by the 'strong institutionalisation of continuing vocational training' (Géhin and Jobert 2001, 81), the latter being regulated by law and involving dialogue with the social partners (as discussed below). The school-based model is built around initial vocational and technical training and pupils are offered three routes: general, vocational and technological education. The latter two lead to Diplomas (Certificat d'Aptitude Professionnel (CAP)) which provide evidence of competency in the basic skills for employment. Although apprenticeships do exist, these tend to be few (Leat 1998), partly perhaps due to the historical attitude of disdain towards them as they have been viewed as being geared towards low academic achievers or those from socially disadvantaged backgrounds (Géhin and Jobert 2001).

Méhaut describes France as having 'a training position without parallel in Europe' (2005, 304). There are two main tenets of training in France; the first of these is employer levies, first introduced in 1971 and described by Leat as 'the most notorious feature of the French [training] system' (1998, 252). Employers who employ more than 10 employees are statutorily required to pay a training levy of 1.5 per cent of the wage bill (Goetschy and Jobert 2004). The levies are for continual vocational training and on-the-job training with some of the money set aside for the training of young people and for external training for employees (Leat 1998). The money is paid into a mutual industry-wide fund from which the employers are then able to draw; those employers who spend more than the regulatory 1.5 per cent are eligible to claim money back from the fund. The second tenet is the company training plan which is produced annually by employers and discussed with the Works Council (which usually has a training committee). However, the views of the latter do not have to be taken into account by the company (Méhaut 2005).

Alongside the levies and training plans employees are also given the right to up to one year's paid (between 80 and 100 per cent) training leave. This allows employees to follow a course of their choice which is outside the company's training plan (Ministère des Affaires Étrangerès 2007). In practice, however, this is an option which, due to cost, relatively few employees are able to take up (Méhaut 2005).

French companies generally spend around 3.2 per cent on employee training (Goetschy and Jobert 2004). Nonetheless, whilst training in France is escalating provision differs between sector and size of organisation with employees of smaller organisations, particularly in low-skilled areas such as construction and hotel and catering losing out (Géhin and Jobert 2001). In fact, it appears that employers in such industries may well be willing to pay the levy rather than allow their workers to gain transferable skills which they could then take to other employers (Leat 1998).

A feature of training in France is that it forms part of the multi-industry bargaining agenda between the trade unions and employers organisations (Goetschy and Jobert 2004). It was the inequality in training as discussed above that formed the basis of a dialogue involving the social partners between 2001 and 2004, which led to the signing of a national inter-sector agreement on employees' lifelong access to training. The outcome of the agreement became law in May 2004 (Méhaut 2005).

The discussions were initiated by the growing contention that the training system which had been in place since 1971 was now inadequate (Méhaut 2005). The employers in particular were reluctant to have the government take an interventionist approach to training and the trade unions were likewise determined not to be marginalised in such matters. It was against the backdrop of the threat by the government that they would legislate if the social partners failed to reach an agreement that the discussions began in 2001. Although the negotiations were by no means straightforward (see Méhaut 2005) the parties finally came to an agreement in 2003. The main provisions were that: individual employees would have a right to vocational training; employers would make a larger financial contribution; and individuals should also share the cost of training – although this may be by undertaking the training outside of normal working hours. Much emphasis was placed on the development of transferable skills and career development.

What is of relevance with regards to trade union involvement in the agreement is that the extent of its implementation at workplace level will depend on both industry and company level negotiations, thus possibly giving the unions a greater role in the workplace than they previously enjoyed (or wished for).

A particularly interesting factor that was evident in the negotiations leading up to the signing of the agreement was the apparent (and unusual) solidarity of the unions. Having previously been in dispute regarding the signing of the unemployment insurance agreement with the government, the unions were determined to show a united front.

With regard to the training of trade union members and activists, this is also underpinned by legislation. Since 1957 a series of laws have been passed, culminating in December 1985 with legislation which grants paid trade union training leave (with various stipulations) to employees in private sector organisations with 10 employees or more (Geoffroy 2000). Public sector employees are also entitled to paid leave but under a different statute. Although it is illegal for employers to refuse trade union training leave without due course apparently avoidance tactics are frequently employed (Geoffroy 2000).

Due to the ideological bases on which French trade unions are formed, their training tends to be union-specific. There are usually two forms of training: firstly, general union education which is for all activists and provides them with an understanding of the union's culture and with basic skills (e.g. negotiation skills) and secondly, specific training for the roles and duties they undertake (e.g. as a member of a tribunal) (Geoffroy 2000).

The French trade unions have connections with universities through Labour Institutes such as the Institut du Travail in Strasbourg which was established in 1955 in order to educate trade unionists. The Boards of the institutions, which are partly financed by the state, are comprised of both trade union representatives and university academics, whilst the curriculum is delegate driven and tailored towards specific requests (Geoffroy 2000). Although the aim of the institutions is to provide education for the union activists, this is based on union ideologies and doctrines and not on providing a general education.

As with all aspects of employment relations in France, vocational education and training is covered by legislation. Policy making at this level entails dialogue between the social partners, thus legitimising trade union involvement and reducing the scope for conflict. The role of the trade unions is, however, interesting. At the industry and sector level where they have strong bargaining mechanisms in place they are clearly keen to be involved and vocational training has become part of the bargaining agenda. At the local level they face a paradox. Here, partly as a result of their historically weak representation levels, they have resisted engaging in employment relations matters. The change in policy with regards to training may inadvertently put pressure on the unions to provide greater workplace representation as individual workers are claiming their right to training leave. As a result, unions will have greater exposure at the workplace level. This leaves us with the question as to whether in France the issue of vocational training could lead to union growth (rather than renewal) at the workplace level.

Germany

The case of Germany is interesting in that it is the only one of the countries covered here which can demonstrate an element of 'industrial democracy' in the organisation of their national employment relations system. Established following the upheaval of the Second World War, the German system is built around the notion of 'social partners' and based upon the dual system of interest representation with both Works Councils and trade unions involved in worker representation. A further notable feature of the German system is the extensive juridification of employment relations practices, processes and procedures.

Works Councils are, as in France (above), elected from the workforce to represent workers at the workplace level but in Germany their roles are strengthened by the system of co-determination which allows for (at least in principle) employee participation in management decision making. The Works Council has varying statutory rights to information, consultation or co-decision making and represents employees on company 'supervisory boards'. They are involved in production issues, individual worker grievances and implementing collective agreements; they are not permitted to engage in collective bargaining which is the domain of the trade unions and which is enshrined in law.

Post-war trade unions in Germany were formed around two principles (Keller 2004). Firstly, as industrial unions with only one union per enterprise they represent workers by industry rather than craft or trade, and secondly they are unitary, or non-partisan, and therefore not affiliated to any political party. Although they received a boost in membership levels following reunification in 1989 (Keller 2004), as with other countries around the world trade union membership in Germany began to decline and by the end of the 1990s it was less than thirty per cent (Keller 2004). Whilst one report suggests that density had fallen to eighteen per cent by 2004 (EIRO 2007b), others suggest that it is closer to the twenty per cent mark (Addison *et al.* 2006). Again, membership levels have remained stronger in the 'traditional' areas of manufacturing and public sector and amongst white males and full-time employees (Keller 2004). The fall in union membership levels has brought pressure to bear on the principle of industrial unions and thus we have seen, since the mid 1990s, a series of takeovers and mergers (Addison *et al.* 2006; Keller 2004) which have led to 'multi-sectoral' unions (Keller 2004, 217).

The majority of German trade unions have traditionally united under the 'comparatively weak' (Keller, 2004, 217) main association, the German Trade Union Federation (DGB) established in 1949. Recently, the decline in the number of trade unions, combined with the creation of Vereinigte Dienstleistungs-gewerkschaft (Ver. di) which incorporates five public and private sector unions (making it the largest trade union in the world (Keller 2005)), puts doubt over the 'continuing purpose' of the DGB (Hyman 2001, 136) and its influence and power (Keller 2005). Thus, the DGB is currently reassessing its role and purpose.

German employers are affiliated to different associations according to their trade and geographical location. Like the trade unions they also have one main overarching representative body, the Bundesvereinigung Deutscher Arbeitgeberverbände (BDA). This covers all private sector employers (excluding the iron and steel industry which is prohibited from joining due to its unique extensive system of co-determination). Organisation amongst German employers is high at around eighty per cent (Eurofound 2007a).

The idea of Germany's dual system was to separate the collective bargaining machinery from workplace representation of worker interests in order to remove conflict from the workplace. Since its earliest days the system has come in for both scepticism and criticism and more recently there have been questions as to the ability of it to survive in the present day economic, political and social climate. Although initially viewed by trade unionists as a mode of divide and rule (Gumbrell-McCormick and Hyman 2006), arguably this did not prove to be the case as trade unionists are frequently voted onto the Works Councils, with eighty per cent of Works Council's elections coming from a union list (Klikauer 2004). It has also been noted that a mutual support mechanism often exists between trade unions and Works Councils; not only do the former tend to supply the delegates for the latter, they also provide training for these delegates (Klikauer 2004). For trade unions, the mutual gain is in the access to information that the Works Councils provide (Gumbrell-McCormick and Hyman 2006) and their assistance in recruiting union members (Addison *et al.* 2006). Indeed, Klikauer describes how Works Councils 'are inextricably linked to the union movement, even though both are structurally separated' (2004, 2). Hyman (2001) identifies how the dual system promotes a consensual rather than adversarial approach to bargaining within carefully defined parameters; shop-floor representation tends to be participative rather than conflictual (Klikauer 2004).

Arguments put forward regarding the inadequacy of Works Councils have gathered momentum more recently. Although mandatory, their creation is not automatic (Addison *et al.* 2006) and their existence has been noted as sparse amongst the smaller organisations (Addison *et al.* 2004; Gumbrell-McCormick and Hyman 2006; Keller 2004). Such smaller organisations (which are increasing in number (Keller 2004)) also tend to lack trade union representation, leading commentators to suggest that there is an 'exclusion zone' (Kommission Mitbestimmung 1998 quoted in Gumbrell-McCormick and Hyman 2006, 480) or a 'representation gap' (Keller 2004, 226) where employees have neither Works Council nor trade union representation.

There has been much debate over recent years as to the stability of the 'German system' of employment relations. Although some (Hassel 1999; 2002) argue that it is under threat, others (Klikauer 2002) suggest that although changing, or 'transforming' (Keller 2004, 251) the dual system is intact and 'remains the key institutional benchmark' (Addison *et al.* 2006, 2) in German employment relations.

Regardless of the debates surrounding the durability of the German system however, as with France, the trade unions still remain as social partners and are given a voice when it comes to national policy making. They are viewed as a significant actor in the German employment relations system. Having said this, on the whole their role tends to be non-confrontational and somewhat passive; thus it is necessary to question the extent to which they have any real input into the 'social dialogue', including learning and training initiatives.

German Workplace Learning and Training

Underpinning the German system of employment relations is the national approach to training and development which, it is argued, 'was integral to the phenomenal success' (Hollinshead and Leat 1995, 185) of the economy up until the social (reunification) and economic challenges of the 1990s. The German approach to training continues to be viewed as providing the country with competitive advantage over many of its European counterparts. Despite this, the Association of German Chambers of Industry and Commerce (Deutscher Industrie und Handelskammertag (DIHK)), warns of a forthcoming skills shortage (EIRO 2006).

As with its employment relations system, the German training system is underpinned by a tri-partite (or quad-partite if one takes State and Federal governments as separate entities – both having separate voting rights) social partnership approach with representation of the partners on the Federal Institute for Vocational Education and Training. The institute was founded by statute in 1970 and is a government-funded body, the main role of which is to research and advance vocational education and training and promote good practice across industries. Eaton describes the German system as 'more corporatist than interventionist' with both 'written and unwritten agreements between employers and trade unions' on the regulation of training (2000, 85). He also identifies how the centralised collective bargaining system helps remove the incentives for poaching trained workers by the non-training organisations although arguably, this has changed in recent years with the growth in small, non-unionised organisations who are likely to view poaching as the cheaper (or in their view more affordable) option.

The German training system is based around a 'dual approach' which places emphasis on both formal education and vocational training, with apprenticeship schemes being 'at the heart' of the latter (Leat 1998, 252). These schemes combine on-the-job practical training with more formal training in basic skills such as German and maths. Highlighting the positive effect this dual system of training has on reducing youth unemployment, Keller (2004) points out that it also provides a large pool of qualified young people on which employers are able to draw. He goes on to state that the resulting 'acquisition of broad skills constitutes a prerequisite for a 'high-skill/high-wage' economy' (2004, 224). Keller also identifies how the system provides potential for creating multiskilled, and thus flexible, workers which can be utilised to the advantage of German employers. It is also suggested by Bean that more 'cooperative industrial relations' emanate from the 'common values and orientations' created by the dual system (1994, 233).

The system is not only supported practically by organisations, they also contribute towards the cost. Needless to say it has come under strain in recent years due to a general downturn in the German economy. There has been a decline in the number of apprenticeship places offered, partly as a result of cost but also due to structural changes in industry from manufacturing and mining (areas which offered the greater number of apprenticeships) to service-related employment. Also, the growth of small enterprises has had a negative effect on apprenticeships as these firms are less willing (or perhaps unable) to finance training. As a result of this decline, in the spring of 2004 the German government threatened to introduce (by statute) a training levy on companies who did not demonstrate that they were providing sufficient training places for young people. The law which was welcomed by the DGB but dismissed as 'bureaucratic' by the DBA (EIRO 2004b) was to come into effect in autumn 2004. It was shelved, however, when the government enjoined a voluntary pact with the employers who undertook to increase training opportunities for young people but without the threat of a training levy. The pact which was to cover three years was, by December 2004, being hailed as a success by the government and employers, although less so by trade unions who felt that not enough apprenticeship training contracts had been entered into. More recently (2007) the Association of German Chambers of Industry and Commerce called for a review and re-organisation of the dual system; this was supported by the DGB (EIRO 2007c).

Apart from the apprenticeship training schemes, Germany has an advanced vocational training system, the 'Meister' system, which concentrates on advanced technical skills for post-apprentice workers (Leat 1998). These workers, who also have several years' workplace training, continue their studies and eventually take on an apprenticeship training role (Rose 1991).

As noted above, Works Councils have co-determination rights with regard to workplace training, rights which were further strengthened under the revised Works Constitution Act 2001. As part of the tri-partite 'Alliance for Jobs' forum (established in 1998) which considers national vocational training and competitiveness, trade unions have a voice in the planning and implementation of training policies and practices and are involved at all levels of the training process. One of the objectives of the Alliance was to address the inequality of provision of organisation-level training so that older, women, low-skilled and blue-collar workers would also benefit. One sticking point for the Alliance is the extent to which training should become a bargaining issue at the local level. Individual unions have since successfully negotiated time-off for training and other training rights for their members.

Time-off for training is mandatory for Works Councillors many of whom are also trade union members and/or activists. Trade unions provide educational courses for Works Council delegates (Klikauer 2004) thus ensuring that the philosophy of the union is taken into the workplace even where there is a low level of union membership. Hence, although Works Councils were initially seen as a way of 'taming' the trade union movement, as discussed above, they can provide union members with a voice, albeit in a more inhibited setting.

The legislation regarding the provision by employers for time-off for educational leave varies between different Länder (states) but tends to be four or five days, depending on certain conditions (e.g. length of working week). This leave allows for the furthering of employees' vocational or political education and is paid for by the participants. Some Länder have provided statutory rights to paid leave for training (Eurofound, 2007b). Employers are known to contest these rights, particularly where the educational courses are political, and can make it difficult for employees to participate (Romer-Karrasch *et al.* 2000).

There was a strong post-war movement by trade unions to become involved not only in training and educating their own activists, but also in adult education in general and adult education academies were developed and have continued to this day (Romer-Karrasch *et al.* 2000). Trade unions, and the DGB in particular, view social education as one of their important union mandates. In line with this, the trade unions have recently voiced concern as to the level and extent of training provided for immigrant workers, calling for more apprenticeship places to be made available to them (EIRO 2007d).

With regard to training provided by trade unions for their members, as in other countries this is taken seriously by the DGB and individual trade unions with both educational and skills courses being provided. Indeed, due to the wide-ranging union delegates on DGB programmes, they are able to use their educational courses 'to develop perspectives which go beyond the problems relating to the sector and the firm' (Romer-Karrasch *et al.* 2000, 148), again allowing for the wider ideology of the trade union movement to be disseminated.

Although declining in numbers and despite the extent of their influence being disputed, due to the nature of the employment relations system in Germany trade unions are still recognised as a social partner and as such are involved in the setting and regulation of vocational education in workplaces. Training initiatives are usually agreed on a national, regional and sector basis and then rolled out to the enterprise level where involvement in training matters tends to be the responsibility of the Works Councillors. Despite trade unions being heavily represented on Works Councils, the latter do not have the right to engage in bargaining; trade unions should, therefore, be wary of considering Works Council membership as significant in representational terms.

Although there is some movement by trade unions towards getting vocational training seen as a collective bargaining issue, employers are resisting this. In the present climate with all social partners recognising the need for maintaining and developing a skilled labour market, this is less of an issue. Nonetheless, the fact remains that with their high levels of Works Council members trade unions are in a position to influence workplace training in the future if they seize the initiative.

It needs to be recognised that the dual system is not representative of all workers. Those in many small firms are protected neither by trade unions nor by Works Councils and it is the skills of these workers with which trade unions need to be concerned. Their position as social partners on the tripartite training forum provides union leaders with an opportunity to promote training in small firms and to those less advantaged in the skills market such as women and immigrant workers, thus allowing them to reach out to these workers who may well respond by joining a trade union. A failure on the part of the unions to gain support from managers and the government with regard to the learning and training of these workers, may well give strength to the argument that the dual system of interest representation in Germany merely pays lip-service to the role of trade unions as an equal social partner. This could result in further decline in membership levels.

Japan

The post-war growth of the Japanese economy is well versed. In recent years, however, we have seen stagnation and decline in growth as the 'bubble economy' collapsed and in the 1990s Japan entered their 'ten lost years' (JILPT 2006) phase. This has had a knock-on effect on Japanese employment systems. Although the notion of 'lifetime employment' and seniority-based wage systems remain (Inagami 2004), arguably these are becoming the exception rather than the rule (Rebick 2005)[3] and arguably only ever existed in the larger organisations.

Since 1955, with only a brief break in 1993–4 when the Japanese Socialist Party (JSP) took power, the Liberal Democratic Party (LDP) has governed Japan. There has, therefore, been a fairly stable political climate over the past fifty years, albeit more recently through a three-party coalition (LDP, Social Democratic Party of Japan (formerly JSP) and Sakigake (Harbinger)). The government has tended to take a non-interventionist approach towards employment relations although since 1945 employees have been protected by the Trade Union Law which gives them 'rights to organise, bargain and take collective action including strike action' (Hollinshead and Leat 1995, 265).

Trade unionism in Japan is organised around the business with all employees (both manual and white-collar workers, but not managers) usually belonging to the same union, rather than specific occupational unions; anyone who leaves the organisation also loses union membership (Kuwahara 2004). Such 'enterprise unionism', which promotes the well-being of the organisation, often meets with criticism as it is seen as being too hand-in-hand with employers. Alternatively, some see it as an advantage in that issues are enterprise specific and employment relations are more flexible than might be the case with craft or general unions (Kuwahara 2004). Due to the number of unions in existence, the union movement is severely fragmented and hence industry wide it tends to be weak.

Trade union membership in Japan has declined over the past three decades from a peak of 35.4 per cent in 1970 to only 18.7 per cent in 2005 (figures from the Ministry of Health, Labour and Welfare, quoted by Morito 2006). Manufacturing and the public sector are the more highly unionised areas, whilst part-time workers and those working in small firms are less likely to be in a union (Morito 2006). As enterprise unions, the Japanese unions draw most of their members from the larger organisations.

Although characterised by fragmentation, the unions unite firstly under their industrial federations (unions within the same industry) and then under the Japan Trade Union Confederation (JTUC), known as RENGO and which has forty-seven local operations throughout the country (RENGO 2006). The industrial federations look to solving industry-specific issues whilst RENGO focuses on employment issues at the national level. The main 'power' of the unions, however, lies at the enterprise level where they tend to take 'a cooperative attitude towards management' (Kuwahara 2004, 285). This cooperation is seen to benefit the well-being of the workers; with lifetime employment and seniority-based wage systems being core

---

3   There is much debate as to the extent of long-term employment and seniority pay in Japan. Rebick, for instance, argues that the extent of both has always been limited (2005) whereas Inoue (1999) and Morito (2006) suggest that both still exist, albeit in a changing employment market.

features of employment practices (Inoue 1999; JILPT 2006), the belief is that if the enterprise prospers so too do the workers (Morito 2006).

Employers in Japan associate at regional and industry level with most uniting under the Federation of Employers' Associations, Nikkeiren, founded in 1948 (Hollinshead and Leat 1995). Nikkeiren does not have a direct role in collective bargaining but draws up wage bargaining guidelines (Bean 1994), has a co-ordinating function with the member associations and provides advice. The organisation was founded to combat post-war communist influence in trade unions and was a major factor in influencing the formation of enterprise unions who, it was deemed, would be easier to control. This gives some substance to the earlier argument that Japanese trade unions are too cosy with management.

Clearly, most Japanese trade unions have no real independent power. Their role appears to be one of accommodating rather than resisting management and they are highly unlikely to challenge government policy making and employment relations initiatives. Their main aim is to mediate any effects of economic downturn on their members; as shown in the following section, this may include supporting the casualisation of employment for non-unionised workers.

Japanese Workplace Learning and Training

Learning and training in Japan is very much enterprise-focussed. This is due to the notion of long-term employment and seniority-based wage systems. However, as discussed above, such employment practices are not as all-embracing as we are sometimes led to believe. In fact, it would appear that it is only in large organisations that these practices still exist and, since the downturn in the economy in the 1990s, only for the core workers of these organisations (JILPT 2006). A response to economic downturn by Japanese organisations has been to employ more temporary and part-time staff (Inagami 2004) and to promote retirement at the national retirement age of sixty.

Large Japanese organisations see no real need to promote individual skills as they employ young employees (from school or university) whose career movement throughout their working lives will generally be in the internal market of the enterprise. Training will be job specific as employees move up the seniority ladder for more money, rather than following a carefully planned career path. Job promotion and increased wages are linked to the development of enterprise skills (JILPT 2006). Thus, employees do not see the need to develop skills other than those which will move them up the wage-ladder. They have little intention of moving outside of the organisation – which provides them with employment protection – and therefore concentrate their energies on gaining company-specific knowledge and skills. Indeed, workers who join an organisation mid-career find conditions in their new position less favourable, and those seeking work mid-career find it difficult to get a position (Inoue 1999).

On-the-job training is the method preferred by Japanese organisations with, in 2003, nearly forty-seven per cent of organisations utilising this method (Ministry of Health Labour and Welfare figures quoted by JILPT). Training is provided hierarchically as lifetime employment provides a natural form of job transition.

As job security (and lifetime employment) is paramount to the unions, job relocation is often a key to workplace restructuring. In this case 'workers must therefore be highly adaptable. Multiskilling through in-house job training programmes is thus an essential prerequisite for relocation' (Inoue 1999, 23). We can see, therefore, that the unions promote enterprise specific skills development of their members. It is perhaps not coincidental that these members are mostly drawn from the core workers of the larger organisations and who are ordinarily more protected in the employment market.

Thus, we have in Japan a system whereby skills are acquired specifically for the organisation and this can be seen to raise a number of issues. Firstly, it is only in the larger organisations that lifetime employment is anywhere near permanent and this is only for the core workers. This results in non-core, temporary workers who are trained with job-specific skills which are not transferable when they attempt to move job. Secondly, employees of smaller firms, who are more likely to be released into the labour market when cost cutting is required, have non-transferable skills. Thirdly, a method employed by the large firms of maintaining the lifetime employment practices is to retire people as they reach the mandatory retirement age of sixty[4]; many of these retirees are subsequently in the labour market looking for work, but without the necessary skills to attain this. Finally, Japan have recognised that they have a forthcoming problem as in 2007 the post-war 'baby-boomers' will be coming up to retirement and entering the labour market without the necessary transferable skills.

In 1995 the Institute of Labour Education and Culture (ILEC) was established by RENGO and is affiliated to the IFWEA. The main aim of the Institute is to promote educational activities and training programmes to union members and their leaders. In conjunction with ILEC, RENGO has established an academy which provides training courses for trade union officials.

Although RENGO and their affiliated unions promote the training of activists, little attention seems to be paid to the transferable skills of workers, who due to the employment practices discussed above, tend to have company specific skills. The extent to which RENGO does address this issue is in arguing for the continuation of the practice of lifetime employment. Thus, they promote the:

> long-term, stable employment of regular workers [as this will ensure] a labour system that combines contemporary technological innovations with human skills. Namely, it can help provide effective future-oriented training schemes that enable to supply high performance labour, or required skills. High performance labour can not be materialized under short-term, unstable employment (quoted in Inoue 1999).

Being mostly enterprise based, Japanese unions appear somewhat comfortable with training directed at this level. With their focus being on full-time, core employees, they are content to allow market forces to prevail with non-core workers left to fend for themselves. Although the unions make some overtures with regard to skills training, this is couched in the rhetoric of long-term employment contracts.

---

4   Over ninety-five per cent of companies have a mandatory retirement age and ninety-one per cent have set this at sixty (JILPT 2006).

There is clearly a potential source of membership recruitment amongst those more vulnerable employees who do not have permanent contracts and who are due for re-deployment in the labour market. RENGO and its associated trade unions would do well to consider campaigning for training for these workers. Under the country's current employment relations system whereby challenging either government or management appears not to be an option, this is, however, unlikely to happen.

United States of America

Employment relations in the USA is characterised by the historical anti-union stance of employers (Hollinshead and Leat 1995; Katz and Wheeler 2004). Although, following a period of industrial unrest in the 1930s, pro-union legislation was enacted under the 1935 National Labour Relations Act (the Wagner Act), this was later watered down following opposition from employers and the Labour-Management Relations Act (Taft-Hartley) in 1947 gave states their own authority to introduce 'right-to-work' legislation (Hollinshead and Leat 1995). Despite the 1935 Act giving workers the right to unionise, it is notable that employers did, and still do, flaunt the legislation and engage with anti-union practices (Hollinshead and Leat 1995; Katz and Wheeler 2004). Such practices include intimidation and dismissal of union members and a so-called 'runaway-shop' approach by employers whereby they relocate their business in states where union membership is less strong (Eaton 2000). Although employers tend not to have employers associations (such as the Confederation of British Industry (CBI) in the UK), they do combine in order to engage in union avoidance (Katz and Wheeler 2004). As part of their 'union avoidance' tactics US managers engage in practices such as teamworking. There is a unitarist approach to people management, from which devolved the origins of Human Resource Management and the belief in union-free working environments.

The trade union movement dates back to the 1860s and although originally formed around crafts and then later industries (Katz and Wheeler 2004), unions are now similar to those in Japan in so far as they are viewed as 'business unions' (Hollinshead and Leat). They tend to focus on general workplace issues such as local benefits and terms and conditions, rather than wider economic concerns of the nation. Unions in the USA generally do not affiliate to a particular political party, although they do engage in lobbying for social welfare policies. Unionisation is fragmented and is focussed in the more traditional industries. As in other countries, there has been a sharp decline in union membership from around 20 per cent in 1980 to 12.4 per cent in 2003 (Visser 2006). Again, as we have seen across the world, trade unionism is strongest in the public services sector.

The enterprise focussed nature of American trade unions is widely reported to stem from a number of factors. Not only is there an absence of the 'feudal' tradition (as often found in Europe) thus making class distinctions somewhat less obvious, there is a very diverse population engaging in struggles independent of one another. Also, the nature of capitalism in the USA has allowed for more widespread prosperity. These factors combined provide for a less unified working class solidarity.

Trade unions in the USA unite under the American Federation of Labor and Congress of Industrial Organizations (AFL-CIO). This institution was created through the amalgamation of the two previously individual organisations in 1955 and was due to the efforts of George Meany (its first president) who fought to unite the divided labour movement at that time (AFL-CIO 2007a). It now has fifty four affiliated unions.

The anti-union stance taken by both government and employers prohibits union intervention with regard to employment policies and practices at either the national or the local level. The very low union density figures exacerbate this situation. As the next section will show, union activity in the USA tends to focus around providing benefits and assistance for their members.

American Workplace Learning and Training

As with other countries, the United States government has, in recent years, focussed policy on raising the skills levels of the workforce (Marquardt *et al.* 2000). There are two Government departments (Labor and Education) charged with the responsibility for policy implementation with regard to training and development. One of the remits of the former is to promote training to unemployed people which will, in theory, enable them to enter into the workforce. Recent legislation promoting this policy is the Personal Responsibility and Work Opportunity Reconciliation Act (1996), the aim of which is to remove people from government benefits by 'promoting job preparedness' (Marquardt *et al.* 2000, 140).

Although many organisations invest in training, Marquardt *et al.* (2000) highlight the fact that it is the 'leading edge' organisations that spend the most on developing their workers. In fact, research has shown that the lower paid and less educated workers are missing out on training opportunities in the workplace (Marquardt *et al.* 2000).

Within organisations, the evidence all points to on-the-job training with little direct involvement of the trade unions in workplace skills related training; this is unsurprising considering the union avoidance tactics employed by US employers.

The AFL-CIO are more directly involved in worker education and learning through the 'Education Services' branch of their 'Union Plus' benefits for members programme. They have established the Union Plus Education Foundation which offers scholarship funding for union members and their families for the purpose of continuing their educational studies at post-school level; they also offer low interest loans for education-related expenses. The AFL-CIO website also provides a database of information on scholarship funding provided by their affiliated unions. Alongside this, there is an online College Planning Centre which is aimed at helping students choose the correct career path for themselves (AFL-CIO 2007b).

Possibly due to the history of college fees in the USA, the scholarship system of supporting trade union members and their children appears to be widely adopted by the trade unions. For example, the Glass Molders, Pottery, Plastics & Allied Workers International (GMP) promote their Memorial Scholarship Fund which provides $4,000 per year for a four-year college tenure for thirty two students (GMP 2007).

During his time as president of the AFL-CIO, in an effort to provide union activists with appropriate skills George Meany created the Labor Studies Centre which has since developed into the National Labor College (NLC). The college offers residential union skills courses alongside fully accredited graduate and post-graduate degree courses for trade union members. Many unions have links to the NLC website on their own website.

Individual trade unions have provided training for their own officials since the 1920s when residential schools were established for this purpose (Nesbit 2002). More recently, trade unions have their own training establishments or their officers attend local college or university courses (Nesbit 2002).

As a result of declining union membership in 1989 the AFL-CIO established the Organizing Institute (OI) 'to promote and foster union organizing' (AFL-CIO 2007c). The OI offers both residential and field training to union organisers in all areas relating to trade union organising and recruitment.

The strong anti trade union stance of the US employers, which is generally supported by the government, makes it extremely difficult for unions in the USA to influence the national vocational training of the workforce. Nonetheless, in line with the servicing model approach to trade unionism, unions do offer assistance towards educational fees to their members as part of the benefits packages they promote. In this way, they encourage people (many of them young) from less advantaged backgrounds into the educational arena, no doubt hoping that they will remember their affiliation with trade unions in future careers.

Conclusions

This chapter has taken an international perspective on union involvement in education, training and learning. It has set each of the countries in their own national employment relations environment, thus demonstrating how national systems of employment relations impact upon the ability of trade unions to influence education and training policy making at the macro level. It is evident that a change in government and/or a change in employment relations practices can have severe implications for trade unions with regard to their involvement in education and training policymaking. In those countries where a more consensual approach to employment relations is practiced, the trade unions are allowed greater scope to influence workplace education and training.

It is apparent and perhaps expected that where unions are weak, as in the USA, or enterprise-based as in Japan, they have little say in national education and training systems. The former are positively sidelined by employer anti-trade union strategies and government unwillingness to involve them whilst the latter work in such close contact with management at the enterprise level that they show little inclination for involvement at the national level. In the USA the unions use training as part of a servicing model approach to trade union recruitment, particularly aimed at young people and those from more disadvantaged backgrounds, whilst in Japan the unions continue to focus on enterprise training and use their voice to call for more stable employment as it is the 'core' workers who benefit from skills development.

What the chapter has also demonstrated is that low union density is not always synonymous with 'weak' unions. A good example of this is in France where, despite many changes of government over the years, a social model of employment relations remains intact. Although unionisation is extremely low and severely fragmented, the trade unions are seen as one of the social partners and alongside employers are given a voice in developing national education and training policy. Therefore, although numerically weak, the unions are able to maintain their position as a social partner. This is due to a highly interventionist approach by the government which in effect 'forces' the social partnership to work. Nonetheless, any involvement of the social partners needs to be considered within the context of the highly developed vocational education and training system already in existence. On the face of it, the French workforce are benefiting from the partnership by better access to training, however, as we see in the other countries, such training may well be limited to the 'core' employees of larger organisations with those in small workplaces losing out.

France also provides us with an example of a changing employment relations system and the impact of this on the trade union movement. Having become entrenched in the long-standing system of bargaining at national or sector level, French trade unions are now in the position of having to adjust to local level bargaining involving training issues. On the one hand this could put pressure on the weak workplace representation, on the other it could strengthen it as more workers turn to unions for support.

Despite the government taking an interventionist approach as in France, the German system is different in that a form of industrial democracy is practiced with worker representation mandatory. Although declining in numbers trade union representation is more complex in that Works Councillors are frequently trade union activists, so representation may take place on two fronts – but not, as we have seen, in organisations where neither trade unions nor Works Councils exist. Again as in France, the vocational education and training system in Germany is highly developed; unions are recognised at national level in policy making but have little input at enterprise level. German trade unions are now concerned with getting training and skills development on the bargaining agenda, a move being resisted by employers.

Australia has gone through a transformation in its employment relations system with, as in the UK, trade unions being marginalised by government. The Australian trade union movement seized the training agenda initiative whilst a more sympathetic Labour government was in power, however, their involvement failed to survive an incoming conservative administration. Having been used to a centralised system of collective bargaining, the Australian unions appear to have been unready when training matters were decentralised to a local level. In a country where skills development is at the forefront of the national agenda the unions clearly feel that they have something to offer. It is apparent that this view is not shared by government or employers and the unions have remained sidelined.

Although each country offers different challenges for trade unions, there are also some similarities. It is clear that even in countries such as France and Germany where there are well developed vocational training frameworks those workers who are not 'core' fall into a training gap which neither government nor organisation fills; a similar situation exists for those who work in small enterprises. It would seem that these workers provide opportunity for trade unions to engage with the training agenda both from both a social advancement viewpoint and from union growth potential.

With regards to training of their own activists, it would appear from the sample countries that trade unions across the world take this seriously, offering both skills training and a wider educational underpinning. In all of the countries, the content of the skills training is similar, focussing on the practical aspects of trade union organisation and representation. In this the countries could, to some extent, be interchangeable. When it comes to the political education of activists, however, we see some differences. In France, for example, due to the ideological underpinning of the individual unions, this aspect of trade union education is separated out. Here, the union officers at national level seek to ensure that the doctrines of their union are adhered to in the education process. Another interesting aspect of activist learning and training is the fact that in Germany the trade unionists broaden their training to include Works Councillors, albeit that many of these are also union members.

References

Australian Government (2007), *WorkChoices: A new workplace relations system.* <http://www/workchoices.gov.au/ourplan/overview?Anewworkplacerelationssytem.htm>

ABS (2006), *Labour Force Survey* Australian Bureau of Statistics <http://www.abs.gov.au/ausstats/abs@.nsf/productsbytitle/99E56147 83415356CA25713E000F92B1?OpenDocument 6202.0>. Labour Force, Australia, Nov 2006. Latest ISSUE Released at 11:30 AM (Canberra time) 07/12/2006.

ACTU (2006a), *Why is Our Prime Minister Celebrating Workers Losing Their Pay & Conditions?* ACTU Media Release, October 5th 2006.

——, (2006b), Education and Campaign Centre. <http://www.actu.asn.au/ unioneducation/default.aspx>.

Addison, J.T. Schnabel, C. and Wagner, J. (2006), *The (Parlous) State of German Unions.* Discussion Paper No 2000. March 2006. (IZA: Institute for the Study of Labour: Bonn, Germany).

Addison, J.T., Bellmann, L., Kölling, A. (2004), 'Works Councils and Plant Closings in Germany', *British Journal of Industrial Relations* 42:1, 125–148.

AEU (2006), *Campaign Facts Sheets 2006* Australian Education Union. <http://www.aeufederal.org.au/Tafe/cfs2006.html>.

AFL-CIO (2007a), *George Meany.* <http://www.aflcio.org/aboutus/history/history/ meany.cfm>.

——, (2007b), *Union Plus Education Services.* <http://www.unionplus.org/benefits/ education>.

——, (2007c), *Organizing Institute.* <http://www.aflcio.org/aboutus/oi/faqs.cfm>.

Australian Government (2007), 'WorkChoices: A New Workplace Relations System'. <http://www.workchoices.gov.au/ourplan>.

Bamber, G.L., Lansbury, R.D., and Wailes, N. (eds.) (2004), *International and Comparative Employment Relations*, 4th Edition. (Sage: London).

Bean, R. (1994), *Comparative Industrial Relations: An Introduction to Cross-national Perspectives,* 2nd Edition. (Routledge: London).

Bridgford, G. and Stirling, J. (eds.) (2000), *Trade Union Education in Europe.* (European Trade Union College: Brussels).

Brown, T. (2006), 'From Union Inspired to Industry Led: How Australian Labour's Training Reform Experiment Turned Sour, *Journal of Industrial Relations* 48:4, 491–505.

Buchanen, J., Schofield, K., Briggs, C., Considine, G., Hager, P., Hawke, G., Kitay, J., Meagher, J., Mounier, A. and Ryan, S. (2001), *Beyond Flexibility: Skills and Work in the Future.* (Sydney: New South Wales Board of Vocational Education and Training).

Buchanen, J. (2006), *From 'Skill Shortages' to Decent Work: The Role of Better Skill Ecosystems.* (Sydney: New South Wales Board of Vocational Education and Training).

Eaton, J. (2000), *Comparative Employment Relations: An Introduction.* (Polity Press: Cambridge).

EIRO (2004a), 'Collective Bargaining Reform Law Passed', *European Industrial Relations Observatory,* EIRO online. <http://www.eurofound.europa.eu/eiro/2004/04/feature/fr0404105f.html>.

——, (2004b), 'Parliament Passes Law on Training Levy', *European Industrial Relations Observatory*, EIRO online. <http:eurofound.europa.eu/eiro/2004/06/inbrief/de0406103n.html>.

——, (2006), 'Companies Intend to Overcome Skills Shortages by Providing More Training', *European Industrial Relations Observatory,* EIRO online. <http://eurofound.europa.eu/eiro/2006/02/inbrief/de0602103n.html>.

——, (2007a), 'France Industrial Relations Profile', *European Industrial Relations Observatory,* EIRO online. <http://eurofound.europa.eu/eiro/country/france_3.html>.

——, (2007b), 'Germany Industrial Relations Profile', *European Industrial Relations Observatory,* EIRO online. <http://eurofound.europa.eu/eiro/country/germany_3.html>.

——, (2007c), 'Chambers of Commerce Association Calls for Reform of Vocational Training System', *European Industrial Relations Observatory,* EIRO online. <http://eurofound.europa.eu/eiro/2007/02/articles/de0702029i.html>.

——, (2007d), 'Union Calls for More Training Opportunities for Immigrants', *European Industrial Relations Observatory,* EIRO online. <http://eurofound.europa.eu/eiro?2006/12/articles/de0612059i.html>.

Eurofound (2005), 'Report Examines Bargaining under the 2004 Social Dialogue Reform Law', *European Foundation for the Improvement of Living and Working Conditions.* <http://eurofound.europa.eu/eiro/2005/07/feature/fr0507104f.html>.

——, (2007a), 'Employers' Association: Germany', *European Foundation for the Improvement of Living and Working Conditions.* <http://www.eurofound.eu.int/emire/GERMANY/EMPLOYERSASSOCIATION-DE.html>.

——, (2007b), 'Educational Leave: Germany', *European Foundation for the Improvement of Living and Working Conditions.* <http://eurofound.europa.eu/emire/GERMANY/EDUCATIONALLEAVE-DE.html>.

Géhin, J-P., and Jobert, A. (2001), 'International Briefing 8: Training and Development in France', *International Journal of Training and Development* 5:1, 81–93.

Geoffroy, M. (2000), 'France', in Bridgford and Stirling (eds.).

Gumbrell-McCormick, R. and Hyman, R. (2006), 'Embedded Collectivism? Workplace Representation in France and Germany', *Industrial Relations Journal* 37:5, 473–491.

Goetschy, J. and Joben, A. (2004), 'Employment Relations in France' in Bamber, Lansbury, and Wailes (eds.).

GMP (2007), *GMP Memorial Scholarship Fund,* Glass, Molders, Pottery, Plastics & Allied Workers International. <http://www.gmpiu.org/pages/scholarships.aspx>.

Hassel, A. (1999), 'The erosion of industrial relations in Germany', *British Journal of Industrial Relations* 37, 483–505.

Hassel, A. (2002), 'The Erosion Continues: Reply', *British Journal of Industrial Relations* 40:2, 309–317.

Heery, H., Conley, H., Delbridge, R. and Stewart, P. (2004), 'Beyond the Enterprise: Trade Union Representation of Freelances in the UK', *Human Resource Management Journal* 14:2, 20–35.

Holland, C. and Castleton, G. (2002), 'Basic Skills and Union Activity in the UK and Australia' in Spencer (ed.).

Hollinshead G. and Leat, M. (1995), *Human Resource Management: An International and Comparative Perspective.* (Pitman Publishing: London).

Howard, J. (2006), *Transcript of the Prime Minister the Hon John Howard MP Skills for the Future Ministerial Statement to Parliament.* Prime Minister of Australia web site. <http://www.pm.gov.au/news/speeches/speech2175.html> 12th October.

Hyman, R. (2001). *Understanding European Trade Unionism: Between Market, Class & Society.* (Sage: London).

IFWEA (2007), *An Introduction to IFWEA: Who We Are, What We Do,* International Federation of Workers' Education Associations. <http://www.ifwea.org>.

ILO (1988), *Trade Unions and the ILO: A Workers' Education Manual.* 2nd Edition. (International Labour Office: Geneva).

Inagami, T. (2004), 'Changes in the Employment System and Future Labor Policies', *Japan Labor Review.* 1:1, 39–51.

Inoue, S. (1999), *Japanese Trade Unions and their Future: Opportunities and Challenges in an Era of Globalization.* Discussion paper DP/106/1999, ILO Labour and Society Programme. (International Institute for Labour Studies: Geneva).

JILPT (2006), *Labor Situation in Japan and Analysis: General Overview 2006/2007.* (Japan Institute for Labour Policy and Training: Tokyo).

Keller, B. K. (2004), 'Employment Relations in Germany' in Bamber *et al.* (eds.).

Keller, B. (2005), 'Union Formation through Merger: The Case of Ver.di in Germany', *British Journal of Industrial Relations* 43:2, 209–232.

Klikauer, T. (2002), 'Stability in Germany's Industrial Relations: A Critique of Hassel's Erosion Thesis, *British Journal of Industrial Relations* 40:2, 295–308.

– (2004), 'Trade Union Shop Floor Representation in Germany', *Industrial Relations Journal* 35:1, 2–18.

Katz, H.C. and Wheeler, H.N. (2004), 'Employment Relations in the United States of America', in Bamber, G.L. *et al.* (eds.).

Kartaş-Özkan, M. (2005), 'The Global Workforce', in Özbilgin, M. (ed.).

Kuwahara, Y. (2004), 'Employment Relations in Japan', in Bamber, G.L. *et al.* (eds.).

Lansbury, R.D. and Wailes, N. (2004), 'Employment Relations in Australia', in Bamber, G.L. *et al.* (eds.).

Leat, M. (1998), *Human Resource Issues of the European Union.* (Financial Times/ Pitman: London).

Marquardt, M.J., Nissley, N., Ozag, R. and Taylor, T.L. (2000), 'International Briefing 6: Training and Development in the United States, *International Journal of Training and Development* 4:2, 138–149.

Méhaut, P. (2005), 'Reforming the Training System in France', *Industrial Relations Journal* 36:4, 303–317.

Ministère des Affaires étrangerès (2007), *Vocational Training in France,* <http://www.diplomatie.gouv.fr/en/france-priorities_1/education-university_2274/study-in-france-grants_2275/vocational-training-in-france_2277/index.html>.

Morito, H. (2006), 'Decentralizing Decentralized Industrial Relations?: The Role of Labor Unions and Employee Representatives in Japan', in *Decentralising Industrial Relations and the Role of Labor Unions and Employee Representatives – JILPT Comparative Law Seminar.* (The Japan Institute for Labour Policy and Training Report No.3: Tokyo).

Nesbit, T. (2002), 'Education for Labour's Professionals: Britain, Canada and the USA' in Spencer (ed.).

OECD (2000), *Literacy in the Information Age: Final Report of the International Adult Literacy Survey.* (Organisation for Economic Co-operation and Development Publication Service: Paris).

Özbilgin, M. (ed.) (2005), *International Human Resource Management: Theory and Practice.* (Palgrave: London).

Parliament of New South Wales (2005), 'Industrial Relations Reforms: The Proposed National System. Briefing Paper No. 11/2005'.<http://www.parliament.nsw.gov.au/prod/parlment/publications.nsf/0/CD0630B625F4C788CA2570AC0017F742>.

Rebick, M. (2005), *The Japanese Employment System: Adapting to a New Economic Environment.* (Oxford University Press: Oxford).

RENGO (2006), *JTUC-RENGO: Role and Function.* <http://www.jtuc-rengo.org/about/index.html>.

Romer-Karrasch, M., Gehrmann, A. and Wienold, H (2000), 'Germany', in Bridgford and Stirling (eds.).

Rose, R. (1991), 'Prospective Evaluation through Comparative Analysis: Youth Training in a Time-Space Perspective', in Ryan (ed.).

Ryan, P. (ed.) (1991), *International Comparisons of Vocational Education and Training for Intermediate Skills.* (Falmer Press: London).

Spencer, B. (ed.) (2002), *Unions and Learning in a Global Economy: International and Comparative Perspectives.* (Thompson Education: Toronto).

Visser, J. (2006), 'Union Membership Statistics in 24 Countries', *Monthly Labor Review* 129:1, 38–49.

Chapter 4

Tackling the UK Skills Problem: Can Unions Make a Difference?

Caroline Lloyd and Jonathan Payne

Introduction

Since the late 1980s, training and learning has become an increasingly important topic on the agenda of British trade unions. The development of a range of union learning programmes, the creation of the union learning representative (ULR), and the forging of new 'learning partnerships' with employers, have been celebrated as a union 'success story' and a potential force for renewal. The current 'new' Labour government, committed to developing Britain as a high-skills, 'knowledge-driven' economy (see DTI 1998; DfES *et al.* 2003), has supported these developments through the creation of the Union Learning Fund (ULF) in 1998 and the provision of statutory backing for ULRs. Unions have also been offered a new position as 'stakeholders' or 'partners' within the vocational education and training (VET) system, a role they have welcomed after years of marginalisation under Conservative governments in the 1980s and 1990s.

These developments have attracted considerable academic attention, particularly from those within the employment relations field. Much of this literature has been concerned to explore unions' ability to advance an *independent* union learning agenda at workplace level, centred on employee needs, and, in doing so, capitalise on such initiatives to attract new members and activists. These are, of course, vitally important matters for a British union movement that has suffered severe decline and membership loss since the late 1970s. Not surprisingly, debates around such issues are on-going, as many chapters in this book illustrate.

Where there has been less discussion, however, is around the role that unions might play in helping to develop Britain as a 'high skills society', a concept which, as Green and Sakamoto (2001) note, lacks precise definition and is open to contestation (see also Lloyd and Payne 2003). In so far as British unions have embraced a 'high skills vision', they have tended to look mainly towards the European 'social model' and, in particular, the examples of Germany and Scandinavia. In these countries, strong trade unions, well-regulated labour markets and a robust welfare state have helped 'close-off' low wage strategies, thereby forcing employers to compete more on the basis of product quality and skills. For British trade unions, the attraction of these examples lies both in the position unions have within their social institutions and in their historical deliverance of sound economic performance together with relatively good social and distributional outcomes.

This vision has not proved attractive to the UK Labour government, however, which remains firmly wedded to flexible labour markets, arguing that 'social Europe' is too over-regulated and 'sclerotic' and must become more like Britain and the US if it is to survive in the current global economy (see Coates and Hay 2001). A convert to 'new growth theory', 'new' Labour seeks to advance its vision of a 'strong economy' and 'fairer society' through an essentially neo-liberal model of political economy that privileges investment in human capital (skills and training), whilst preserving 'the most lightly regulated labour market of any leading economy in the world' (Blair 1998, see Lloyd and Payne 2002).

This chapter begins by critically interrogating the Labour government's skills strategy, arguing that there is a tendency to load unrealistic policy expectations onto education and training, both in the economic and social spheres. Attention is drawn to the narrowness of the current policy agenda which focuses mainly on measures aimed at improving the supply of skills/qualifications, despite evidence to suggest that many British employers continue to be wedded to models of competitive advantage which limit their demand for skilled workers. The chapter then moves on to examine the way in which trade unions are positioned within this skills strategy, probing the limits of their role as both 'stakeholder' within VET institutions and 'evangelist for learning' at the workplace. While trade unions can do a great deal to help motivate, encourage and support workers in taking-up learning opportunities at work (thereby boosting skills supply), we argue that the shift towards a more inclusive high skills society requires that they challenge current policy assumptions and advance a broader agenda aimed at raising employer demand for skill. The rest of the chapter explores the extent to which UK trade unions have sought to do this, highlighting the obstacles they face and the possibilities for success.

The UK Skills Problem

Having committed itself to developing Britain as a 'knowledge economy' (see DTI 1998), 'new' Labour has joined a near universal policy consensus across the developed world (see Crouch *et al.* 1999; Brown *et al.* 2001). The core argument has been that advanced industrialised countries must seek competitive advantage on the basis of high quality, high value-added goods and services or else risk being undercut by low wage competition from abroad. For 'new' Labour, this is seen to depend critically upon developing a highly skilled and adaptable workforce that can attract high-quality inward investment as well as enable indigenous firms to pursue 'high road' business strategies. As the government's skills strategy makes clear:

> Competing on the basis of low wage costs is not an option. We must compete on the basis of our capability for innovation, enterprise, quality, and adding greater value through our products and services. *All that is dependent upon raising our skills game* (DfES *et al.* 2003, 11 [our emphasis]).

Feeding into this agenda is a range of specific UK policy concerns. These include relatively low levels of productivity, a persistent 'skills gap' with France and Germany, the exclusion of large sections of the adult workforce from education and training, limited investment in capital, R&D and innovation, and skill shortages and gaps in the labour market (see HM Treasury *et al.* 2004). The current policy narrative presents skills as one of the five drivers of productivity alongside competition, investment, innovation and enterprise. However, whereas these other elements have largely been promoted through deregulatory mechanisms, small scale incentives and a 'stable macroeconomic environment', education and training are a key target of active policy intervention and control (see Keep 2006). As the Prime Minister, Tony Blair, stated, 'education is the best economic policy we have' (DfEE 1998).

For 'new' Labour, skills are not only seen as essential for economic success, they are also regarded as fundamental to achieving a fairer and more inclusive society (see DfES *et al.* 2003; DTI 2004). In this view, it is education and training which gives individuals the ability to escape poverty, to find a job and, ultimately, to access high-quality, high-waged employment. By extending the opportunities to develop marketable skills to everyone, particularly the disadvantaged, the 'new' Labour government seeks to promote social mobility as well as address rising levels of income inequality that have blighted the UK since the late 1970s (eg. HM Treasury *et al.* 2004). The emphasis given to education and training is reflected in a plethora of initiatives aimed at raising school standards, expanding participation in post-compulsory and higher education, reforming the qualifications structure, revamping apprenticeships and changing the way in which VET is managed, delivered and funded. Current policy priorities focus on increasing the proportion of the adult workforce qualified to level two (five 'good' GCSEs or their equivalent) and meeting a 50 per cent target for the proportion of the 18–30 age cohort entering higher education by 2010.

Given the sheer scale of government activity in this area, it is perhaps hardly surprising to find that the UK has made considerable headway over the last decade in terms of the supply of skills, at least as measured by formal qualifications (for a more detailed discussion, see Keep *et al.* forthcoming). Between 1994 and 2004, the proportion of the working population in the UK qualified to degree or sub-degree level increased from 19 per cent to 26 per cent (Leitch 2005). There has also been a marked reduction in the share of adults with no qualifications, dropping from around one fifth of the working population in the mid-1990s to 14 per cent. Meanwhile, the proportion of people who lack a qualification at level two fell over the same period from 43 per cent to 33 per cent. Despite such improvements in the supply of qualifications, policy makers insist that much more still needs to be done. Other major competitors have also been investing in education and training, frequently from a higher base, while new players, notably China and India, are said to be rapidly catching up in terms of their national skill stocks. According to the Leitch Review, 'Being world class is a moving target' (Leitch 2005, 1), its authors insisting that:

> This current ambition will not go far enough to improve the UK's comparative skills base or ensure that the economy is well positioned to operate in increasingly competitive global markets. It will not go far enough to improve social justice (Leitch 2005, 11).

While skills clearly have an important role in improving economic performance, there is a real danger that their contribution becomes overplayed to the neglect of other factors that are also needed. Research indicates that for effective utilisation, skills must be combined with other elements, such as investment in innovation and research and development, high quality product market strategies and appropriate forms of work organisation and management approaches (Keep and Mayhew 1998; Brown *et al.* 2001). Where these wider elements are lacking or deficient, providing firms with a more highly skilled or qualified workforce may produce, at best, only very limited results.

British policy makers have tended to assume, however, that the UK is confronted with a major 'skills crisis', and it is the lack of skills supply which hinders performance and prevents firms from adopting new technologies and moving into higher value added product markets (HM Treasury and DfES 2002). The evidence for such convictions, however, remains questionable. Are UK firms really being held back by a lack of skilled workers? According to the 2005 National Employer Skills Survey (LSC 2006a), just 4 per cent of the firms surveyed reported having any 'skill shortage vacancies'. The incidence of 'skills gaps', where members of the workforce are deemed to lack sufficient skills for their current job role, fell from 22 per cent of establishments in 2003 to 16 per cent in 2005, accounting for just 6 per cent of the workforce. Furthermore, nearly three quarters of these 'skill gaps' were transitory in that they applied to new recruits or recently promoted staff.

Furthermore, evidence indicates that many employers may be failing to make full and effective use of the skills already available to them. According to WERS 2004, over half of employees surveyed considered that the skills they possessed were higher than those required to do their current job (Kersley *et al.* 2006). Other research indicates that the workforce is becoming increasingly overqualified (Green 2006). The 2001 UK Skills Survey estimates that there were 6.4 million people qualified to level 3 but only 4 million jobs in the economy that demanded these qualifications on entry (Felstead *et al.* 2002). With the expansion of higher education, there has been some concern as to whether there are sufficient 'graduate' jobs for the current cohort, let *al.*one for a world of 50 per cent participation (Wolf 2002; Keep and Mayhew 2004). In one of the few qualitative studies undertaken, Mason (2002, 454) found that in parts of the UK service economy, the under-utilisation of graduate skills may already be something of a problem, noting that:

> ... the scope for new job upgrading of a permanent kind in service industries now appears to be limited. Large numbers of jobs filled by non-mainstream graduates have not been modified in response to the greater availability of graduates.

It seems that employers are not necessarily adjusting the way they utilise their employees in response to improvements in their qualification or skill levels. On the basis of current evidence, the supply of skills in the UK, though still lagging behind competitors such as France and Germany, would seem to be broadly in line with, if not actually higher than, the underlying level of employer demand across the economy as a whole.

Rather than the UK 'skills problem' being simply one of a poorly educated and trained workforce, some commentators argue that it reflects deep structural weaknesses in the British economy that serve to limit or depress employer demand for higher level skills (see Keep and Mayhew 1998; Coffield 1999; Lauder 1999; Brown *et al.* 2001; Lloyd and Payne 2002). As a recent DTI report observes, outside of pharmaceuticals and aerospace, the bulk of large UK firms are located in sectors that are low or very low in research and development intensity (DTI 2005). These sectors, such as food production and hotels and hospitality for example, tend to have higher concentrations of low skilled workers. At the same time, there is evidence to suggest that a relatively high proportion of UK firms continue to compete through 'neo-Fordist' production approaches centred on standardised goods and services delivered by a predominantly low skill, low wage workforce (Keep and Mayhew 1998), and are trapped in, what Finegold and Soskice (1988) originally labelled, 'the low skill equilibrium'. Porter and Ketels' (2003) report into the UK's productivity problem also drew attention to the dangers of the UK's reliance upon being a relatively low cost base for production in Europe and argued that there was a need for a 'step-change' to a new business model competing primarily on innovation and value-added.

Firms adopting cost-driven strategies are not necessarily pursuing an irrational approach as many are successful and have little incentive to change. As a recent study makes clear:

> ... for many of these organisations, their current strategies are, at least for the time being, delivering the desired results, in terms of profitability and business success. They are not failing businesses ... The research indicates that, currently at least, there is a thriving marketplace for goods and services sold on the basis of low cost and supported by low wages (Wilson and Hogarth 2003, 10).

If these firms are doing reasonably well where they are, then it seems unlikely that simply supplying them with more skilled or qualified labour will encourage any substantive shift towards innovative or quality-based business strategies. Furthermore, it would be mistaken to assume that such companies will necessarily be compelled to change as a result of global competitive pressures. Many sectors, for example hotels, predominantly operate in national or local markets that are rarely exposed to international competition (Mason 2004). The latest WERS findings report that only one quarter of workplaces face competition from overseas-based suppliers (Kersley *et al.* 2006).

Current labour market trends also cast doubt on the view that low skilled work is gradually being phased out as Britain enters a new era of knowledge-driven growth. On the contrary, while there has certainly been an expansion of professional and managerial occupations, this has occurred alongside a rapid increase in jobs affording low pay, little training, and few progression opportunities, prompting some commentators to speak of the emergence of a polarised or 'hourglass economy' (see Nolan 2001; Goos and Manning 2003). Indeed, the fastest growing jobs (in absolute numbers) in the 1990s were not those of highly skilled, semi-independent 'knowledge workers' but shelf-stackers, sales assistants, hairdressers, nursery nurses, prison officers and domestic house-keepers (Nolan 2000).

Other evidence indicates that the UK retains significant numbers of jobs that demand less than a Level 2 qualification, regarded by government as the minimum platform for 'employability'. The second UK Skills Survey estimated that in 2001 there were 6.5 million jobs in the UK, or over one quarter of the total, that did not require a single qualification to obtain them (Felstead *et al.* 2002, 11). A more recent survey of 412 employers for the Learning and Skills Council (LSC) found that nearly three quarters of companies would consider hiring staff who did not have five good GCSEs or their vocational equivalent (LSC 2006). Moreover, with retailing and personal and protective services also predicted to be major areas of job growth for the foreseeable future (Campbell 2001), low skilled work looks set to maintain a sizeable presence within the UK economy.

Given the increasingly bifurcated labour market, it is all the more important to consider how far education and training can function as the principal mechanism through which to solve the problems of income inequality and social mobility. If the supply of 'good jobs' remains finite, the best that education may be able to do is move certain individuals up and down the job queue (Brown 2003). Its ability to transform current labour market structures, either by reducing the proportion of low skill, low wage jobs on offer within the economy or raising the pay and quality of those jobs at the bottom end, would seem extremely limited. As long as 'bad jobs' exist someone will inevitably have to do them. Furthermore, despite improvements in educational attainment at all levels, inter-generational social mobility has actually declined over the last twenty years (Blanden *et al.* 2005). This has been linked to rising levels of income inequality, together with the ability of the middle-classes to play the new 'market for education' and ensure that their offspring continue to gain access to elite schools and universities that are often a ticket to the 'best' jobs in the labour market (Wolf 2002; Brown 2003; Keep and Mayhew 2004).

The limitations of the government's skills strategy has led several commentators to argue for a much broader range of policy interventions, including measures designed to impact on the 'demand-side' of the skills equation (see Coffield 1999; Keep 2000; Lloyd and Payne 2002; Wilson and Hogarth 2003). A recent report for the Sector Skills Development Agency, concludes that:

> … although supply-side improvements in the provision of education and training are no doubt a prerequisite [for a high skills economy in the UK], the more important factor is stimulating the demand among employers for more highly skilled workers, with concomitant changes in training and product strategy that this implies (Beaven *et al.* 2005, v).

The kind of policy interventions that might be deployed to stimulate employer demand for skills remains controversial, even among those academics who subscribe to the general principle (see Coffield 2004; Lloyd and Payne 2006). Arguments have been made in favour of licence to practice, the use of public procurement to raise standards, and an industrial strategy aimed at promoting investment and research and development in innovative and quality-based sectors and companies.

Some commentators, however, also claim that a fundamental part of the problem resides with the UK's flexible labour market and weakened trade unions, and that there is a need for government to deploy stronger regulatory levers aimed at denying employers the opportunity to compete through low wage, low skills strategies

(Keep 1999; 2000; Lauder 1999; Lloyd and Payne 2002). Beaven *et al.* (2005, 51) conclude, for example, that although the state may be able to use 'demonstration, promotion and exhortation' to encourage employers to take the 'high road', 'some sticks and carrots may be needed as well. This might include raising the minimum wage to force employers to move to ways of working that are high skill rather than low skill'. Attention has also been drawn to the detrimental role played by the UK's financial markets in encouraging employers to pursue short-term profit maximisation at the expense of the long-term investment that might enable firms to move to more innovative and quality-based business strategies (Hutton 1995). Shareholder-driven capitalism is not necessarily an obstacle to a high skills route for some firms (as the example of California's high skill clusters demonstrates), but it may still act as a powerful constraint for the overwhelming majority (Streeck 1989).

While academics have put forward various policy recommendations aimed at addressing employer demand for skill, they inevitably clash with the current skills supply orthodoxy and the more neo-liberal elements within the Labour government's political economy. The result is an impasse or stalemate, with a meaningful debate on the issues impeded by the prevailing ideological and political parameters within which policy is constructed (for a discussion, see Keep 2006). This is not only a problem for many within the academic community; it is also a challenge for trade unions seeking to advance their vision of an inclusive 'high skills society' in the UK. The next two sections explore the extent to which trade unions have been willing and able to engage policy makers on these issues.

Trade Unions and the 'Supply-side'

We begin by examining the role and influence that trade unions currently have within the VET system and workplace learning (i.e. on the 'supply-side' of the skills equation), focusing mainly on the situation in England. The discussion is structured around three questions. First, how far have unions been able to influence the direction and delivery of VET policy through their new institutional position? Second, what challenges have unions faced in terms of developing an independent learning agenda at workplace level? Third, having embraced their role as partner or supporter of the government's skills strategy, have unions been able to avoid dependence upon state funding and retain a critical voice within skills policy?

Unions and the VET System

Unions emerged from a long period of Conservative rule at the end of 1990s to find themselves almost completely marginalised within VET institutions. The corporatist training system, developed since the 1960s, had been dismantled, as tripartite structures, such as Industrial Training Boards, with their powers to levy firms and give grants, together with the Manpower Services Commission, were abolished in the 1980s. The election of 'new' Labour to government in 1997, promised a new style of politics and a government at least willing to engage with trade unions (amid the rhetoric of 'social partnership'), even if it had rejected any return to the quasi-corporatism of its 'old Labour' past. There were two key elements to unions' role within skills policy - as 'stakeholders' within the VET institutional framework and as 'brokers' to encourage learning within the workplace.

Today, unions are represented on most of the new VET institutions created by the Labour government. These include the Learning and Skills Council (LSC) and the 47 local LSCs, established in 2001 with overall responsibility for funding post-compulsory education and training (excluding higher education). The newly-formed Sector Skills Councils (SSCs), although designed as 'employer-led' bodies, allow for a relevant trade union to have a seat on the board and, in sectors where unions have an established presence, they have also been involved in the formulation of new 'sector skills agreements' as well as Regional Skills Partnerships. Alongside these regional and sector bodies, the TUC has also been given a role in the national Skills Alliance, established in 2003 to advise government on the progress and implementation of its skill strategy and promoted as an example of the government's new 'social partnership' approach (DfES *et al.* 2003, 22).

While unions now have a higher profile in VET than they did before 'new' Labour entered office, the extent of their current engagement falls far short of what might reasonably be described as social partnership (at least as far as that term is understood in the rest of Europe). It is clear from the skills white paper (DfES *et al.* 2005), for example, that the VET system was never intended to be genuinely tripartite or partnership-based, with the government's main aim being to work 'in partnership with employers by putting *their* needs and priorities centre stage in the design and delivery of training for adults' (part 1:9). Although the TUC initially welcomed their new institutional role, it now openly concedes that there is a 'lack of a robust social partnership approach to skills' (TUC 2006a, 15), insisting that a stronger trade union voice is needed.

Having just one seat on key institutions, such as SSCs, is considered by the unions to be a serious constraint, although it is unclear how much of a difference simply boosting union representation would make. The very way in which these bodies are funded, together with their terms of reference, indicate that, despite the rhetoric of an 'employer-led' training system, it is the state which is the dominant player. As Keep (2006, 51) argues, the SSCs are 'state-licensed entities, receiving their core funding from government and expected to respond (positively) towards delivering national programmes and targets, the design and setting of which they have played no role'. Similarly, the LSCs exist to meet central government targets and to deliver pre-determined policy objectives. The same may also be said of the Skills Alliance which meets but twice a year, and whose remit is to act as a 'high profile champion for the Skills Strategy'.

A brief glance across the channel to the role that trade unions play within most other European nations identifies the UK's continued exceptionalism and the weakness of British-style social partnership. In Germany, the Netherlands and the Nordic countries, for example, corporatist structures mean equal representation for both employers and trade unions on bodies that are established to deal with skill and training matters (Crouch *et al.* 1999; Sung *et al.* 2006). Although company-level collective bargaining over training is relatively rare, unions play a substantial role in the management of the training system whether in tripartite or bipartite bodies at national and/or sectoral level in France, Germany, the Netherlands, Belgium, Sweden and Norway (amongst others). The unions receive an equal number of seats or an equivalent role to employers, even when the VET system is essentially managed by the state and the social partners act in an advisory capacity, as in the case of Greece and Portugal (see Noble 1997; EIRO 1998; Crouch *et al.* 1999; Sung *et al.* 2006). The most extensive engagement would appear to be at sectoral level, particularly in those countries that have industry-level collective bargaining arrangements. It is primarily at this level that issues around occupational requirements, the teaching and certifying of training and qualifications and the definition of training standards are addressed.

Workplace Learning

While UK unions may be somewhat disappointed with their limited involvement at a strategic and policy-making level, they have nevertheless been keen to celebrate their new role in promoting learning at the workplace. The central union innovation has been the establishment of a new cadre of union lay official – the union learning representative (ULR) – which received statutory backing in 2002 and has drawn major financial support through the Union Learning Fund (managed by the LSC). As the government has stressed on a number of occasions, the essential role of the unions is to 'encourage and enable adults to learn' (DfES *et al.* 2003, 42; 2005 Part 1:9*)*. The TUC estimates that 13,000 ULRs have been trained and over 450 ULF projects covering over 3000 workplaces have received funding, with more than 67,000 learners able to access courses each year through these projects (TUC 2006b). In 2006, Unionlearn was established, with funding from the DfES, to take over the management of the ULF as well as run union representative training and wider learning.

The main role allotted to unions at the workplace has been that of an evangelist for skills, encouraging and supporting individuals' access to learning, particularly disadvantaged groups who have often fared badly within mainstream schooling and who may receive few, if any, training opportunities from their employer. Many unions have been keen to embrace this role both on equity grounds and because it is seen to offer a window for union revitalisation and renewal (Sutherland and Rainbird 2000). A key question has been the extent to which unions have been able to withstand and broaden a narrow employer-driven agenda around the skill needs of the firm and create opportunities for workers to access broader forms of learning that support employability, progression to better jobs and personal development (see Munro and Rainbird 2004a).

There is no denying that in terms of forging an *independent* union learning agenda around worker needs, there have been some notable successes. As many other chapters in this book demonstrate, unions have been able to open up learning opportunities that can have a genuinely transformative effect on people's lives. The programmes run by the public sector union, Unison, such as Return to Learn, sometimes in partnership with employers, are among the best and most frequently cited examples (see Kennedy 1995; Munro and Rainbird 2004b). Recent evaluations of the ULF as well as TUC case studies indicate that there are also many other areas where unions can demonstrate good practice (Thompson *et al.* 2006).

Yet, such successes should not blind us to the limited nature and extent of unions' ability to influence levels of training and learning in the UK. Although nearly 40 per cent of employees have access to a union lay representative, employers only negotiate in 3 per cent of workplaces and consult in a further 13 per cent of workplaces over training issues (Kersley *et al.* 2006, 194). In smaller workplaces and across large parts of private sector services, such as hotels, hospitality, leisure and entertainment, where skills levels are often fairly basic, unions are simply not present to make a difference. Even where unions are recognised, many private sector employers are resistant to learning agreements, with ULRs finding it difficult to challenge employer attempts to steer the learning agenda towards their own priorities (see Wallis *et al.* 2005; Calveley *et al.* 2003; Moore and Wood 2005).

Union calls for a new 'post-voluntary' or statutory framework (Unison 2003; TUC 2005) places a right to bargain over training as a key demand. Even if unions were to achieve this, however, to be truly effective such a right would still need to be backed up with organisational capacity at the workplace and bargaining strength. Furthermore, it may be recalled that in other European countries with the relevant legal rights, collective bargaining over training at workplace level is relatively rare. Training and skills are normally considered to be sectoral issues which, if devolved to the firm, can lead to predominantly narrow firm-specific training (Culpepper 1999). It is questionable whether British trade unions are in a strong enough position to avoid such problems. Moreover, following the collapse of multi-employer bargaining in Britain in the 1980s, the idea of a return to any form of sectoral engagement with trade unions, even over relatively 'safe' issues like training, remains an anathema to most employers (see Terry 2003).

Retaining a Critical Union Perspective on Skills Policy

While unions have welcomed government funding for union learning activity, being dependent upon the public purse poses further difficulties and challenges. The budget for Unionlearn in 2006–7 stood at over £10m and is expected to rise to £22.5m in 2008–9, by which time it will be receiving 95 per cent of its funds from the state and its various quangos (TUC 2006c). Such dependence upon state support questions the sustainability of union learning activity which would be threatened were a Conservative government to return to power or 'new' Labour decided to reduce or sever funding.

Linked to this is the question of how far unions, in embracing their role as 'partners' in the government's skills strategy, may have restricted their ability to critique policy initiatives the purpose and rationale for which remains seriously in doubt. A good example is the Treasury's Employer Training Pilots (ETPs) currently being rolled out nationally through the National Employer Training Programme ('Train to Gain'). ETPs were originally designed as a way of addressing alleged 'market failure' by offering public subsidies to employers who allowed workers 'time off' to acquire basic skills or a first Level 2 qualification (see HM Treasury 2002). Official evaluations indicate that ETPs have generated high levels of 'deadweight', estimated at anywhere between 60–100 per cent (see Abramovsky *et al.* 2005), effectively subsidising training that employers would have paid for in any case. Despite this, such initiatives continue to draw an enthusiastic response from the TUC. In addition, some commentators have expressed concerns that the TUC has focused too much energy on supporting the take-up of low level NVQs in accordance with government targets (see Munro and Rainbird 2004a), despite these qualifications attracting no discernible wage premium (Dearden *et al.* 2004) and being mainly concerned with the accreditation of prior learning rather than 'training'.

The absence of a critical union voice in respect of the more questionable aspects of current skills policy raises the danger of unions becoming trapped, or ghettoised, within the government's skills supply strategy. Does being a partner in skills policy require unions to share many of the assumptions that drive policy in this area? Alternatively, can unions challenge such assumptions and push for policies that move beyond simply boosting the supply of qualifications and address issues of skill demand and utilisation? The next section explores how far unions have sought to do so and what further scope there might be for trade unions to advance a 'demand-side' approach to the UK skills problem.

Fronting Up to the 'Demand-side'

Trade unions have long criticised the weakness of the UK VET system, yet it is only recently that the problem of employer demand for skill has figured prominently in their policy analyses. In response to the 2003 Porter report, the TUC acknowledged that government needed to do more to tackle weak employer demand for skill 'through support for innovation and through encouraging organisations… to raise their game, including a higher national minimum wage to wean management off its low pay crutch' (TUC 2003,18). The UK's weak regulatory and institutional framework and the short-termism of the business environment were also emphasised as detrimental to shifting businesses onto the 'high road'. More recently, the TUC has argued:

> we know that upskilling the workforce is just one side of the coin. Effective skills utilisation is the other side of the coin and varied research has highlighted that there is a 'low skills equilibrium' in the UK, with too many employees trapped in low-spec jobs with limited opportunities for development in their particular workplace even if they do receive training (TUC 2005, 8).

Some constituent unions, such as Amicus, the GMB and Unison have also picked up on elements of the low skill equilibrium analysis (Unison 2003; Amicus 2003; GMB 2004). Amicus, a union that represents many members in the manufacturing sector, has the most comprehensive analysis, arguing for a broad range of policies designed to shift the UK to a high value-added economy. These include establishing a national investment bank, increasing expenditure on research and development, providing support for exporters and strengthening labour market regulations. On the latter point, Amicus insists:

> if the UK is to stop competing on a low-cost, low-quality basis, it must stop making it so cheap and easy to fire its workers' (Amicus 2003, 28).

In the same vein, the GMB argues for a higher National Minimum Wage 'to address the low pay, low skill, low productivity vicious circle' (2004, 1).

Despite acknowledging the validity of the demand-side analysis, unions have not found it easy to advance a consistent and coherent argument in favour of a demand-side agenda. There are times, for example, when the TUC appears to accept the conventional policy wisdom that an increase in the supply of skills and training might jolt the UK out of the low skills equilibrium:

> To break out of this trap the UK desperately needs to develop a consensus that employers have an obligation to train their employees to meet the requirements of the present jobs (TUC 2006d, 23).

There seems to be an acceptance of the argument that the UK suffers from widespread 'skills shortages' and 'market failures', alongside general praise for Employer Training Pilots and the 50 per cent higher education target (Unison 2003; TUC 2006a; 2006e; Clough 2004). The latter is particularly surprising given that one consequence of such a target maybe to further weaken and undermine the UK's already marginalised and low status work-based route for young people (see Keep and Mayhew 2004). The general view appears to be that, in the area of qualifications, more is necessarily better. Recently, however, Amicus (2006) has voiced strong criticism of the weakness and paucity of some low level NVQs, accusing the government of adopting 'a 'Tesco' approach to skills training – stack them high and sell them cheap'. Even so there is no clear trade union voice which consistently argues that improving the supply of qualified labour will only make a fundamental difference if there are jobs created at the requisite level for these workers to fill. Indeed, in embracing their role as a partner and supporter of the government's skills supply strategy, it remains difficult for unions to make this case without being seen to undermine, or be in opposition to, the strategy itself.

How might trade unions adopt an alternative approach towards the skills agenda and what could be achieved? To explore these possibilities, it is helpful to examine the role of trade unions in other countries with more success in developing higher skilled work and higher value added production strategies. In countries, such as Germany and Scandinavia for example, strong trade unions and sectoral wage bargaining, underpinned and supported by the state, have played a vital role in forcing employers to adopt high quality, skill-intensive production strategies that can absorb and accommodate relatively high labour costs. As Streeck (1992, 31–32) has argued:

> … whereas German institutional rigidities have largely foreclosed adjustment to price-competitive markets, they have at the same time and instead forced, induced and enabled managements to embark on more demanding high value-added diversified quality production strategies.

In Germany, training is subject both to codetermination at the level of the firm and to corporatist governance structures at the national level that ensure standardised and rigorously enforced curricula and rules regarding the organisation of work (see also Culpepper 1999).

In the UK, such 'beneficial constraints' (Streeck 1997), aimed at supporting 'high road' approaches, are either absent or relatively weak. The lack of sectoral collective bargaining and codetermination arrangements within the firm, combined with the current weakness of workplace organisation, severely constrain the ability of unions to block-off low wage routes to competitiveness. The limited nature of collective institutions of both unions and employers, particularly at sectoral level, has long been considered a major barrier to a restructuring of the UK economy based on high skills and high wages (see for example Nolan 1989; Soskice 1993). More recently, Keep (1999, 343) has argued that the capacity of British unions to act as an agency for intervention in raising the demand for skills is problematic as they are 'weak and lack the support of any statutory model of social partnership'.

An alternative approach is one in which the state plays a more prominent role in shaping firms' competitive and production approaches. In France, for example, in the frequent absence of social partners willing to 'bargain in good faith', the state has been forced to step in to ensure industrial and social stability. This has resulted in relatively high labour costs, the 35 hour working week, strong employment regulations, a training levy and the extension of collective bargaining agreements to non-participatory firms. In addition, a long-term industrial policy provides support for key companies and strategically important industries. These incentives and constraints, together with a robust welfare state, have combined to produce consistently high levels of productivity, alongside lower levels of poverty and inequality than those found in the UK. The question is how might unions go about this within the UK, confronted with a Labour government firmly wedded to a neo-liberal growth paradigm centred on flexible capital and labour markets and a marginal role for the state in areas such as industrial policy. This challenge is made harder still by the decline that trade unions have suffered since the late 1970s, and a weakening union-Party link under 'new' Labour, with unions repositioned as simply 'one pressure group among many' (see Ludlam *et al.* 2002).

Can unions, then, advance a 'demand-side' agenda *within* existing political and policy constraints, what might this consist of, and what are the limits of such an agenda likely to be? One starting point could be to encourage policy makers to adopt initiatives, similar to those found in some other European countries, aimed at developing innovative forms of work organisation that may make for better use of workers' skills and capabilities. The Finnish Workplace Development Programme, launched in 1996 with the support of the social partners, provides a useful example of what can be done in this area, albeit within a different institutional context (Payne 2004; Alasoini 2006). The Programme funds the use of external experts in various projects aimed at achieving a holistic change in an organisation's entire mode of operation (management approaches, work design, HR practices, skills and training), involving the whole workforce in the process.

Another interesting innovation for unions to draw upon is that of Australia's 'skills-ecosystem projects', which explicitly target productivity and performance, skill development and decent work in specific sectors or regions (Buchanen *et al.* 2001; Buchanen 2006; Windsor 2006). A key aim of the pilot projects is to encourage investment not in skills alone but in bundles of innovative practice that help develop and utilise a skilled workforce. The projects seek to join up the design and delivery of business support and skills support for firms, so that skills are linked into broader issues of business strategy, technology, job design and employment systems. The idea is to encourage industry stakeholders to take ownership of skill development rather than rely on the state to simply supply them with more skills through the VET system. As such it favours solutions that focus on the type and level of skills that are likely to be required in particular sectors and firms. This kind of targeted approach may offer an important corrective to the UK's blanket 'one-size fits all' policies aimed at simply increasing the stock of graduates or those holding a Level 2 qualification (see Keep *et al.* forthcoming).

Another option is for unions themselves to engage directly with employers by attempting to integrate workplace learning with job redesign. The public sector has already seen a major innovation in this area with the NHS's 'skills escalator' and Changing Workforce Programme (CWP). The former links training explicitly into career development, while the CWP was aimed at redesigning actual job roles in order to improve patient care and to expand the skills and autonomy of workers. However, despite union representation at a national level, very few of the thirteen CWP pilot sites had any trade union involvement (McBride *et al.* 2005). With the project ending in April 2006, there appears to have been little promotion of the programme by the unions involved or evaluation of the lessons that could be learnt.

A disappointment for unions must be the lack of engagement of workplace union representatives in the majority of the NHS pilot projects on job redesign. Union Learning Representatives ought to be in the ideal position to link these wider issues of skill utilisation, job design and progression opportunities to their current activities around workplace learning. To date, their role has not been identified in this way, reflected in the lack of courses and guidance for learning reps in terms of how they might seek to raise issues with management over the way that jobs could be reconfigured to utilise higher levels of skill. Providing ULRs with an awareness and training in this area, however, does not mean that management will respond positively. Some employers are already hostile to learning reps and many may not welcome an enlargement of their role to include issues of job redesign. In addition, previous experience of general partnership agreements indicates that success is unlikely to be forthcoming if based upon union weakness (Martinez Lucio and Stuart 2002; Kelly 2004; Oxenbridge and Brown 2004). Despite these challenges, it would seem essential that unions strive to link up their learning activities to a wider agenda around workplace and work organisation development.

By focussing greater attention on issues of business strategy, job design and management approaches, unions could help prise the policy debate on skills away from the existing supply-side mentality. After a quarter of a century of skill supply initiatives (see Mansfield 2000), this would be no mean achievement. However, the difficulties of advancing the policy agenda even this far are considerable given current political and policy assumptions. Moreover, even if such gains were achieved these types of approaches would not establish the 'beneficial constraints' that are also necessary to push firms to 'raise their game', nor would they address the problems of a highly polarised labour market and rising social inequality. This would require a break with the neo-liberal growth model and a much stronger regulatory approach on the part of government, something a weakened trade union movement has found difficult to advance in the face of opposition from both state and capital (see Lloyd and Payne 2002).

Conclusion

In recent years, British trade unions have presented themselves as an active force for learning within the workplace, a role that has been welcomed and supported by the 'new' Labour government as part of its mission to develop the UK as a 'high skills economy'. While their position within the VET system remains far weaker than that of many other continental European countries, the unions can still identify many examples of where they are making a real difference to people's lives by helping them to access learning opportunities. Indeed, there is evidence to suggest that such initiatives can be a potential force for union revitalisation and renewal, although much would seem to depend on strong workplace union organisation already being in place.

In policy terms, the main role allotted to unions has been that of promoting training and learning at work, or boosting the supply of skills. Despite this, unions have been receptive to arguments that the UK suffers from a problem with employer demand for skill, linked to institutional and labour market factors that help support and sustain low wage routes to accumulation. The examples of countries such as Germany and Scandinavia, where strong trade unions and regulatory regimes help close-off 'low road' competitive strategies, have been central to the unions' own economic and social vision for Britain, inspired by 'social market Europe'. A major obstacle to this project has been 'new' Labour itself which has tied its colours to an American business model of labour market flexibility and untrammelled global competition, and has been extremely reluctant to confront business interests. This is the interface at which the tensions between 'new' Labour's 'high skills' project and that of British trade unions are most apparent.

In accepting their role as 'stakeholder' or 'partner' with the government's current skills supply strategy, unions have often found it difficult to advance a consistent and coherent argument in favour of a broader 'demand-side' approach to the UK's skill problem. There has sometimes been a confusion of message, with unions accepting the policy rhetoric of a 'skills crisis', in one breath, and arguing that there is a 'low skills equilibrium' problem and a crisis of employer demand for skill, in the next. Policy assumptions have been left unchallenged, while the merits of publicly-subsidised employer training through ETPs and 'Train to Gain' have not been subject to full critical scrutiny. To move the agenda forward requires unions to be more discerning, being supportive of programmes for labour up-skilling where they are positive and well thought through, but also insisting that additional courses and qualifications are not going to have a fundamental impact on labour market structures, income inequalities or the quality of jobs at the bottom end. While unions have voiced demand-side arguments, they have found it difficult to direct them into a sustained critique of the limitations of 'new' Labour's skill supply strategy, fearing perhaps that to do so would jeopardise their current position and risk further marginalisation.

The chapter has highlighted some ways in which unions might attempt to advance a limited demand-side approach, by focusing policy attention on issues such as job design, management and the utilisation of skill, and ensuring that their own learning representatives are trained to deal with such issues at the workplace. A further possibility is that unions may seek to use the new framework of devolved government in the UK in a bid to shape policy discussions in Scotland, Wales and Northern Ireland, where political actors may be more open to new ideas and directions. Even if unions could help to secure progress on this agenda, however, it would still be within the constraints imposed by the current neo-liberal growth model and a UK labour market increasingly polarised in terms of job quality and incomes. It is vitally important, therefore, that unions continue to highlight the long-term economic and social implications of the present model, the limitations of 'new' Labour's supply-side project and the range of reforms that are necessary to develop a genuinely inclusive high skills society in the UK.

Acknowledgement

The authors which to acknowledge that this research was financially supported by the ESRC centre on Skills, Knowledge and Organisational Performance.

References

Abramovsky, L., Battistin, E., Fitzsimons, E., Goodman, A. and Simpson, H. (2005), *The Impact of the Employer Training Pilots on the Take-up of Training Among Employers*. Research Report No. 694. (Nottingham: DfES).

Alasoini, T. (2006), 'In Search of Generative Results: A New Generation of Programmes to Develop Work Organization', *Economic and Industrial Democracy*, 27, 9–37.

Amicus (2006), 'Taxpayers 'mugged' on skills says Amicus', Press release 13 September. (London: Amicus).

——, (2003), *Rebuilding UK Manufacturing*. (London: Amicus).

Beaven, R., Bosworth, D., Lewney, R. and Wilson, R. (2005), *Alternative Skills Scenarios to 2020 for the UK Economy: A report for the Sector Skills Development Agency, as a Contribution to the Leitch Review of Skills*. (Cambridge: Cambridge Econometrics).

Blair, T. (1998), 'Foreword', DTI White Paper, *Fairness At Work*. (London: HMSO).

Blanden, J., Gregg, P. and Machin, S. (2005), 'Social Mobility in Britain: Low and Falling', *CentrePiece*, Spring.

Brown, P. (2003), 'The Opportunity Trap: Education and Employment in a Global Economy', *European Educational Research Journal*, 2:1, 142–180.

Brown, P., Green, A. and Lauder, H. (2001), *High Skills: Globalisation, Competitiveness and Skill Formation*. (Oxford: Oxford University Press).

Buchanen, J., Schofield, K., Briggs, C., Considine, G., Hager, P., Hawke, G., Kitay, J., Meagher, J., Mounier, A. and Ryan, S. (2001), *Beyond Flexibility: Skills and*

Work in the Future. (Sydney: New South Wales Board of Vocational Education and Training).

Buchanan, J. (2006), *From 'Skill Shortages' to Decent Work: The Role of Better Skill Ecosystems*. (Sydney: New South Wales Board of Vocational Education and Training).

Calveley, M., Healy, G., Shelley, S., Stirling, J. and Wray, D. (2003), 'Union Learning Representatives – A Force for Renewal or 'Partnership'? Working Paper Ref: UHBS 2003:10. (Business School, University of Hertfordshire).

Campbell, M. (2001), *Skills In England 2001 – The Key Messages*. (Nottingham: DfES).

Clough, B. (2004), 'From Spearholders to Stakeholders. The Emerging Role of Unions in the UK Learning and Skills System', in Cooney and Stuart (eds.).

Coates, D. and Hay, C. (2001), 'Home and Away? The Political Economy of New Labour', paper presented to the ESRC Labour Studies Seminar: The State and Labour, University of Warwick, 28–29 March.

Coffield, F. (1999), 'Breaking the Consensus: Lifelong Learning as Social Control', *British Journal of Educational Research*, 25:4, 579–497.

——, (2004), 'Alternative Routes out of the Low Skills Equilibrium: A Rejoinder to Lloyd and Payne', *Journal of Education Policy*, 19:6, 733–740.

Cooney, R. and Stuart, M. (eds.) (2004), *Trade Unions and Training: Issues and International Perspectives* (Caulfield, Australia: National Key Centre in Industrial Relations, Monash University).

Crouch, C. Finegold, D. and Sako, M. (1999), *Are Skills the Answer? The Political Economy of Skill Creation in Advanced Industrial Societies*. (Oxford: Oxford University Press).

Culpepper, P. and Finegold, D. (eds.) (1999), *The German Skills Machine*. (New York, Berghahn Books).

Culpepper, P. (1999), 'Individual Choice, Collective Action and the Problem of Training Reform' in Culpepper and Finegold (eds).

Dearden, L., McGranahan, L. and Sianesi, B. (2004), 'An In-depth Analysis of the Returns to National Vocational Qualifications obtained at Level 2' Centre for the Economics of Education Discussion Paper No. 46. (London: LSE).

DfEE (Department for Education and Employment) (1998), *The Learning Age: A Renaissance for a New Britain*. (Sheffield: DfEE).

DfES, DTI, HM Treasury and DWP (2003), *21st Century Skills: Realising Our Potential: Individuals, Employers, Nation*. (London: HMSO).

——, (2005), *Skills: Getting on in Business, Getting on at Work*. (London: HMSO).

Dickens, R. Gregg, P. and Wadsworth J. (eds.) *The Labour Market Under New Labour*. (London: Palgrave).

DTI (Department of Trade and Industry) (1998), *Our Competitive Future: Building the Knowledge-driven Economy*. (London: HMSO).

——, (2004), *Department of Trade and Industry Five Year Programme: Creating Wealth from Knowledge*. (London: DTI).

——, (2005), *R&D Intensive Businesses in the UK*, DTI Economics Paper No.11. (London: HM Treasury).

EIRO (European Industrial Relations Observatory) (1998), *Collective Bargaining and Continuing Vocational Training in Europe.* www.eiro.eurofound.eu.int.

Felstead, A., Gallie, D. and Green, F. (2002), *Work Skills in Britain 1986–2001,* (Nottingham: DfES).

Finegold, D. and Soskice, D. (1988), 'The Failure of Training in Britain: Analysis and Prescription', *Oxford Review of Economic Policy*, 4:3, 21–53.

GMB (2004), *Evidence to the Low Pay Commission's fifth review of the National Minimum Wage.* (London, GMB).

Goos, M. and Manning, A. (2003), 'McJobs and MacJobs: The Growing Polarisation of Jobs in the UK Labour Market', in Dickens *et al.* (eds.).

Green, F. (2006), *Demanding Work: The Paradox of Job Quality in the Affluent Economy.* (Woodstock: Princeton University Press).

Green, A. and Sakamoto, A. (2001), 'Models of High Skills in National Competition Strategies', in Brown *et al.* (eds.).

Healy, G., Heery, E., Taylor, P. and Brown, W. (eds.) (2004), *The Future of Worker Representation.* (London: Palgrave/MacMillan).

HM Treasury (2002), *Developing Workforce Skills: Piloting a New Approach.* (London: HM Treasury).

HM Treasury and DfES (2002), *Developing Workforce Skills: Piloting a New Approach.* (London: HM Treasury).

HM Treasury, DfES, DWP and DTI (2004), *Skills in the Global Economy.* (London: HMSO).

Hutton, W. (1995), *The State We're In.* (London: Jonathan Cape).

Keep, E. (1999), 'UK's VET Policy and the 'Third Way': Following a High Skills Trajectory or Running up a Dead End Street?', *Journal of Education and Work*, 12:3, 323–346.

——, (2000), 'Creating a Knowledge-driven Economy – Definitions, Challenges and Opportunities', *SKOPE Policy Paper* 2. (Coventry: SKOPE, University of Warwick).

——, (2006), 'State Control of the English Education and Training System – Playing with the Biggest Train Set in the World', *Journal of Vocational Education and Training*, 58:1, 47–64.

Keep, E. and Mayhew, K. (1998), 'Was Ratner Right?', *Economic Report*, 12:3, Employment Policy Institute.

——, (1999), 'The Assessment: Knowledge, Skills and Competitiveness', *Oxford Review of Economic Policy*, 15:1, 1–15.

Keep, E. Mayhew, K. and Payne, J. (forthcoming), From Skills Revolution to Productivity Miracle: Not as Easy as it Sounds?, *Oxford Review of Economic Policy*.

Kelly, J. (2004), 'Social Partnership Agreements in Britain: Labour Cooperation and Compliance', *Industrial Relations,* 43:1, 267–292.

Kennedy, H. (1995), *Return to Learn: UNISON's Fresh Approach to Trade Union Education.* London: UNISON.

Kersley, B., Alpin, C., Forth, J., Bryson, A., Bewley, H., Dix, G. and Oxenbridge, S. (2006), *Inside the Workplace: Findings from the 2004 Workplace Employment Relations Survey.* (London: DTI).

Lauder, H. (1999), 'Competitiveness and the Problems of Low Skills Equilibria: a Comparative Analysis', *Journal of Education and Work*, 12:3, 281–294.

LSC (Learning and Skills Council) (2006a), *National Employers Skills Survey 2005: Main Report*. (Coventry, LSC).

——, (2006b), 'GCSE drop-outs "unemployable"', News Release, 24 August. (Coventry: LSC).

Leitch, S. (2005), *Leitch Review of Skills: Interim Report*. (London: HM Treasury).

Ludlam, S., Bodah, M. and Coates, D. (2002), 'Trajectories of Solidarity: Changing Union-party Linkages in the UK and the USA', *British Journal of Politics and International Relations*, 4:2, 222–244.

Lloyd, C. and Payne, J. (2002), 'On "the Political Economy of Skill": Assessing the Possibilities for a Viable High Skills Project in the UK', *New Political Economy*, 7:3, 367–395.

——, (2003), 'What is the 'High Skills Society'? Some Reflections of Current Academic and Policy Debates in the UK', *Policy Studies*, 24:2/3, 115–133.

——, (2006), 'The High Skills Project and the Limits of Possibility: A Response to Coffield', *Journal of Education Policy*, 21:4, 471–483.

Mansfield, B. (2000), *Past Imperfect?* (Harrogate: PRIME Research and Development Ltd, (mimeo)).

Martinez Lucio, M. and Stuart, M. (2002), 'Assessing Partnership: The Prospects for, and Challenges of, Modernisation', *Employee Relations*, 24:3, 252–261.

Mason, G. (2002), 'High Skills Utilisation under Mass Higher Education. Graduate Employment in Service Industries in Britain', *Journal of Education and Work*, 15:4, 427–456.

——, (2004), 'Enterprise Product Strategies and Employer Demand for Skills in Britain: Evidence from the Employers Skill Survey', *SKOPE Research Paper*, No 50. (Coventry: University of Warwick, SKOPE).

McBride, A., Hyde, P., Young, R. and Walshe, K. (2005), 'How the "Customer" Influences the Skills of the Front-line Worker' *Human Resource Management Journal*, 15:2, 35–49.

Moore, S. and Wood, H. (2005), *The Union Learning Experience: National Survey of Union Officers and ULRs*. (London: Working Lives Research Institute, London Metropolitan University).

Munro, A. and Rainbird, H. (2004a), 'The Workplace Learning Agenda. New Opportunities for Trade Unions?', in Healy *et al.* (eds.).

——, (2004b) 'Opening Doors as well as Banging on Tables. An Assessment of Unison/employer Partnerships on Learning in the UK Public Sector', *Industrial Relations Journal*, 35:5, 419–433.

Noble, C. (1997), 'International Comparisons of Training Policies', *Human Resource Management Journal*, 7:1, 5–18.

Nolan, P. (1989), 'Walking on Water? Performance and Industrial Relations under Thatcher' *Industrial Relations Journal* 20:2, 81–92.

——, (2000), 'Back to the Future of Work', Paper presented to the BUIRA Conference, Coventry: University of Warwick.

——, (2001), 'Shaping things to come', *People Management*, 27 December, 30–31.

Oxenbridge, S. and Brown, W. (2004), 'Achieving a New Equilibrium? The Stability of Cooperative Employer-union Relationships', *Industrial Relations Journal*, 35:5, 388–402.

Payne, J (2004), 'Re-evaluating the Finnish Workplace Development Programme. Evidence from Two Projects in the Municipal Sector', *Economic and Industrial Democracy*, 25:4, 485–524.

Porter, M. and Ketels, C. (2003), *UK Competitiveness: Moving to the Next Stage*, DTI Economics Paper No. 3.

Rainbird, H. (ed.) (2000), *Training in the Workplace.* (Basingstoke: MacMillan).

Rogers Hollingsworth, J. and Boyer, R. (eds.) (1997), *Contemporary Capitalism: The Embeddedness of Institutions.* (Cambridge: Cambridge University Press).

Soskice, D. (1993), 'Social Skills from Mass Higher Education. Rethinking the Company-based Initial Training Paradigm', *Oxford Review of Economic Policy*, 9:3, 101–113.

Streeck, W. (1989), 'Skills and the Limits of Neo-liberalism. The Enterprise of the Future as a Place of Learning', *Work, Employment and Society*, 3:1, 89–104.

——, (1992), *Social Institutions and Economic Performance.* (London: Sage).

——, (1997), 'Beneficial Constraints: On the Economic Limits of Rational Voluntarism', in Rogers Hollingsworth and Boyer (eds.).

Sung, J., Raddon, A. and Ashton, D. (2006), 'Skills Abroad: A Comparative Assessment of International Policy Approaches to Skills Leading to the Development of Policy Recommendations for the UK', SSDA Research Report 16.

Sutherland, J. and Rainbird, H. (2000), 'Unions and Workplace Learning: Conflict or Cooperation with the Employer?' in Rainbird (ed.).

Terry, M. (2003), 'Can 'Partnership' Reverse the Decline of British Trade Unions?' *Work, Employment and Society*, 17:3, 459–472.

Thompson, P., Findlay, P. and Warhurst, C. (2006), 'Organising to Learn/Learning to Organise. Three Case Studies on the Effects of Union-led Workplace Learning' SKOPE Research Paper 68, (Oxford University: SKOPE).

TUC (Trades Union Congress) (2003), *UK Productivity: Shifting to the High Road. A Response to the Porter Report.* (London: TUC).

——, (2005), *Skills White Paper: TUC Response to Skills White Paper.* (London: TUC).

——, (2006a), *2020 Vision for Skills. Priorities for the Leitch Review of Skills.* (London: TUC).

——, (2006b), *Changing Lives Through Learning. A Guide to Unionlearn.* (London: TUC).

——, (2006c), *Strategic Plan for Unionlearn 2006–2009.* (London: TUC).

——, (2006d), *Globalisation and the Comprehensive Spending Review.* (London: TUC).

——, (2006e), *Further Education White Paper: TUC Response to the Further Education White Paper – Further Education: Raising Skills, Improving Life Chances.* (London: TUC).

Unison (2003), *Learning for Life. Learning for Everyone: A Unison Report: In*

Response to the Government's Skills Strategy. (London: UNISON).

Wallis, E., Stuart, M. and Greenwood, I. (2005), 'Learners of the Workplace Unite!' An Empirical Examination of the UK Trade Union Learning Representative Initiative', *Work, Employment and Society*, 19:2, 283–304.

Wilson, R. and Hogarth, T. (2003), *Tackling the Low Skills Equilibrium*. (London: DTI).

Windsor, K. (2006), *Skills Ecosystem National Project: Mid-term Evaluation Report*. (New South Wales Department of Education and Training).

Wolf, A (2002), *Does Education Matter?* (London: Penguin).

SECTION II

UNION LEARNING:
ACTIONS AND OUTCOMES

Chapter 5

A Beneficial Combination?
Learning Opportunities from Union
Involvement in Career
and Pay Progression

Anne McBride and Stephen Mustchin

Introduction

Writing in 1992, Seifert noted that a central element of industrial relations in the UK National Health Service (NHS) is the 'existence and influence of powerful trade unions and professional associations' (1992, 3). This still holds true in 2006 when unions have been intimately involved in an extensive pay modernisation project. Seifert also argued that the managerial imperative to raise labour productivity in the NHS ensures that wage determination (denoted as market relations) and performance controls (denoted as managerial relations) lie at the heart of operational needs. With regard to the latter, he indicated the overwhelming concern of NHS managers to 'control the work effort and direction of their workforce' (1992, 3).

The last two decades have seen substantial changes in the governance and management of public services by successive governments which has often been termed 'new public management' (Ferlie *et al.* 1996), and 'modernisation'. In the HR context, Bach (2002) notes that 'modernisation' has generally been used in policy discourses to describe increased private sector involvement in public services, as well as attempts to reform pay, working conditions and work practices. Seifert and Sibley (2005, 234) note that notions of '"modernisation" have been used repeatedly in government derived statements on improving public services to mean "modernisation" of the workforce and of their terms and conditions of employment apparent in the NHS, as well as local government and the Fire Service'. They also argue that '"modernisation" is not a neutral step forward but a highly coloured version of progress rooted in market-style efficiency' (2005, 226).

The Government has argued that pay modernisation is very necessary in the NHS since the determination of pay has been tied to an antiquated, and now outdated, set of structures and processes which 'imposes artificial career ceilings and frustrates changes to ways of working' (Department of Health 2003, 21). Until recently, pay was determined through a system of Whitley Councils. The Whitley Council system of managing industrial relations derived from the Whitley Committee on the Relations of Employers and Employed in 1917, which led to Whitley councils being set up in public employment, in the Post Office, civil service and Royal Dockyards (Pelling 1976). When the NHS was set up, there was a commitment from government that 'there would be "set up some machinery of the Whitley council type" for dealing with pay' (Clegg 1976, 384).

While the original vision of the Whitley Committee envisaged these bodies dealing with a broad range of issues affecting employment, national negotiations were largely restricted to pay and conditions with non-pay issues (which would include training) being determined locally (Bain 1986). This system of eleven Whitley Councils for different NHS staff groups involved bargaining with professional unions, which operated solely in healthcare, and larger, general unions (Burchill and Casey 1996). Whitley Councils, subsequent pay reviews and the influence of the state led to considerable differences in pay, terms and conditions for staff within the NHS, within staff groups and compared to comparable workers in other industries (Seifert 1992). In the context of a gendered segmentation of the workforce, this has led to numerous (successful) equal pay for work of equal value claims. There have also been considerable differences in access to learning opportunities, as funding has historically been spent on pre and post-registration training of staff, rather than non-qualified, non-registered staff.

Collective activity around training gained prominence in the 1990s with the TUC's Bargaining for Skills project (Dundon and Eva 1998). The focus of this chapter is the introduction of a range of measures concerned with reforming NHS pay, such as Agenda for Change, the Knowledge and Skills Framework (KSF) and the Skills Escalator which have been introduced in partnership with the professional and general health service unions. This has enabled the definition of skill requirements; processes for determining learning needs; and implications of not meeting those needs, to be the subject of extensive negotiation. In unionised workplaces in Britain, this is relatively rare. The Workplace Employment Relations Survey (WERS) 2004 indicated that only 8 per cent of employers negotiated over training with 38 per cent of employers consulting unions, and 26 per cent providing information to employee representatives concerning training (Kersley *et al.* 2006). The development of the above measures, which affect the majority of the 1.3m health service workers in the NHS, is therefore worthy of consideration.

Of particular importance is the manner in which pay reform has been explicitly linked with learning and development initiatives in the NHS. As indicated by the Department of Health (2003, 21) 'pay reform will underpin the Skills Escalator, facilitating new types of skill mix and providing stronger incentives for staff to acquire new knowledge and skills…strong national standards to ensure consistency with increased flexibility for local employers'. This emphasis on linking pay reform to performance reflects the shift towards a performance management culture identified in Bach's (2004) study of three NHS Trusts over the period from 1995 to 2001.

Another management change noted by Bach related to the increased interest Human Resource (HR) managers had in developing partnership working with trade unions. This reflects the strategy at a national level. However, a heavy cost at a local level appeared to be that 'HR specialists increasingly viewed trade unions as an adjunct to the management process rather than as an important source of independent employee voice' (Bach 2004, 189). Whilst literature on partnership working raises concerns for broader issues of independence and influence (see Kelly 1996; Martinez Lucio and Stuart 2002; Heaton *et al.* 2002), Forrester discusses the dangers of partnership for learning. He notes the danger that shared commitments to learning could risk such activities becoming 'sophisticated elements in persuading 'colleagues' to work harder or longer' (Forrester 2001, 324). He also raises concerns that the language and framework for union involvement in learning 'derives more from a human resource development discourse than from a distinctly union, or even adult, learning perspective' (Forrester 2004, 416). All these concerns about partnership are in contrast to the trade union Unison's literature which portrays such processes as allowing the union 'to raise concerns about how the scheme is working in practice. If parts of the new system are not working out for staff, Unison will seek further negotiations to put things right' (Unison 2004).

A Department of Health-commissioned study by the authors of skills development in the NHS (McBride *et al.* 2006) provides some further insights into these complex issues. The study identified the nature, progress and outcomes of the Skills Escalator concept, with an emphasis on how it was being applied and implemented at a local level within NHS Trusts. The authors have argued elsewhere (Mustchin and McBride forthcoming) that unions had a limited role in the interpretation and implementation of this concept – due partly to their heavy involvement in negotiating and implementing Agenda for Change. However, respondents did feel that the new structures would provide a good basis for increasing staff input into the learning agenda – and it is this potential that is the focus of this chapter. It begins by providing an overview of learning opportunities in the NHS. It then introduces three features of pay modernisation, Agenda for Change; KSF and the Skills Escalator. Following a brief outline of the research methods, we indicate how unions are pursuing staff development through these structures. Given that KSF development was still on-going during the study, it is not possible to assess its full contribution. The article finishes with a discussion of how this unique set of measures could be an opportunity for unions to co-determine performance controls at the same time as leading to narrowly focused, job-related learning.

Contemporary Learning Opportunities in the NHS

Although the service sector has been typified as consisting of jobs that require fewer skills, the NHS spends over £4 billion in education and training every year (Department of Health 2005a). There is also evidence to suggest widespread participation in training and learning activities within the NHS. This means that in some respects it may have less far to travel in developing workforce skills than organisations in other sectors which lack strong underpinning regulation that often stimulates the provision of learning opportunities (for further discussion, see Green and Felstead 1994). The National Employer Skills Survey 2004 noted that health care and other public sector employers 'show the highest levels of training engagement', being more likely to train the majority of their staff, to have organised job-specific training and to have scheduled training away from the workplace (National Learning and Skills Council 2005, 92).

This is endorsed by the experience of employees themselves; data analysed by Skills for Health from the Labour Force Survey 2001/2 showed that workers in the health and social care sector reported being much more likely to receive training in the past four weeks than other industries (Skills for Health 2003) and data from the Employer Skills Survey indicated that staff were more likely to experience all categories of training from induction to management development, except IT, than any other sector. High levels of training in health care are likely to derive from the prominent value attached to clinical skills in occupations such as medicine and nursing, the presence of professional regulation which sets standards for post-qualification training and a well-developed provider infrastructure to deliver them. Indeed, a significant proportion of the £4 billion is spent on salaries for clinicians in training. This explains how nearly three-quarters of a million NHS staff are qualified to graduate level, equivalent or above (Fryer 2006).

However, 40 per cent of NHS staff are qualified to National Vocational Qualification (NVQ) Level 2 or below, and 25 per cent are qualified at NVQ1 or below (Fryer 2006). In addition, the Audit Commission (2001) study of education, training and development for NHS healthcare staff indicated that Trusts had very different levels of involvement in NVQs. A small number of Trusts had no NVQ schemes and 45 per cent of Human Resource Directors surveyed said that NVQ use was limited to some parts of their Trust. In common with earlier work by Thornley (1998), the Audit Commission (2001) confirmed that nursing auxiliaries and assistants were less likely to have their development taken seriously than qualified healthcare professionals. The study also indicated that part-time workers, staff with domestic caring responsibilities and those working non-standard hours or shifts tended to report receiving and taking up fewer training opportunities.

In recognition of an imbalance of provision, the NHS Plan (Department of Health 2000) made a commitment to all staff without a professional qualification that they would have access to a Learning Account of £150 per year, or dedicated training to NVQ Level 2/3. Adult literacy and numeracy provision was also promoted in concert with Learning and Skills Councils in a later document (Department of Health 2001). Learning accounts and NVQs were described by the Department of Health in the 'Framework for Lifelong Learning' as 'key to our commitments to staff without professional qualifications' (Department of Health 2001, 17). This Framework also set out the vision for all NHS organisations to be 'learning organisations' so that 'learning and effective use of knowledge is at the heart of their business' (2001, 53). The NHS Learning Account Scheme was introduced in April 2001 and the requisite finances were ring fenced for this commitment to March 2006. Table 5.1 shows an overview of the Learning Accounts and NVQs taken up in NHS England over the last four years.

It is to be noted that NHS Learning Accounts survived the discontinuation of the wider Individual Learning Account scheme in 2001[1] and trade unions have played a key role in their use. Indeed, a Unison officer was seconded to the Department

---

1   The Individual Learning Account (ILA) scheme, administered by Capita, involved little regulation of providers leading to widespread mis-selling and fraud. Other criticisms include their focus on ICT (Information Communication Technology) and maths training, and that two-fifths of people taking up ILAs had degree or equivalent level qualifications already (Clough 2004, 17, 18).

Table 5.1   Learning Accounts and NVQs for the NHS England, 2002–2006

	Learning Accounts	NVQs
2002/2003	22,000	21,000
2003/2004	65,000	34,000
2004/2005	75,551	34,252
2005/2006	61,953	32,544

Source: Department of Health, personal communication

of Health to assist with the NHS Learning Accounts scheme, and Unison provided courses in a pilot project sponsored by the NHS University (NHSU) to enhance take-up of Learning Accounts. NHSU was part of the Government's agenda to 'ensure that access to learning and development is available 24 hours a day, and 365 days a year, to every member of staff' (Department of Health 2001, x). Much of the emphasis of the NHSU initiative related to widening participation in learning, in part through the use of distance learning, with a target to support 250,000 staff on an NHSU 'learning pathway' by 2008 (Johnson 2004, 547). Launched in 2003, it was closed in 2005 with its responsibilities subsequently being taken on by the NHS Institute for Innovation and Improvement and the Widening Participation in Learning Strategy Unit.

A report evaluating the NHSU pilot projects indicated the important role of Union Learning Representatives (ULRs) in encouraging non-traditional learners to participate in learning activity through the NHS Learning Accounts (Aldridge *et al.* 2005). By their very nature, professional associations and unions have a history of involvement in training and education issues. COHSE and NUPE set up their own trade union education departments from the early 1970s, albeit initially to train activists to deal with government imposed reforms within the sector (Munro and Rainbird 2000a). More recently unions have become heavily involved in the personal development of their members, and work by the above authors (Munro and Rainbird 2000b; Rainbird *et al.* 2003; Rainbird and Munro 2003; Munro and Rainbird 2004) provides considerable evidence of the nature and beneficial outcomes of learning partnerships in the UK public sector.

Career and Pay Progression in the NHS

As noted above, pay and conditions in the NHS have been radically overhauled. The eleven Whitley Councils for a range of staff groups have now been rationalised into single bodies for pay and consultation. Agenda for Change is the name given to the collective agreement covering the pay and terms and conditions of all staff, with the exception of consultants and General Practitioners (GPs). The key features of the Agenda for Change are the equalisation of terms and conditions across staff groups; comprehensive job evaluation across all jobs; and career and pay progression. This chapter is concerned with the latter, which applies to over one million NHS staff from October 2006.

Prior to the introduction of Agenda for Change, annual pay progression had been the norm. Although annual increments are still the norm for health service workers, there are two 'gateway' points at which entitlement to progression rests on a proven ability to meet the job needs identified by the Knowledge and Skills Framework (KSF). The KSF consists of a set of knowledge and skills identified for general and role-specific working in the NHS, connected to the new pay and grading structures. It has a set of six core dimensions and 24 specific dimensions 'designed to be applicable and transferable across the NHS' (Department of Health 2004). The intention is that each job has a KSF outline, and staff have an annual Personal Development Review (PDR) at which their work is compared with the KSF outline. From this, Personal Development Plans (PDPs) are jointly produced to identify learning and development needs and how these will be met. There seems to be less clarity about how often (if at all) a KSF outline may change.

If a KSF subset is met at the 'foundation gateway' (12 months in post) or the full KSF is met at the 'second gateway' (towards top of pay band), staff continue to the next increment, or top of the pay band respectively. This creates an explicit connection between the development of skills and remuneration – for both employees and managers. If an employee is not able to demonstrate the application of skills at the gateway, and this is due to an organisational issue such as lack of resources for training or assessment, then the employee will progress through their gateway. Once individuals have passed through the second gateway, 'the focus may shift to career development' (Department of Health 2004, 17).

As indicated by Bach (2004, 192), the six core knowledge and skills dimensions place an emphasis on 'softer interactive competencies' which in turn can be linked to the servicing of internal and external 'customers'. They require all individuals (to a lesser or greater degree), over six levels, to be involved in:

- communication;
- contributing to their own personal development;
- assisting in maintaining their own and others' health, safety and security;
- making changes in their own practice and offer suggestions for improving services;
- maintaining the quality of their own work;
- acting in ways that support equality and value diversity.

A third important component of workforce modernisation was the introduction of the Skills Escalator. It is important to note that trade unions were involved in the conception of the idea. A Department of Health policymaker indicated how the idea came from discussing workforce strategy with trade unions. A Unison representative involved in research into public sector reform in other countries arranged for the policymaker to meet up with a Danish trade union involved in a city-wide approach to developing generic skills and giving people the opportunity to move up the career ladder through job rotation.

When first introduced, the Skills Escalator was described in relation to a number of management interventions, lifelong learning; career development; widening participation and skill mix changes. It was described in the Framework for Lifelong Learning (Department of Health 2001, 17) as a means of supporting those 'who wish to develop their careers and make an increasing contribution to improvements in service delivery'. The Department of Health's first depiction of the Skills Escalator is given in Table 5.2 below:

Table 5.2   The Skills Escalator approach from 'Working Together, Learning Together' (Adapted from Department of Health 2001: 18)

Level	Category	Means of career progression
1	Socially excluded individuals	6 month employment orientation programmes
2	The unemployed	6 month placements in 'starter' jobs
3	Jobs/ roles requiring fewer skills and less experience	NVQs, Learning Accounts, appraisal, PDP
4	Skilled roles	NVQs or equivalent
5	Qualified professional roles	Appraisal and PDP to support career progression
6	More advanced skills and roles	As above, role development encouraged in line with service priorities/ personal career choices
7	'Consultant' roles	Flexible 'portfolio careers' informed by robust appraisal, career and PDP

A critical review of its introduction and policy documentation provides three alternative interpretations of the Skills Escalator concept (McBride *et al.* 2006). First, following the HR 'best practice' literature (for example, Pfeffer 1998), it could be interpreted as a holistic 'best practice' workforce strategy to grow and change the workforce. Second, following the HR 'best fit' literature (for example, Boxall and Purcell 2003), it could be interpreted as a 'brand' to cover a portfolio of interventions, only some of which will be selected to meet the needs of the organisation. Third, grounded in industrial relations literature (for example, Thornley 1996; Seifert and Sibley 2005) it could be interpreted as a strategy of labour substitution.

A government employee interviewed as part of the project was keen to stress the important relationship between Agenda for Change and the Skills Escalator:

Agenda for Change was basically designed for the Skills Escalator and the Trade Unions understood that position as well. Agenda for Change is a pay reform, which links learning and pay together and is entirely about giving people the opportunity to take on extra roles and responsibility and to be rewarded for it ... Because, in terms of pay, it's not a huge amount of increase in your pocket, if you get Agenda for Change, so that it wasn't the deal to the staff, I mean there is more money in your pocket, but the deal really is, the opportunities for careers that it presents, rather than the actual pay deal that you're getting straight away.

However, this respondent did also indicate that:

we're saying to every member of staff, that if you're prepared to do the learning and if you want the career opportunity, then you have the chance to move up to the next level of the

Skills Escalator, but also the benefit to the system is that by developing this much greater role flexibility, we can have work done by the person who is a) safe to do the task but b) the most economically efficient to do so.

It has been argued that through involvement in learning at work, 'unions help workers sustain a cultural life in the workplace and beyond that positively expresses, throughout its diversity, the unique economic and political standpoint of workers' (Bratton *et al.* 2003, 162). An approach to learning concerned with citizenship has been advocated as a means of broadening 'narrow' agenda of employability focused lifelong learning provision (Forrester 2005, 264). However, the learning generated by the KSF could fall short of these more aspirational conceptions of lifelong learning, and may be more likely to reflect Streeck's (1989) observation that employer dominated training systems will mainly generate narrow, job specific skills.

In their guide to the KSF, Unison (2005) indicate that the KSF 'represents the largest commitment to training and development ever seen in the United Kingdom'. This raises some important research questions in the context of the above literatures, such as, what role do unions play in the process of KSF implementation? What are the links between KSF and learning and development? Does the KSF enable union involvement in managerial relations to the extent that unions are co-determining them to the benefit of their members? Could this be at the expense of broader learning opportunities?

Research Methods

The authors were commissioned by the Department of Health to examine the structure, process and outcome of the Skills Escalator and associated activities over the period December 2003 to June 2006. This involved identifying how the Skills Escalator was understood; what Skills Escalator activities looked like in an organisational context; why these activities were being introduced; what the impact of them was on individuals, teams and organisations. The study took place in two stages. Phase 1 involved 48 semi-structured telephone interviews in England with learning managers in the Workforce Development Directorates of Strategic Health Authorities and staff involved in delivering workplace learning within a variety of healthcare organisations (see McBride *et al.* 2006).

Phase 2 involved seven case studies in three Acute Trusts; two Primary Care Trusts (PCTs); one Mental Health Trust and one Ambulance Trust across a range of geographical locations across England. These sites were chosen because of their known Skills Escalator activity – with a range of apparent progress – and the selection provided a range of organisational contexts (as differentiated by size, corporate status, financial status, judged performance). This research involved 187 interviewees including managers, registered staff, ancillary staff, contracted out support workers, healthcare assistants, admin and clerical staff and trade union stewards, regional officers, and Learning Representatives. Requests were also made for quantitative data on training budgets; numbers of staff participating on a range of learning activities; attrition and completion rates; numbers of staff without a qualification. Union officers and lay activists were asked about their involvement, and influence, in lifelong learning; career development; widening participation; skill mix changes – any activities which could be construed as Skills Escalator activities. They were also asked about their involvement in broader workforce issues such as pay modernisation and large-scale workforce changes. Managers and employees were asked about their experience of trade union involvement in these activities too. This work was supplemented with interviews with five 'subject matter experts' who held responsibility in governmental organisations for developing the Skills Escalator at a strategic or operational level. The Skills Escalator concept had been introduced to the Health Service several years before the start of the research. The KSF was being introduced during the study and was due to be completed in the year after the collection of the empirical data.

The main focus of this chapter will be on the case study data from eighteen union respondents (a mixture of Branch Secretaries, Branch Executive members, Union Learning Representatives, Regional Educational Officers from Amicus, RCN and Unison) interpreted within the overall context of the project and individual case studies (see McBride *et al.* 2006). The following section provides an overview of union involvement in the learning agenda across the seven case sites – which have been numbered for means of anonymity. This is followed by a more detailed account of union involvement in the KSF and the implications of this for staff development.

Union Involvement in Learning

With the exception of one Trust, there was a maximum of three ULRs within each case site. Three of the organisation's sites had no ULRs at all at the time of the research. At one site respondents indicated that such activities had been limited by the work on Agenda for Change; at another, that the role had not initially been understood by the Branch; and the third had tried to recruit ULRs without success – leading to a network of non-union learning representatives instead. This picture would seem to confirm the comments of a UNISON regional education officer that:

> It would be wrong to say that because we've got 15, 16, 20 years history of membership development, then we've cracked it. And clearly we haven't. There's still a lot more work that we have to do to get a lot more buy-in by our branches.

The exception was a Trust with a network of ten ULRs – although these were co-ordinated at a regional level. This was a large organisation of approximately 5,000 employees which was explicitly developing a partnership approach to employment relations to overcome a history of poor industrial relations and high numbers of grievances. The Trust had developed a partnership agreement and appointed a staff side representative to the Board of Directors to oversee employee relations.

Notwithstanding the seemingly slow development of ULRs in the case study sites, respondents did believe that once the administration of Agenda for Change was completed, more staff would come forward to take on the ULR roles. In the meantime, unions were able to talk about their involvement in their organisations' learning agenda – which often included the provision of courses. Several themes arose from this provision. First, unions felt it was important that they were providing something different to management. In Trust 2, they acknowledged that the employers were providing a number of courses but felt that some staff might not want to go through the formal Trust system. They noted that their own assertiveness course situated in a pleasant hotel for the weekend was something that the Trust would never do, even though it encouraged staff to get involved in their own development for the first time. Another example was provided of the supportive nature of union learning centres:

> people at those learning centres are very, you know confidential, very supportive and that really benefits people who can't go to the managers about that sort of thing.

A second theme raised by union respondents was that union provision was usually of no cost to the employer. This was seen as an important motivator to encourage both individuals and the employer to engage in learning. One union representative noted how their course on the European Computer Driving Licence would save the Trust money, whilst they were 'supporting the Trust ... with the learning that we're providing'. Indeed, as one regional education officer noted, Trusts were quite interested in union provision 'because it means they don't necessarily have to pay for people'.

All respondents noted the importance of the line manager in encouraging, and supporting, staff to take up learning opportunities. As well as negotiating with line managers on behalf of members for time off for learning, respondents were also keen to enlighten line managers as much as possible as to the benefits of developing their staff, and changing the line manager's perception of their own role. They also understood that managers were constrained too, and 'under the pressures you know, to meet ... their targets'.

Workplace Learning and the KSF

As noted above, the KSF process was still in development during this study, so the following relates to initial preparations and perceptions of potential. The existence of explicit criteria for each job (as articulated through the KSF outlines), alongside the annual PDR, was seen as the beginning of a number of important processes concerning workplace learning. First, the exercise enabled the identification of knowledge and skill requirements for individuals in particular jobs. Representatives in several Trusts indicated the benefits of gathering evidence for the annual PDR. As one representative noted, once staff had the competence to carry out their job they would have written documentation 'very similar to a certificate, to say this person has achieved the necessary requirements to fulfil the post in which they are employed'. Another representative noted how such a process could run alongside NVQs, or even replace them if the NVQs were 'just about gathering evidence in your own workplace'. A union colleague within the same organisation, referred to this evidence as 'a passport of skills' that staff had developed each year. For this interviewee, the existence of this evidence in the context of all jobs having a KSF outline, was the ability to 'look at other roles ... look at developing towards them' and asking the organisation for support. To illustrate this point, an example was given of a KSF workshop participant whose application to be a theatre technician had been rejected because he would have to retrain, but who now appreciated that he could gather evidence of the skills that he applied in his job and from that base only develop skills which were not part of his current job.

Table 5.3   Selected results of staff survey for case study trusts

		% staff appraised in last 12 months	% staff with PDPs from last 12 months	% staff received any training in last 12 months	% staff receiving at least 1 day's training on taught course in last 12 months
Trust 1 (Acute)	05/06	49	40	92	n/a
	04/05	50	50	94	78
	03/04	42	41	82	70
Trust 2 (PCT)	05/06	71	62	97	n/a
	04/05	78	64	100	81
	03/04	76	64	94	83
Trust 3 (PCT)	05/06	42	36	93	n/a
	04/05	57	53	100	73
	03/04	54	56	89	76
Trust 4 (Mental Health)	05/06	72	64	96	n/a
	04/05	72	63	100	86
	03/04	67	59	94	89
Trust 5 (Ambulance)	05/06	35	24	97	n/a
	04/05	50	46	98	87
	03/04	42	33	93	81
Trust 6 (Acute)	05/06	68	57	96	n/a
	04/05	66	49	100	74
	03/04	78	60	92	83
Trust 7 Acute	05/06	60	49	91	n/a
	04/05	62	50	89	66
	03/04	53	47	86	69

Source: Websites of CHI (for 2003 figures), and Healthcare Commission (for 2004, 2005 figures)

Second, the exercise identifies the skills and knowledge required by each individual for their job and hence the responsibility of the organisation to support individuals in gaining those skills. This is important for two reasons. The volume of appraisals conducted in the 7 case sites indicates the extent to which learning needs are not currently being systematically identified. Table 5.3 indicates that Trusts 1, 3 and 5 are only providing appraisals to 50 per cent or lower of their staff, and that Trusts 1, 3, 5 and 7 are only providing PDPs to 50 per cent or lower of their staff. Given that all staff should now have an annual PDR and PDP, this illustrates the magnitude of the task, and the extent to which these requirements may encourage better management practice. In addition, union respondents in one Trust noted how they were prepared to monitor the extent to which organisations were fulfilling this responsibility, and how they would use the disciplinary route if management were not supporting staff as indicated in the PDR.

Third, unions perceived that the collection and synthesis of this individual data on skill requirements would provide an effective needs assessment across organisations. In language that could easily have been spoken by a learning and development manager, one of the union representatives noted how, once they had got the KSF outlines in place, they would be able to determine 'in a very structured way' what their training and development needs were. Noting that this was the first time this had ever happened, this interviewee argued that mapping current training and development opportunities against the KSF requirements, would ensure 'that we can be responsive as an organisation to what is actually coming from the KSF reviews'. This implication of common needs and interests will be returned to later. In the meantime, it seems to be assumed by many union respondents that this needs assessment will lead to a change in the traditional prioritisation of funding, which will be towards members of general rather than professional unions. Indeed, one interviewee felt that their Trust had started spending more money on staff groups traditionally excluded from learning opportunities in preparation for the KSF process.

A fourth link between the KSF process and learning opportunities was related by the representative in the Ambulance Trust (Trust 5) as starting once staff had proved that they were competent in their roles and 'could set themselves new challenges'. He felt that the KSF was indicating to staff that responsibility was being handed back to them to lead their own training and development. He believed that staff:

> very quickly ... start to look at different avenues of enhancing their own skill base, because they see a changing service, they want to be entering into that as the strength and not weakness of feeling that they're not highly, you know, well enough skilled to take on the challenges of it ... [they ask] can I do something better, is there somewhere else in the organisation I can access, can I do a better job in another role? Do I want another role?

The interviewee argued that such questions were not broached before, but believed that once it started, 'it's irreversible'. He felt that the organisation would gain some big benefits 'without a lot of outlay' because the process could be used to 'remodel and reshape' the workforce and organisation to where 'you want it to go' and where the Department of Health needed 'to see change', needed to see a 'sharpening of the process' and patient improvement. This response resonates with the policy documentation from the Department of Health which notes the links to service improvement, increased flexibility and improved patient care. However, as representatives in Trust 2 noted, having specific job outlines could be used to ensure that staff were not expected to do work that was not included in their KSF. This in effect could curtail previous informal, but potentially exploitative flexibilities, when staff could be asked to take on anything that was 'commensurate' with their job. So, whilst the representative in Trust 5 thought it would empower staff to be open to new challenges, one representative in Trust 2 noted how if 'it's not in that job description, it doesn't happen'. Another, how they had told staff that as long they completed their KSF requirements, 'nobody can come back and say that you haven't done anything'. These latter comments echo an earlier observation by Burchill and Casey (1996, 181) that the use of detailed job descriptions could create a situation where 'staff become less flexible and management are reluctant to change job content, because of the impact of re-evaluations'.

This potential for using the process to 'police' employee relations came up in other interviews. One interviewee noted that if organisations were not looking at their training needs, then 'our local branches will make them look at it ... because if they're not doing that, then it doesn't fit in to the new NHS model'. The implication that unions could use it to ensure that organisations were working to requirements was picked up by a representative in Trust 5. They noted how the process could 'ask very searching questions of effective management and the absence of it', which the Department of Health 'really could do with analysing ... fairly quickly'. They added that if the Department of Health used their incentives creatively they would be able to send a message to everyone to take development review and KSF seriously.

Union Involvement with the Knowledge and Skills Framework

Munro and Rainbird (2000a; 2000b; 2004) have previously noted the potential for jointly managed systems of workplace learning. As one interviewee noted with learning and training, 'there's no excuse not to work together'. Indeed, they felt it was a huge opportunity for Trusts and unions to 'put aside all the rubbish from years gone by and actually get on with some good work that benefits everybody'. However, as noted elsewhere (Mustchin and McBride forthcoming), unions in the case study organisations were often so involved in the technicalities of pay modernisation that they were not explicitly engaged in interpreting or implementing the Skills Escalator concept. Nor, as noted above, was there an abundance of union learning representatives. As one interviewee noted, 'people are very concerned about their grades and their positions within the trust, nothing is straightforward or planned properly so they're more concerned about where they're at'. However, unions were involved in KSF project management; raising awareness and developing linked programmes of study. In this respect, their actions seemed to reinforce Bach's (2004, 189) earlier comment that trade unions were seen as 'an adjunct to the management process'. However, it did also give them considerable access to the determination of managerial relations in their organisations.

The national requirement for Agenda for Change and the KSF process to be introduced in partnership was adhered to at a local level such that one interviewee noted that 'we're effectively project managing the KSF jointly'. This was not seen as problematic because 'everything's been thrashed out there. Realistically, it's worked reasonably well'. Another representative in Trust 4 noted the 'massive piece of work' that was involved in developing the KSF outlines and as KSF Lead appeared to be taking responsibility for putting together the structure and implementation plan for the whole process. This notion of taking, or sharing, responsibility was also evident in Trust 5:

> We also collectively between us share the responsibility for delivering the staff awareness, the reviewer training and the appeals process if staff have any particular problems with development review or, or reviewers, I would say.

A respondent in Trust 6 noted that there was 'no obvious difference as to who's management and who's staff side. They're working extremely well together and very much within the partnership'. This almost echoed a respondent in Trust 2 who noted: 'I wouldn't know who was the manager or who was the staff side, that never ever even came into [it], you know, it was a real show of partnership working'. In addition, a regional educational officer felt there had been 'a real blurring of role and responsibility and in some places … there's a blurring of who is staff side and who is management because the staff side have actually led on the KSF.'

This was also apparently to be found at a national level, where this regional education officer noted that:

> it's very difficult for me to tell who's the union and who's an independent consultant or Department of Health Organisational Agency member of the group because everybody works very well together. And we all understand the benefit of working together you know rather than sort of any quibbles that you might have …

Raising awareness of the KSF, and its implications, was seen as a key role of union representatives. As one union respondent noted 'there's still a huge amount of ignorance about how the Knowledge and Skills Framework can help' and 'a lot of myths about how it works'. Another noted that a lot of staff tended to think that Agenda for Change was just about pay and assimilation to another pay band and forgot that the KSF was part of it. Respondents were delivering, or gearing up to deliver, workshops to both staff and management on KSF, with one noting how they 'probably ran parallel with the training department on most things nowadays because of the KSF work'. For staff, such workshops were about making staff aware of the KSF process and indicating how it could affect their career progression, and access to learning opportunities. In the Ambulance Trust, the union representative appeared to be using such workshops to change the culture of the organisation:

> we clearly say on the Knowledge and Skills [training], you've always been spoon-fed your education to the point where you've become dependent on it. Now we're looking for a culture change where we want you to lead on your own training and education and development, but without pulling the rug from under you, there needs to be a concerted effort to gradually move you into a new system.

For line managers, workshops were also about raising awareness. Several respondents noted the importance of educating managers to 'see the importance of the KSF and Agenda for Change, so that they can release staff and encourage staff'. Line managers and supervisors hold an important role in the KSF process. They will be involved in the development of KSF outlines for individual jobs; they will probably be responsible for conducting PDRs and will be the gatekeepers to learning opportunities. As a regional officer noted, if they did not sign up to the idea and encourage the development of their staff, then it would be a waste of a good idea. The officer continued:

> We cannot expect management, line management, to take that role on unless they are given training, unless they understand that's part of the process. And those managers will need learning opportunities themselves because within the KSF framework, they're going to be required to identify skill need ... identifying where a person is, in terms of the levels, whether they are in entry or level one or two, is not necessarily a given for everybody.

One union representative also noted how they provided training to managers as to how to put together KSF outlines. The importance of this was illustrated in another Trust where we were told of managers who issued forms to staff asking them to fill out the KSF outline which defeated the object of having a dialogue between the manager and the staff as to the requirements of the job and how the outline should be put into practice.

Unions were also being proactive in developing learning opportunities linked to the KSF. As noted earlier, there are 6 core KSF dimensions which all staff are required to apply in their jobs. Unison branch officers indicated how they were working with a local education provider to support learning around these dimensions, cross referencing the knowledge and skills that are required in posts within the Trust with courses that they offer. Unison is also proactive at a national level in matching the core dimensions to their educational programmes which are accredited through the Open College Network.

Immediate Benefits from Union Involvement in KSF

Given that KSF outlines were being developed, rather than used during this research, it is too soon to know the effect they will have on identifying and supplying workforce learning needs. Thus far, unions have tended to talk about potential. However, the exercise was clearly having personal benefits for union respondents, and the wider union. One representative noted how they had been 'quite rooted in trade unionism, staff representation' and that since they had got involved with the KSF process, they were 'rolling out quite in-depth sessions on a regular basis' on modernisation and many other aspects of the NHS, to the extent that their confidence and skill base was 'light years away from when I started'. Another commented how all staff side representatives involved in the KSF had had to learn quickly and 'hit the ground running', to the extent that 'they've had a great sort of remodelling of their careers':

> because they've had to learn to present, they've had to learn to roll out awareness sessions, develop outlines. So it's been a development of their own but so much so the staff side have moved into different areas now, and all quite confident and competent at delivering different aspects of Knowledge and Skills.

Another representative noted how they now tended to be co-opted onto modernisation project groups – although as noted elsewhere (Mustchin and McBride forthcoming), union involvement in role redesign projects was the exception, rather than the rule.

As noted above, there was only one site which had a network of union learning representatives. There appeared to be none at three sites, and only a few at the remaining three. However, it was felt that the KSF would lead to there being more learning representatives in the future. Indeed, one noted how prior to the KSF they would very rarely see any applications for learning representatives. However, since they had held awareness days and staff had been involved in debates about modernisation, education, training and development, staff had started to ask how they could get involved, and the representative had received a number of applications. One of the regional officers was explicitly using the KSF to encourage senior representatives to find people who could help them. Only one representative however noted how Agenda for Change and KSF was a potential hook for membership recruitment.

Discussion

The dismantling of the Whitley Council system in the NHS provided an opportunity for unions to influence the restructuring of market relations. In the context of partnership working, unions negotiated the equalisation of terms and conditions across staff groups, job evaluation, and career and pay progression. The 2004 Workplace Employment Relations Survey (WERS) (Kersley *et al.* 2006) indicates the uniqueness of this level of influence. This chapter has indicated the pivotal role of the KSF, a process which describes the knowledge and skills which NHS staff need to apply in their work. Unions have been very much involved in thinking through the use of KSF to improve learning opportunities for their members. Given the above noted expressions of the potential that unions see in the KSF process, it is perhaps not surprising to see the depth of their 'embeddedness' in the process. There is a heavy emphasis on working in partnership – and common descriptions of unions and management as 'we'. The potential for unions to monitor the KSF could ensure a rebalancing of learning opportunities between registered and non-registered staff. Clear outlines of what staff are expected to do may protect against work intensification. In addition, if the KSF is to be used as a means of managing performance, unions are ensuring that they are co-determining how it will be used and exerting some influence on managerial relations. This appeared to be very much the approach of the union representatives in Trust 2, a Primary Health Care of 3,800 staff.

A different philosophy, however, was expressed in Trust 5. This was an Ambulance Trust of 1,400 staff. Here, representatives discussed the potential for 'culture change'. It will be remembered that one of the core KSF dimensions was the contribution to one's own personal development, and this was felt to be an important signifier to staff that they were no longer going to be 'spoon-fed' training. From this perspective, requiring all staff to contribute to their personal development, make changes in their own practice (dimension 4) and maintain the quality of their own work (dimension 5) could be a powerful way of changing people's ways of working.

It has been noted earlier that unions seemed to have little workplace involvement in the development of the Skills Escalator model of workplace learning. The KSF, and provisions for development within it, seems to offer the possibility of unions ensuring that staff receive their developmental entitlements. This raises the question of whether it matters that they had been less involved with the Skills Escalator itself. On the one hand, the KSF enables staff to receive training appropriate to their PDR, build up 'a passport of skills', and once competent look to where they might wish to move to within the Skills Escalator. Within this scenario, unions are determining the role of the KSF in managerial relations. However, this process of drawing up rules beyond which staff members should not work is likely to be fragile due to a number of factors, including extra tasks being taken on within teams due to staff shortages, redundancies and other localised pressures that increase people's workloads. While there is considerable potential for the KSF to act as a stimulus to workplace learning, there are also considerable risks that the KSF will only serve to promote narrower, job-related concerns (Forrester 2005). There is no guarantee that once competent in one's own job, one could learn how to develop the skills and knowledge required for other jobs. Indeed, line managers are under constant pressure to restrict learning opportunities to what is legitimate and affordable (McBride *et al.* 2006). The limited involvement of unions in interpreting and implementing the Skills Escalator would then become an issue.

As noted earlier, there are three interpretations of the Skills Escalator – as holistic 'best practice'; as 'best fit' practice; or as labour substitution. Of the seven Trusts, one could be said to be implementing the Skills Escalator as 'best practice', such that if the aggregation of individual KSFs were used to map skills and needs across the organisation, there would be potential for developing individuals within the organisation at all levels, and to all levels. Four Trusts were implementing the Skills Escalator in a 'pick and mix' manner to meet organisational and labour market needs. Two Trusts appeared to be using the Skills Escalator as a way of delegating tasks through paraprofessional roles. One of these was the Ambulance Trust which was adopting the Emergency Care and Assistant Practitioner roles encouraged by the Bradley Report (Department of Health 2005b) into ambulance services in England. The other was an Acute Trust with a considerable financial deficit. In the former, the union representatives were keen to get involved in a 'culture change'. In the latter, there was only one ULR for 4,500 staff and the union representatives were heavily involved in the practicalities of implementing Agenda for Change.

The dilemma of having influence at the same time as being incorporated into the managerial agenda is not a new phenomenon. However, this chapter has sought to indicate the unique potential of union involvement in the NHS and how they have 'seized the moment'. Danford *et al.* (2004) note how employees reject partnership strategies that solely address the needs of the organisation. It is only through future research with employees, when the KSF has been fully introduced and pay 'gateways' have been negotiated, that the full implications of this union involvement in the NHS will be seen.

Acknowledgements

This article is based on research gathered during the study of Skills Escalator activities commissioned by the Department of Health, Policy Research Programme. The article represents the views of the authors and not the Department of Health. The full research team comprises Anne McBride, Annette Cox, Stephen Mustchin, Marilyn Carroll, Paula Hyde, Elena Antonacopoulou, Kieran Walshe and Helen Woolnough.

References

Ackers, P., Smith, C. and Smith, P. (eds.) (1996), *The New Workplace and Trade Unionism.* (London: Routledge).

Aldridge, F. and Dutton, Y. with Robinson, D. and Tackey, N. (2005), *NHS Learning Accounts – the NHSU Project.* (Leicester: NIACE).

Audit Commission (2001), *Hidden Talents, Education, Training and Development for Healthcare Staff in NHS Trusts.* (London: Audit Commission).

Bach, S. (2002), 'Public-sector Employment Relations Reform under Labour: Muddling through on Modernisation?' *British Journal of Industrial Relations* 40:2, 319–339.

——, (2004), *Employment Relations and the Health Service: The Management of Reforms.* (London: Routledge).

Bain, G. S. (1986), *Industrial Relations in Britain.* (Basil Blackwell: Oxford).

Boxall, P. and Purcell, J. (2003), *Strategy and Human Resource Management.* (Basingstoke: Palgrave).

Bratton, J., Helms-Mills, J., Pyrch, T. and Sawchuk, P. (2003), *Workplace Learning: A Critical Introduction.* (Toronto: Garamond Press).

Burchill, F. and Casey, A. (1996), *Human Resource Management: The NHS – A Case Study.* (Basingstoke: Macmillan Business).

CHI (Commission for Health Improvement), NHS National Staff Survey 2003 accessed from <http://www.chi.nhs.uk>.

Clegg, H. (1976), *The System of Industrial Relations in Great Britain.* (Oxford: Basil Blackwell).

Clough, B. (2004), *From Spearholders to Stakeholders. The Emerging Role of Unions in the UK Learning and Skills System.* (London: TUC).

Crompton, R., Gallie, D. and Purcell, K. (eds.) (1996), *Changing Forms of Employment.* (London: Routledge).

Danford, A., Richardson, M., Stewart, P., Tailby, S. and Upchurch, M. (2004), 'High Performance Work Systems and Workplace Partnership: A Case Study of Aerospace Workers', *New Technology, Work and Employment* 19:1, 14–29.

Department of Health (2000), *The NHS Plan.* (London: Department of Health).

——, (2001), *Working Together, Learning Together: A Framework for Lifelong Learning for the NHS.* (London: Department of Health).

——, (2003), *HR in the NHS Plan: More staff working differently.* (London: Department of Health).

——, (2004), *The NHS Knowledge and Skills Framework (NHS KSF)*. (London: Department of Health).

——, (2005a), *National Framework to Support Local Workforce Strategy Development: A Guide for HR Directors in the NHS*. (London: Department of Health).

——, (2005b), *Taking Healthcare to the Patient: Transforming NHS Ambulance Services*. (London: Department of Health).

Dundon, T. and Eva, D. (1998), 'Trade Unions and Bargaining for Skills', *Employee Relations* 20:1, 57–72.

Ferlie, E., Ashburner, L., Fitzgerald, L. and Pettigrew, A. (1996), *The New Public Management in Action*. (Oxford: Oxford University Press).

Forrester, K. (2001), 'Modernised Learning: An Emerging Lifelong Learning Agenda by British Trade Unions?' *Journal of Workplace Learning* 13:7/8, 318–325.

——, (2004), '"The Quiet Revolution'? Trade Union Learning and Renewal Strategies', *Work, Employment and Society* 18:2, 413–420.

——, (2005), 'Learning for Revival. British Trade Unions and Workplace Learning', *Studies in Continuing Education* 27:3, 257–270.

Fryer, B. (2006), 'Learning for a Change in Healthcare', presentation by National Director, Widening Participation in Learning, 19 October.

Green, F. and Felstead, A. (1994), 'Training During The Recession' *Work, Employment and Society* 8 (2), 199–219.

Healthcare Commission, NHS National Staff Survey 2004 and 2005, accessed from <http://www.healthcarecommission.org.uk>.

Heaton, N., Mason, B., Morgan, J. (2002), 'Partnership and Multi-unionism in the Health Service', *Industrial Relations Journal* 33:2, 112–126.

Johnson, N. (2004), 'Supporting Effective Learning in the National Health Service: The Role of the NHSU', *Education for Primary Care* 15, 543–549.

Kelly, J. (1996), 'Union Militancy and Social Partnership' in Ackers (eds.).

Kersley, B., Alpin, C., Forth, J., Bryson, A., Bewley, H., Dix, G., Oxenbridge, S. (2006), *Inside the Workplace: Findings from the 2004 Workplace Employment Relations Survey*. (London: Routledge).

Martinez Lucio, M. and Stuart, M. (2002), 'Assessing the Principles of Partnership – Workplace Trade Union Representatives' Attitudes and Experiences', *Employee Relations* 24:3, 305–320.

McBride, A., Cox, A., Mustchin, S., Carroll, M., Hyde, P., Antonacopoulou, E., Walshe, K. and Woolnough, H. (2006), *Developing Skills in the NHS*. (Manchester: University of Manchester).

Munro, A. and Rainbird, H. (2000a), 'Unison's Approach to Lifelong Learning' in Terry (ed).

——, (2000b), 'The New Unionism and the New Bargaining Agenda: Unison – Employer Partnerships on Workplace Learning in Britain', *British Journal of Industrial Relations* 38:2, 223–240.

——, (2004), 'Opening Doors As Well As Banging On Tables. An Assessment of Unison/employer Partnerships on Learning in the UK Public Sector', *Industrial Relations Journal* 35:5, 419–433.

Mustchin, S. and McBride, A. (forthcoming), 'Lifelong Learning, Partnership and Modernisation in the NHS', *International Journal of Human Resource Management*.

National Learning and Skills Council (2005), *National Employer Skills Survey 2004 – Main Report*. (London: LSC).

Pelling, H. (1976), *A History of British Trade Unionism*. (Harmondsworth: Pelican).

Pfeffer, J. (1996), 'When it comes to 'Best Practices' – Why Do Smart Organisations Occasionally Do Dumb Things?', *Organizational Dynamics* 25, 33–44.

Rainbird, H. and Munro, A. (2003), 'Workplace Learning and the Employment Relationship in the Public Sector', *Human Resource Management Journal* 13, 30–44.

Rainbird, H., Sutherland, J., Edwards, P., Holly, L. and Munro, A. (2003), *Employee Voice and Training at Work. An Analysis of Case Studies and WERS 98*. (London: Department of Trade and Industry).

Seifert, R. (1992), *Industrial Relations in the NHS*. (London: Chapman and Hall).

Seifert, R. and Sibley, T. (2005), *United they Stood: The Story of the UK Firefighters' Dispute 2003–2004*. (London: Lawrence & Wishart).

Skills for Health (2003), *A Health Sector Workforce Market Assessment*. (London: Skills for Health).

Streeck, W. (1989), 'Skills and the Limits of Neo-Liberalism: The Enterprise of the Future as a Place of Learning', *Work, Employment and Society* 3:1, 89–104.

Terry, M. (ed.) (2000), *Redefining Public Sector Unionism – Unison and the Future of Trade Unions*. (London: Routledge).

Thornley, C. (1996), 'Segmentation and Inequality in the Nursing Workforce: Reevaluating the Evaluation of Skills' in Crompton *et al.* (eds).

——, (1998), *Neglected Nurses, Hidden Work*. (London: UNISON).

Unison (2004), *Agenda for Change: A Summary of the Proposals*. (London: Unison).

——, (2005), *A Unison Guide to the Knowledge and Skills Framework*. (London: Unison).

Chapter 6

Have Laptop will Travel:
Case Studies in Union Learning

David Wray

Introduction

In recent years, challenging social and economic disadvantage through the relationship between trade unions and workplace learning has gained contemporary policy and practical significance. Underpinned by legislation, supported by government funding, and endorsed by employers, workplace learning is now widely recognised as having a unique and positive role, particularly in relation to disadvantaged and excluded workers with basic skills needs. The Union Learning Fund (ULF) has, and continues to be, the principle mechanism challenging disadvantage through learning for workers in all sectors of the economy. This fund has supported and encouraged the development of Union Learning Representatives (ULRs) alongside other learning initiatives such as the creation of union learning centres that have often been developed in association with employers. Given statutory rights in 2002 (Employment Relations Act July 2002), and underpinned by an ACAS Code of Practice in 2003, these initiatives have impacted positively in workplaces throughout the UK. The undoubted success of the ULF, and the projects it has supported, can be seen in the increasing number of very positive evaluative reports that have emerged. All those involved in the projects: ULRs; tutors; employers; and learners; report general satisfaction with the projects they have been associated with. [For a sample of project evaluations undertaken in the North East see York Consulting (2003), Hope *et al.* (2003), Wray (2004)].

However, despite these successes and the general good will of everyone involved, there are some sections of the workforce who, because of structural constraints of their employment, their own individual circumstances or, as we shall see, a combination of both, are 'hard to reach' and as a result may be excluded from the learning opportunities offered by such projects. One significantly large group of workers that can be identified as 'hard to reach' are those who are employed on atypical contracts, particularly those who work part-time for only a few hours per day. Others may be difficult to identify, and thus harder to reach, not through labour market structural difficulties, but though more individual and personal circumstances. Given their marginal connection with the labour market, these groups may well be those with the most to gain from the educational opportunities offered through the ULF. This chapter offers an insight into the problems of three such 'hard to reach' groups, and evaluates their experiences in relation to the educational opportunities offered to them by the ULF. The chapter also highlights the central, and often critical, role of individuals in ensuring that the ULF, and all the training and education it offers, is within the reach of all workers.

The learners concerned in the case studies are: a group of school dinner 'ladies'; Asian factory workers excluded through language problems; and a group of abused women living in a Women's Refuge. All case studies were established through the TUC's Learning for All Fund (LFA) and are located in the north east of England. All individuals and organisations have been given pseudonyms to maintain confidentiality.

Have Lap-top Will Travel: Delivering Learning to School Ancillary Staff

> Dinner ladies make bloody good scones but no one ever asks them if they have essential skills needs. (ULR)

The initial project that generated this case study was established through a partnership between three of the major trade unions and a large Borough Council. The general population of this Borough has low levels of literacy and numeracy skills in comparison to the national average. The initial bid to the LFA (£25,000) was granted in 2003. The initial projects set up through this funding were acknowledged by everyone involved to have been a resounding success. However, the senior ULR and the Project Leader of the programmes set up under the bid, recognised that there were certain sections of the Borough's workforce who, by the nature of their employment, were excluded from the educational opportunities offered to all employees. The groups identified were all employed on part-time and short hour contracts.

The main barriers to learning for this group are not uncommon in the flexible labour market of the twenty-first century, but in terms of taking advantage of educational opportunities offered through the workplace, they can be the most difficult to overcome. Such workers, despite working short hour contracts for one employer may, in fact, have a number of similar contracts with other employers, and may work very long hours. An additional barrier was the fact that these atypical workers tend to be dispersed across the borough and in some cases, may work alone. What mainstream courses were available for these workers through the LFA programmes were often in the wrong place, as well as at the wrong time.

Having identified the problem, the senior ULR approached the Union Learning Committee overseeing the LFA programmes, in the hope that they could collectively develop a solution. Following a successful second bid (£14,000) to the LFA, a pilot project was developed to enable school ancillary staff such as cooks and kitchen staff working in the schools throughout the Borough, to take advantage of the learning opportunities available through the LFA programmes.

The initial problem in engaging these workers with the programmes was to make them aware of the learning opportunities that were available to them. The first attempt at engagement involved brining one individual from each school to a centrally located education centre, where the senior ULR gave a presentation on the educational opportunities available. The intention was that these individuals would then take the message back to their own workplaces to encourage staff to come forward and articulate their own learning needs. This attempt brought no response, not even from the delegates to the meeting. The senior ULR then decided to take matters into her own hands by visiting each of the 34 schools in the Borough to conduct her own survey by talking to each worker individually. The questions 'What do you want to learn?' and 'Where do you want the learning to take place?' brought a much stronger response. The majority of those wanting to take part identified basic computer skills as an area they would be interested in, though none of them used a computer in their work.

With the problem of 'what' solved, the next issue to be addressed was 'where'. The solution, developed by the Union Learning Committee was as effective as it was simple:

> Dinner ladies make bloody good scones but no one ever asks them if they have essential skills needs. If they do and they can't get to the courses at a place and time to suit them, then we'll take the courses to them. For the tutor it has been a case of 'have laptop will travel'. (ULR)

Liaising with the Adult Education Department of the Borough, the decision was taken by the Union Learning Committee to organise the learners from 4 or 5 schools into 3 groups based on a geographical area, and to use a teaching venue in each area. It is worth pointing out that, surprisingly, none of these venues was a school. In response to a question on this apparent anomaly – that people working in a school could not use school facilities for work based learning – a spokesperson for the Borough stated that:

> It makes no difference to the Local Authority if learning is taking place in a private or public organisation, because our remit is to cater for the learning needs of people in the Borough.

The venues were located in: an Educational Development Centre, a library and an Adult Learning Centre. All venues had computers, though the project used laptops to supplement any shortfall in provision. The five week certificated course, initially entitled 'Training for Work' was soon renamed 'Computers for the Terrified' by the learners. Classes were held after the learners' shift ended (2:30 to 4:30pm) and ran weekly, giving a total learning time of 10 hours, and all courses were taught by the same tutor from the Adult Learning Centre.

As the course progressed the (experienced) tutor identified several individual learners exhibiting basic skills needs and was able to use her own skills to begin to address those needs during the Training for Work course. As the course progressed, and confidence had been established in the tutor, each learner was assessed to identify their basic skills needs. This assessment identified that the learners ranged from the Entry Level to Level 1. These results were recorded and fed back to the learners, with most of them progressing to the 'Skills for Life' courses provided by the programme at the Adult Learning Centre, and importantly for these new learners, by the same tutor.

Many of the individual learners, having been out of education for so long, reported initial concerns about starting the course. Some were also worried about the tutor/learner relationship, as often their last experience at school had been a negative one. However, once the learners realised that they were learning in a friendly, helpful and non-judgemental environment those fears were allayed. The relationship that developed between tutor and learner proved to be sufficiently strong for the learners to say that they would like to keep the same tutor if more courses were provided. The tutor reinforced this by saying 'learning is also about establishing relationships and good relationships bring good results'.

This sentiment was also demonstrated by one learner who stated that learning in a group environment, where learners helped each other in a fun environment, was one of the most enjoyable elements of the course. Other learners stated:

> An enjoyable and informative class in an informal atmosphere ... the group help was great.

> It was important meeting people just like myself, who are interested in learning some skills.

Of the thirty women (ranging in age from the mid-20s through to the mid-50s) participating in this initial course, all successfully completed the Learning for Work Course. Listening to the learners during interview, it was obvious that they themselves had benefited in a number of ways, particularly in an improvement in self-confidence, and feelings of self worth, and all those interviewed intend to continue with learning. As one learner recalled:

> I was frightened to death when I put my name down, and panicked when the course started, but it wasn't as bad as I thought it would be. When we completed the course the Chief Executive and our local MP presented us all with certificates. I really felt great because it's the first certificate I've ever had in my life. The tutor often used the word 'empowerment' and now I know why. Now I've taken the first step I don't intend to stop, and I'm looking to see what I can do next.

The tutor also reported surprise in how far these learners had come by the end of what was only a five week course:

> At the end of the course, I was amazed at how far they had come in such a short time. They were able to operate a computer, type, organise and edit text, copy and paste, etc. They were delighted with what they achieved ... most importantly they overcame the barrier of getting back into education and found that it [learning] wasn't difficult ... they'd got over their bad experience of education at school, they had increased their self esteem and moved on as people.

According to the senior ULR, the success of the course was a result of identifying the needs of the learners and taking the learning to them:

> It's about providing them with something convenient that fits in with their lives. Enrolling on a course is a barrier, they don't have the willpower to go to the Local Authority to enrol, but if something was provided through the workplace and made very easy for them then it could continue ad infinitum. It's about creating convenient opportunities.

The prime mover for the majority of these timid and initially reluctant learners was a desire to be able to keep up with their children in the use of computers, a situation that this author has encountered elsewhere (Wray 2004). Having computers in the home, they wanted to learn the skills that would allow them to keep up with their children in the use of IT. The longer term benefits for these women can be seen firstly, in the confidence they undoubtedly gained from the learning experience and secondly, in their ambition to continue with what they see as a second chance to learn.

Since the initial intake, a further 30 learners have now completed the 'Training for Work' course, and on the basis of this successful beginning to the project, home care workers are now being targeted. Home care workers who, by the nature of their work tend to work alone, are another 'hard to reach' group who could benefit from such flexible and innovative provision.

Not Every One is A Winner. Teaching English for Speakers of Other Languages

How can you Integrate if you can't Communicate?

Perhaps the hardest to reach groups in any working situation are those who are excluded because they can not speak the language. This case study is of just such a group of workers whose main (and often only) languages are Urdu and Punjabi. It is a case study unlike the others, in that the story does not begin with a learning project, nor can it be seen as a success. This case study begins with a change of plant ownership and meetings between the workforce and a trade union Full-Time Officer (FTO). The workers concerned were all employed across three branch plants of an international company, all located in one local area, which employed large numbers of Asian workers, both male and female. In two of the branch plants Asian workers represented 10 per cent of the workforce, and in the third represented 90 per cent of the workforce. While many of these Asian workers could speak some English, the main language of communication on the shop floor in the third branch plant was Urdu, with some Punjabi also spoken. This case study also has a serendipitous element to it, in that the FTO with responsibility for this firm was from an Asian background, and fluent in both Urdu and Punjabi. She was also, at this time, her trade union's Race Officer with a special responsibility for recruiting Black and Asian workers throughout the region.

The beginnings of this project came during a meeting between that FTO and a group of Asian workers from the firm:

> I'd said 'I'm sick of repeating everything I say in Urdu, Punjabi...' and they'd said 'well, help us learn English then'. It was because of that, that I made the application for funding and got the project started. Since then I have come to realise just how difficult it must be to be unable to communicate with others if you do not speak the language (FTO)

The case study is based on the resultant (three) attempts to provide courses in English for Speakers of Other Languages (ESOL) to the Urdu and Punjabi speaking employees at this firm.

The first attempt was made in 2000, following a successful bid by the trade union to the European Social Fund aimed at improving the language skills of the primarily Asian workforce at the firm. The trade union received £25,000 to develop and deliver the training, and armed with this funding the FTO gave a presentation of the planned project to the directors of the firm. Despite the justification that an improvement of the language skills of these workers would have many benefits for the firm, not least in terms of health and safety and productivity, the offer was refused. With this negative response, the funding was reluctantly returned, and no language training took place.

In 2003 a second attempt was made by the FTO, with an application to the LFA fund for a 12-month project. As LFA funding requires a minimum number of stakeholders in order to qualify (usually: the TUC, a trade union and an employer) and as in this case the employer did not want to be involved, the FTO proposed that the Asian workers form a 'community', which would effectively replace the employer as the third stakeholder. In this way the employer's veto was circumvented. Following an approach by the FTO, the Local Authority within which the firm is located became an additional stakeholder, and offered the provision of ESOL courses free of charge. With this final part of the project in place, the TUC released funding for a six-month trial period. As a condition of the funding, one ULR had to be identified within the 'community' to undergo ULR training, and 12 learners had to progress to ESOL Entry Level 2. The project started in August 2003 with a grant of £10,000. For the FTO the project was an attempt to widen participation, not just in education or in trade union membership, but in the community as a whole. She believed that breaking down the barriers of language would bring down cultural barriers as well. Her vision saw the project not simply as something for the workplace, but something for the wider community within which the firm was located.

From those workers coming forward to take part in the ESOL courses, the ESOL Coordinator, following an initial assessment, identified two groups with different levels of English: one group for Pre-Entry and Level 1; and the other, more advanced group, to work toward Level 2, demonstrating the need for such language training within this workforce. As the employer was not involved the classes, which lasted two hours, had to be delivered in the worker's own time, and were run over two days. One day for Pre-Entry and Level 1, and the other for Level 2. On each day, classes were delivered twice, (in the morning and afternoon) to fit in with the firm's shift pattern (an eight hour sift rotation, with four days on and four days off). Classes were held at two locations convenient to all learners. The initial intake for Pre-Entry and Level 1 was 10, and the intake for Level 2 was 5. A further 30 learners were recruited to take the courses as the project rolled out. Initially, the project started well, with the learners progressing well, the ULR was selected (Asian male) and trained, and the FTO, despite a heavy workload, continued to support the ULR, who had became involved because:

> When I came to England two and a half years ago I quickly discovered the need to speak English if I was to get on in this country. I became involved in the project because I wished a scheme like this had been available to me, and the opportunity to train to become a ULR offered me the chance to help others in the same situation I had been in. (ULR)

There then followed a series of unfortunate events which delayed the progress of the learners, and ultimately led to the abandonment of the project: at half-term in October there were no tutors available to deliver the classes; then it was Ramadan, so participants found it difficult to attend in the evenings; then it was Christmas and again the tutors were unavailable. To add to these difficulties, in January, the employer switched to a continental shift pattern (12 hours on and 12 hours off) which meant the learners found it very difficult to attend the classes. The management of the firm said the shift patterns were changed to meet the needs of production, though some of the workers believe that it was simply an attempt to hinder the progress of the project. With few learners able to attend, the project could not progress, and it was suspended.

Seeing the change in shift patterns as the main problem, the FTO and the ESOL coordinator approached the Local Authority's Adult Education Service who agreed that the courses could be delivered on site, but the HR Manager refused the offer, stating that 'they could have carried on learning in their own time even with the new shift pattern'.

The third attempt to provide ESOL training to the workers at this firm was made in 2004, and this time the project did not include the trade union. Following a series of meetings between the employer and the Learning and Skills Council (LSC), the firm received £35,000 from the Skills For Life (SFL) programme, a programme with the twin objectives of enhancing the skills base of the workforce, and increasing productivity. The SFL programme funds capital equipment, with the condition that the employer must match the sum received. The targets of the SFL programmes are usually to progress learners through to National Test Level 1 in Literacy or Numeracy, however, the focus of the LSC's grant to this firm was specifically to provide ESOL for their Asian employees, to enable them all to eventually achieve the National Test Level 1 in English.

The funding provided four computers for each branch plant and a training room for six people on the site with the large proportion of Asian employees. Having set these training facilities up, the firm then approached the Adult Education Service at the Local Authority requesting them to provide the ESOL tutors, with the promise that the courses would be delivered at times that would suit the new shift patterns. With these convenient times arranged, posters were displayed around the factory informing employees about the ESOL courses and 80 people showed an initial interest. However, when the ESOL coordinator visited the factory to carry out the ESOL assessment only 20 people attended. Their level of English ranged from Pre-Entry Level to Level 1, again demonstrating the poor standard of English among the Asian employees at the firm. Despite the computers and training room set up via the LSC funding, all courses were to be delivered off site in two centres in the local area supplied by the Local Authority, and again, free of charge. As only two people turned up for the classes, the courses, and the ESOL project was discontinued.

The employer reported that the failure of the project was due to the employees wanting to do the courses in the firms time, despite being told that they would have to be done in the workers own time:

> We continually emphasised the point that the course would have to be done in their own time at all stages of the discussions. The failure is down to the workers wanting to be paid for taking the training.

The ULR believes that the roots of the failure of the project lie in the shift patterns and the low wages paid by the firm:

> The workers are very keen to do the ESOL classes, but it is already hard work carrying out their work with the hours in the new shift patterns and this is made worse if they do overtime. Most want the overtime because of the low wages. If they could do the courses in paid time, there would be more interest in them.

The Human Resources manager reflected that it was unfortunate that the ESOL courses did not run, but went on to say that:

> ... learning has got to fit in with the business plan ... do they have to read or write or speak English to work here?

As the ESOL classes did not materialise, the training resources were used to provide communication courses for team leaders and supervisors (there is approximately a 50/50 split between ethnic minorities and non-ethnic minorities who are team leaders) with the courses delivered on the computers financed by the ESOL project. Given the history of the this case study, it is difficult not to see the final attempt at providing ESOL courses to the workforce as a cynical and opportunistic attempt by the management to gain part funding for a training resource for the firm. Readers can decide for themselves. In doing so they should consider that, given the funding was for capital equipment, (which was set up on the firm's premises) with the aim of providing ESOL for the Asian workers, why then were the courses delivered off site? Even the neutral reader will be brought to speculate on the reasons the senior management at this firm were reluctant to provide their Asian workforce with the language skills that would allow them to assimilate into the general population of workers.

When questioned about the continued offer of free courses, given the circumstances surrounding this case, the Local Authority cited their determination to ensure that everyone has the opportunity and the ability to fully integrate into the wider community.[1]

The Oyster Room: Learning in Refuge[2]

> I passed my driving theory course in the Oyster Room, which is funny really, because the Oyster Room used to be the garage (Resident)

Both case studies outlined above discuss the difficulties in engaging 'hard to reach' groups of workers; in these instances hard to reach as a result of the structural conditions of their employment. This case study concerns a group of individuals not

---

1 Shortly after the research was completed for this case study, the ULR involved in the project left the firm. He declined to give a reason for his leaving.

2 Given the nature of the issues involved in this case study, I would like to acknowledge the contribution of Val Adlparvar, who conducted all the interviews that took place within the refuge. Without her assistance this case study would not have been possible.

in employment, though excluded through the individual conditions of their lives. The group we are concerned with in this case study are women who find themselves in personal crisis; homeless, and with their lives in chaos because they are the victims of domestic violence. Because of the very individualistic nature of this case study, I have given greater 'voice' to the individuals concerned than in the previous case studies.

The project was initiated by the FTO of a major trade union who was also the union's Regional Equality Rights Officer. Part of the remit of this equality role was a specific responsibility for women, and in particular making domestic violence a workplace issue. That role brought her into contact with the manager of the Woman's Refuge that is the focus of this case study. Through discussions on the individual consequences of domestic violence came the realisation that many of the women, on leaving the refuge to reshape their lives, simply transfer dependency for themselves (and their children if they have them) away from an abusive man, on to the state. If this cycle of dependency, and the social exclusion associated with it, was to be broken then those women would need the life skills necessary to gain, and then maintain, employment. Knowing of the availability of funding through the LFA, the FTO saw the solution in terms of a learning centre attached to the Refuge, so that these vulnerable individuals, wanting to improve their life chances through education, would not have to leave the Refuge. As the FTO stated 'one of the main tools in helping these women put their lives back together is education'.

Not knowing if such a scheme would fall under the remit of the LFA, the FTO and the Refuge Manager approached the regional TUC, who were enthusiastic about the plan, and offered support. As a result of this approach, a (successful) bid was quickly put together for the funding for what would turn out to be a fully equipped learning centre in what had been the garage of the Refuge. To ensure that the requirements necessary for the funding were met, the deputy manager of the Refuge (a trade union member), underwent the training to become ULR for the project. Following the opening of the learning centre, a competition was held among the residents of the Refuge to find a name for the facility. The wining suggestion was the 'Oyster Room' because, as the winner explained:

> When you walk into the learning centre you come out of your shell, and you leave with pearls of wisdom.

Given the individual circumstances of these women, and the reasons why they were in the Refuge, learning was a low priority and demand for the Oyster Room was not initially high. However, by holding the weekly house meetings in the Oyster Room, residents were introduced to the facilities available to them. By encouraging a different individual each week to take the minutes, and then edit them on a computer, those individuals started to use the facility in their own time and progress, though slow, was made. As one resident reports:

> When I first came in, D... says, 'Do you want to type the minutes after the meeting', I said 'No, I can't use a computer'. She said, 'There's no such word as can't ... I'll show you'. She switched it on and said, 'If anything goes wrong you press that button'. I kept phoning her up and saying, 'I've done it again, I've wiped it off, I don't know how to get it back'. She says, 'Press this then that', and then the confidence was just there. So now I know how to do it, just my spelling's not up to scratch.

The main problem in delivering formal courses in the centre was numbers. Given the nature of the residents living in the Refuge: the varied length of stay; and of the differing and changing priorities of these individuals; the organisation of formal courses to be delivered by external tutors was difficult, because the 'women often won't undertake courses with strangers at this stage in their lives' (ULR).

The solution partially came through the inclusion of two (female) tutors from a community education project in the local area. These tutors started informal 'tea and talk' sessions twice weekly in the Oyster Room:

> We call it 'tea and talk', but basically it was advice sessions because I am also an IAG worker, and it was advice on learning and work we concentrated on. We try to motivate the women, raise their aspirations, broaden their outlook, engage them in some sort of learning. We put posters around the Refuge, giving dates and times and they can come in when they feel like it (Tutor)

The ULR highlights the extent of these difficulties (and also the successes) through the experience of A:

> When she first attended the centre we gave her a folder and asked her to put a label on it so that she could write her name on it. She almost broke into tears because she couldn't decide where to place it on the folder. She had never been allowed to make even the simplest of decisions. She developed so much while she was here, and since that she is now doing a degree course at university. While A... is not typical of all our learners, all of them leave with a sense of achievement.

By far the most successful initiative undertaken in the centre has been the delivery of the driving theory course. While initially there were problems over confidentiality and men coming in to the Oyster Room to oversee the exam, these were dealt with sympathetically with the organisations concerned, and 10 women successfully completed the course. Provisional licences were paid for through the project, with the women paying for the exam. The incentive for the women is that if they pass they get 10 free driving lessons. This course is also available to women who have left the Refuge, as is the use of the Oyster Room:

> The whole ethos of the Oyster Room is about confidence building, but with a purpose, because if you can get your driving test, you have mobility and independence and the opportunities they provide. It just increases your life chances (Refuge Manager)

Given the constantly changing population of the Refuge it has been difficult for the project leaders to develop any formal and continuing programme of courses. As the Refuge Manager explains:

> It's very difficult to know what course to try and organise because the Oyster Room is needs led. It's whatever the women who come through the door need. It could be courses on assertiveness; or Asian women with issues around forced marriage; it could be asylum seekers with immigration issues. We have one resident with us now with immigration problems as well as a violent husband, and when she came in we were able to get some ESOL support for her. She is learning to develop her English language skills and she's just passed her exams in English, and she is hoping to go on to college and do some courses

there. This is despite everything else that is going on in her life, so it's a huge achievement but it's something that's given her the courage and the strength to be able to continue. If we can't provide the needs, then we'll find somebody who can.

Every new resident, once settled in, is offered a basic skills assessment in literacy and numeracy. They are then encouraged to take the course that the skills assessments suggest would help them develop their life skills.

More important than the passing of tests, success is seen in the increasing confidence of the learners, and the different, more positive, ways they see themselves. According to the Refuge Manager:

> Our success can't be judged by bums on seats, or exams passed. It has to be judged by how many residents take that first step into the Oyster Room. When they come here the last thing on their minds is education, but when things settle down we introduce them slowly to the idea of learning. Once they meet the staff, and see that they can go at their own pace, they soon start to become involved.

Success is also seen in the numbers of ex-residents who continue to use the facilities of the Oyster Room. The ULR feels that ex-residents continue to attend because the service offered is flexible, confidential, and personal, and in a setting within which they are comfortable:

> Individuals keep coming back because we are able to meet their needs. Despite the problems in their lives, they still see learning as important, and they always make time for the sessions. One of the best aspects of being a ULR here, is to slowly see confidence building in people who came here with none.

Due to the nature and practicalities of this project, everyone involved in the project, from its inception to completion, is female, and perhaps because domestic violence resonates more with women than men, all are completely engaged in meeting the needs of the client group. This is a very personal project to all concerned, and not least to the Tutors from the community education project who donated £1,000 to what they described as 'our favourite place', for the purchase of books.

However, it could be argued that the success of this particular project should not simply be judged in terms of engagement with learning. For F... the strength of the Oyster Room is that:

> We can access it at any time of the week when it's open, from first thing in the morning till it closes on a night. Basically we can use it whenever we want, for whatever we want. Some of the women would rather book a session and do it privately, so they can get their own thoughts on the computer, like I did with my experiences of domestic violence and things, like a diary. Other times we all get together just to have a little grumble or we can let our hair down and have an hour away from the kids, and play about on the computers. It's a little bit of breathing space for the women, gives them time to talk, and share experiences.

Perhaps the last word on this project should be left to the ULR:

Overall, the great success of the Oyster Room can be seen through the unique learning opportunity it offers women, at a time of major change in their lives. The dedication, enthusiasm and commitment of all those involved are providing a vulnerable group of women with the confidence, and the tools, to rebuild and significantly change their lives for the better. Exposure to education, at whatever level, gives people feelings of self worth and the ability to make choices, something our clients have been denied within oppressive relationships. Through education we are helping to keep people from being socially excluded.

Conclusion

What can we take from these case studies? As with all case studies they offer very little in terms of a broader understanding of the national project in union learning. Nonetheless, they do offer detailed insights into individual projects that collectively provide a strong qualitative base within which more quantitative research projects can be grounded. The learning experiences of the individuals benefiting from the two successful studies; the dinner 'ladies'; and the women in the Refuge; are similar to those reported from other LFA project evaluations, and are remarkable only in terms of the client groups involved.

Significantly, both of these successful cases demonstrate in their own way, the complexities of ensuring that 'learning for all' means just that: ensuring that the educational opportunities offered through such projects meet the needs of all those who can benefit from them, not just in terms of content, but in terms of availability. 'Hard to reach' groups, excluded either through structural or individual reasons, must be identified and solutions found to overcome the circumstances of their exclusion. While difficult, the examples outlined above demonstrate what can be achieved, if the will is there.

There is another less obvious, though perhaps more important, lesson to be learned from these distinct and very disparate case studies: the central, even vital, role of the individual. It is the individuals involved in the organisation and day to day running of the programmes on whose actions the projects either succeed or fail. With much of the research concerned with quantifying either the numbers of learners; or the nature and form of projects, the contribution and impact of individuals tends to be only implicit, rather than explicitly identified. Where research has previously been concerned with 'structure', it must now seriously consider 'agency' as a factor of evaluation.

In each of the case studies offered here, key individuals, all with the skills, enthusiasm, imagination, inventiveness and drive can be identified as pivotal to the development of the projects. Similar individuals were identified in all of the other ULF projects that were part of the larger evaluative research project from which these three case studies are drawn (Wray 2004). At the heart of each project, a small group of committed individuals could be identified as central to each project and exhibiting all the qualities described above. These individuals were either ULRs, trade union officers or activists, employers, educators, and in some instances non-aligned individuals involved through a commitment to widening participation to learning.

Among the individuals involved in the three case studies offered here, these qualities can be seen in abundance, particularly those of imagination, inventiveness and drive. Even in the failed ESOL project, the qualities and determination of the FTO twice took the project to the brink of success, and was only frustrated by the actions of others beyond her control, who, in the opinion of the author, were working to a different agenda.

The failed ESOL project also raises another question that will be pertinent to all projects that involve the development of a learning centre funded by the ULF. That question is 'who owns the project?'. Or to put it another way: what will happen to the learning centre, and more importantly to the hardware such as computers and printers, when the funding runs out? Will these centres become simply training rooms for the benefit of the firms, as in the ESOL case, or will they continue to be used for the purpose they were created? What happens if the firm closes down? Will the trade union 'partner' be able to remove that hardware to another facility, perhaps in the community?

Finally, for the learners, the benefits they received from the two successful projects are the most obvious achievements, and hardly need repeating here. In both instances, high quality programmes were created that were both flexible and responsive to the disparate needs of the learners, as learning was made both available and accessible. The impact of lifelong learning opportunities for those two particular groups of learners is graphically illustrated in their own words above. Collectively, those statements encapsulate what this author believes to be the key issue for all those involved in developing lifelong learning projects: the need to constantly push open doors to provide learning opportunities is simply the first phase; the second is developing in the individual learner the confidence to continually go through those doors themselves. That final (and vital) phase can only be achieved through the instillation of an enthusiasm for learning that will encourage individual learners to keep doing it for themselves.

References

Hope, R., Stirling J., and Wray, D. (2003), *Promoting Access to Learning: Establishing a Trade Union Learning Centre*. (Unison)

Wray, D. (2004), *Learning to Shine: Case Studies of Trade Union Learning for All Fund Projects in the North East*. (North Region TUC).

York Consulting (2003), *Evaluation of the Learning for All Fund*. (North Region TUC: York Consulting).

Chapter 7

The Outcomes and Usefulness of Union Learning

Steve Shelley

> Our learning is about real learning ... what we want to learn ... and what's useful to us
> (USDAW, Union of Shop, Distributive and Allied Workers 1999, 21).

Such a statement from a trade union's 'lifelong learning' literature is notable in the way it emphasises ownership and usefulness to be something particular to the union and distinct from learning in other contexts. It also raises issues about what 'real' learning means, the extent of distinctiveness that may occur through union learning and, indeed, what 'useful' may mean to the learners involved.

These issues are particularly significant given that, in addition to their own agendas, trade unions now have a heightened role within what may be construed to be the more mainstream public policy arena of 'lifelong learning' in the UK (DfES 2003a; DfES 2005). Within this arena, since 1998 part of the public funding for learning and skills development has been accessed only by trade unions, through the Union Learning Fund (ULF). Funding increased from £2m in 1997 to a current annual budget of £12.5m (Unionlearn 2007) and under the scheme 580 union learning centres had been established by 2006 (York Consulting 2006). National learning and skills policy also supports Union Learning Representatives (ULRs) which are funded partly by the ULF. Appointed from 1998 on a voluntary basis and given statutory recognition for time off to support their activities of advising and providing learning support to workplace colleagues in the Employment Relations Act (2002) (Calveley *et al.* 2003; CIPD 2004), almost 18,000 ULRs were appointed by 2007 (a figure that is due to rise to 22,000 by 2010) and in the year 2006/07 ULRs involved over 150,000 workers in various forms of learning (Unionlearn 2007).

This chapter focuses on these contemporary union learning and ULF activities in the UK, exploring the nature of learning in the public-funded ULF learning centres and in the work of Union Learning Representatives (ULRs). Although the broader range of union education and training, defined to include 'tools', 'issues' and 'labour studies' courses (Spencer 2002) is an important context, these are analysed and brought together with union learning elsewhere in this book. What is necessary in this chapter is to enquire about the meaning of learning and the issues of distinctiveness and usefulness, given trade union roles within the implementation of mainstream learning and skills policy. The chapter draws upon a range of secondary documentary sources in order to gain insights into the subjects learnt, taking account of the learning environment, including the inputs (such as the materials and methods used), the contexts (access, the trainers, the physical environment), and the benefits, reasons and purposes of the learning in the wider work and social environment of the learner.

Interpretations of 'usefulness' are sought firstly in the context of mainstream understandings of learning. Such definitions suggest that learning is a broad process of enquiry and reflection. Ranson and Stewart (1994) build on the work of Argyris and Schon and others in stating that learning is a process of discovery about why things are as they are and how they might become; the ability to undertake such open enquiry forming the basis of the 'learning society'. This 'lifelong learning' approach would appear to be commonly shared by government, trades unions and employers (Rainbird 2000), aiming to achieve individual, organisational, societal and economic benefits in an inclusive and high skill society (Keep and Mayhew 1999; Lloyd and Payne 2002). In this unitarist interpretation all learning is seen to be 'good', to the benefit of all. This prevailing neo-liberal economic approach sees skill development linked to economic growth, so that as:

> businesses become more productive and profitable [they help] individuals achieve their ambitions for themselves, their families and their communities (DfES 2005, 5).

This impression is reinforced by the assertion from the General Secretary of the Trades Union Congress (TUC) that the massive popularity of lifelong learning has proved that economic development can benefit working people:

> The learning agenda has proved that economic progress and social justice are two sides of the same coin (Barber 2004, 10).

Within this policy government rhetoric directs many of these initiatives at the low skilled and disadvantaged, so that they 'make a real difference to the lives of working people' (Clarke 2004, 10). At the same time the trade union movement expresses the advantages to the nation's economy, as Brendan Barber, TUC General Secretary states:

> Unions are using their unique role in the workplace to raise the skills levels of UK workers so that businesses can better compete in the global economy (TUC 2004a).

The established learning and skills rationale for trade union involvement is based on evidence that union members are more likely to receive training than non-union members (TUC 2002; TUC 2004a) and that union representatives seen as trusted colleagues, are thought to be able to encourage learning, overcome organisational barriers and be especially effective in redressing inequality in learning opportunity (CIPD 2004).

However, in understanding the 'usefulness' of trade union learning, the multiplicity of purpose and the assumed unproblematic unitarist nature of learning policy requires further examination. This understanding has to be through consideration of the individual and social context of the learning, the nature of work opportunities, learning diagnosis and development, and the economic contexts and political agendas that may influence the purposes of the learning.

A starting point for such interpretation may be the tradition of 'really useful knowledge' originally expressed through the Chartist movement in the nineteenth century (Ainley 1994). This was seen as learning for liberation, not just for understanding but to change the world for workers' own benefit. Extending this understanding of 'usefulness' in order to better understand the nature of union learning, this chapter uses a framework of analysis compiled from various typologies of union and adult learning, in particular those of Simon (1965), Freire (1972), Elsey (1986) and Taylor (1993). This framework comprises of three categorisations. Firstly, learning of a liberal humanist nature, provided in an impartial context, that is of direct benefit to the individual and to the achievement of their personal fulfilment, largely, but not exclusively, intellectual fulfilment. Secondly, vocational learning that is, in effect, work training and that enables the individual to make economic progress. Thirdly, learning of a more radical nature that is provided with a direct agenda to change society through collective as well as individual action.

Of course, use of such a framework is not itself without problem, as discussion of the multiplicity of union learning outcomes reveals later in the chapter. In addition to drawing upon historically-derived categorisations, there is admittedly a risk of the framework losing its contemporary validity. Notions of radicalism have a contextual interpretation from the nineteenth and early twentieth centuries where social drives for education were closely linked to strong definitions of class (Maheu 1995) and where political and industrial campaigns were often explicitly connected (Pimlott and Cook 1991). There is an increasing recognition that notions of societal divisions now include class and non-class bases, and a more overt recognition of the duality of structure and agency (Urry, 1995). Thus, as the introduction to this book discusses, in contemporary times trade unions have had to consider entering into accommodative partnership arrangements with employers and have had to explore servicing as well as organising models with their memberships (Blyton and Turnbull 2004). Nevertheless, the framework used here enables understanding of learning outcomes both within and outside mainstream policy orientations, and of what has been and what might be, thus opening up opportunities for the potential of union learning that might otherwise be by-passed.

Liberal Humanist Learning

As an earlier chapter of this book details, the trade union movement has historically campaigned for education for all, and as a way out of poverty. One form of this education has been a liberal humanist approach, placing emphasis on transforming the individual for intellectual development and for leisure, rather than directly work-related and vocational outcomes, and in so doing to enable individuals to participate fully in democratic society.

There are currently a number of union learning initiatives which appear to be oriented in this direction. Currently, the most numerous subjects provided by trade union learning initiatives are information and communication technology (ICT) and Basic Skills (O'Grady 2006). Basic skills training centres on numeracy and literacy and is provided free to all who need it under the 'Skills for Life' banner and through the 'learndirect' network, with one way of delivering this being through ULF-funded projects. Other examples include other forms of ICT training such as for digital photography and for computer troubleshooting, learning a language, first aid training, learning to swim, household finance, fitness and nutrition, FA football coaching to train a local youth team, garden design and GCSE, A level and degree courses in, for example, law and social sciences.

The outcomes of these learning provisions are diverse. The Skills for Life programme attempts to enable the learning of basic skills amongst groups who have been disadvantaged by lack of access to these in the past. It aims to enable parents to help educate their children, so that the next generation is not disadvantaged. It provides assistance for everyday life on such issues as not getting into debt, being 'streetwise', avoiding being 'conned', understanding pensions (for those fortunate enough to have one), and to enhance first aid and safety in the home (SERTUC 2004a).

Union reports also highlight the liberating nature of affective outcomes such as self confidence:

> It was excellent and abolished a lot of the negative feelings about learning that I left school with. I realised I wasn't a dunce, that I had got a brain. It was a real confidence booster. These courses have certainly inspired me. Apart from all the skills I learnt, which will help me to progress in my career, I have started doing some creative writing (Unison 2005).

These examples illustrate how workers are enabled to develop discretion in their career and life opportunities.

Nevertheless, there are complications to this liberal humanist agenda, in terms of the nature of learning and its funding, participation, pedagogical approaches and outcomes of individual and societal transformation. Firstly, within a broad definition of liberal humanist education, Elsey (1986) sees a recreational model that is learner self-financing and a liberal progressive model that is publicly funded. In current union learning a clear tension concerns the extent of public funding, currently limited to basic skills learning and free entitlements to level two qualifications. This tension is apparent in the learning that unions broker but are unable to arrange funding for, notably uncertificated learning and qualifications that are outside of the current DfES/ULF public funding entitlements (Shelley 2005). The way in which employers partly fund union learning, through support of work-based learning centres discussed later in this chapter, also distorts the 'pure' liberal humanist interpretation.

A second complication concerns learner and teacher/trainer participation in the setting of the learning agenda and content, and in the pedagogical delivery of the learning. As it stands, and with a few notable exceptions, union learners have choice from a range of pre-determined and pre-structured courses. In addition, these are largely delivered by computer-based learning which brings with it the advantages of access and of learner interaction with the learning materials, but which affords less opportunity for the learner to shape the content of the learning and still less for the tutors or other providers to themselves learn from interaction. Using radical analysis of pedagogy, based on Freire (1972) and extended by Taylor (1993), there are probably two interpretations here. One is a likely emphasis on learning of a 'maintenance' nature (Taylor 1993), with the teacher operating as 'banker' (Freire 1972), as an acknowledged expert providing direction albeit with the learners having a say in the particular content, examples and orientation of the learning. Another is that the teacher is also participating as a learner, but that the content of the learning is constrained by the prevailing institutional agenda, for example with limited choice of courses from a pre-set menu and with a predetermined curriculum.

Although current union learning may have potential for social transformation outcomes beyond the individual and thus be construed as 'reforming' (Taylor 1993) in nature, the extent of this is uncertain given the constraints of the learning provision. Such constraints jeopardise the realisation of liberal humanist education to, as Simon (1965) and Elsey (1986) see it, extend transformation beyond the individual to evolutionary, incremental societal change, for example, through knowledge acquisition, confidence and ability to participate in society at a number of different levels, from family, to local community and to national society through the democratic process. Such have been mainstream aims of the labour and trade union movements since their involvement in education in the early twentieth century.

When wider structural constraints of work and employment are considered, separating out work and non-work related learning is highly problematic. So, although Skills for Life and other seemingly emancipatory programmes can be seen to be about a wider non-work related agenda, the work-related context of such learning is also apparent and the learning topics have applications directly to jobs and tasks within jobs. Thus, the government seeks to convince chief executives and managing directors of the business benefits that arise from improving literacy and numeracy at work (DfES 2003b). Given the prevailing work context of employers seeking to extract surplus value from workers in ever more persistent and ingenious ways (Warhurst *et al.* 2004), such learning provision can also be understood as attempts to engender employee commitment through an appeal to 'hearts and minds' and, more instrumentally, through part of the benefits package. Indeed, almost any learning contextualised in the prevailing (structured) political economy, but particularly that based in any way in the workplace, may be seen as workers (and trade unions) manufacturing their own consent (Burawoy 1979) through undertaking learning that is directly or indirectly to do with work, careers, 'employability' and 'citizenship'. It is thus here that the liberal humanist analysis of union learning overlaps with more explicit vocational outcomes.

Vocational Learning

Vocational learning has outcomes that are directly concerned with work performance and with career progression. Thus Elsey (1986) describes the work/training model of learning as being for economic purpose, financed publicly and/or in partnership with industry and featuring training towards work related skills strategies and competence-based qualifications. From the workers' perspective these should enable the individual to gain better paid employment, make economic progress and to obtain a greater share of the profits of capitalism (Simon 1965; Taylor 1993). The earlier discussion of lifelong learning policy illustrates a rational economic view of such learning outcomes, not only raising the appropriate types of skills in order for the individual to prosper, but also enabling the organisation to become more profitable and to enhance economic growth at national level. This is a rather narrow interpretation of 'useful' learning, with an overall emphasis on performance.

Examples of work-related union learning directly provide key transferable skills, specific task-functional and organisation-specific skills. The basic skills previously discussed are transferable in the way in which they may enable effective communication in the work context. Examples of company-specific training and training related to particular jobs and vocations include the training for print workers managed by the print union GPMU and Leeds College of Technology, including machine printing, print finishing, Mac skills, workflow and digital print (The Learning Rep 2004a):

> With vocational training a major issue in an industry [print] where too many companies plug their skills gaps by poaching from the competition, the centre has been offering courses in industry standard software, including Adobe PhotoShop, Quark Xpress and Microsoft powerpoint, outside of work time (TUC 2004b).

Other examples of vocational training provided by union learning initiatives include health and safety training, job specific qualifications and customer service training.

There are undoubtedly major advantages to be gained by workers involved in such learning, advantages that need recognition of the relationship between economic and humanistic quality of life outcomes. In addition to direct economic benefits, the acquisition of task-functional skills may afford workers' greater control of their labour process at the job level with, as recognised by Grugulis (2003a) and Grugulis *et al.* (2004), discretion of decision-making and use of knowledge in job roles. In terms of workers' broader careers, such learning may enable greater worker control and discretion over their ability to choose jobs both in and outside particular organisations, by promotion and by increasing employability and ability to change employers and indeed other forms of economic activity. In terms of quality of life opportunities there can be broad outcomes including well-being and economic sufficiency. As one learner comments, 'I was previously stuck in secretarial work and I was bored – but no longer' (Unison 2005).

However, in many respects, the outcomes from union learning may be seen to be optimising control on the agenda of employers and capital, with benefits perceived particularly by employers, as a manager at Barking and Dagenham Council said:

> There has been a marked increase in morale, staff have a more positive attitude, and turnover has been reduced (The Learning Rep 2004a, 11).

In the case of the INA Bearing Company, trade union learning is supported in the context of:

> response to increased competition from low-labour-cost countries ... a sustained attempt to upskill the workforce ... the union involvement has been welcomed by management and personnel staff (CIPD 2004, 7).

The economic context shapes the agendas of agencies involved in labour market demand and shortage. So for example, the London Development Agency (LDA) prioritises manufacturing and design; creative and cultural industries; tourism, hospitality and allied sectors (SERTUC 2002), and seeks to harness trade union learning for this end.

There are further tensions concerning trade union involvement in vocational learning. Firstly, low cost employer strategies and control of the labour process restrict opportunities for many workers to maximise their share of capital. The prevailing market-driven approach to vocational training is one in which, despite notable exceptions, prevailing business strategies are towards low cost production and service provision that encourage minimalist and low-skill employer approaches to training (Taylor 2003). Critical views also suggest that the outcomes of vocational learning need to be understood in the context of a class-based social pyramid (Ainley 1999). Both suggest the importance of understanding learning and skill in the context of employers' control of the labour process, in which vocational learning is seen as functionalist with skill incorporated in work design so as to limit workers' task discretion and in a manner that can be defined as narrowly task or firm specific, thus providing an efficient, submissive and obedient workforce (Karabel and Halsey 1977). Thus, for example, whilst Heyes and Stuart (1998) find that trade union participation is associated with improved quality of training, this is nevertheless training that is on the employer's agenda, such as coping with an increased workload. It is argued that the result of a low skill economy approach is the perpetuation of disadvantage (Ashton and Felstead 2001; Nolan 2001; Taylor 2003; Grugulis *et al.* 2004) and a situation that is markedly at odds with the reflective requirements of a learning society propounded by Ranson and Stewart (1994). There are clearly issues here with the provision of union learning that is directly work related, in terms of the relative gains available to workers and employers.

Secondly, this critical analysis extends beyond job-related training to concerns about so-called 'transferable skills'. A feature of union learning is the emphasis on transferable skills and associated credentialism typically based on vocational qualification-based courses through government-sponsored programmes (Forrester 2004), including National Vocational Qualifications (NVQs), learndirect, and the European Computer Driving Licence (ECDL). 'Certified learning' is seen to be a major benefit for the learners involved (CIPD 2004). For example, learndirect programmes focus on diagnosis and testing of basic skills, through the use of national Adult Literacy and Numeracy Tests, awarding certificates that are the equivalent of key skills tests for communication and application of numbers at Level 1 and Level 2 (DfES 2003b).

However, there is well documented evidence that the outcomes of transferable skills training are only partially transferable and that they reinforce low-level multi-function work within organisations (Stevens 1996; Ainley 1999). When linked to qualifications, the 'transferable' (and therefore liberating) rhetoric of credentialism appears stronger. Yet reports of trade union learning indicate that employers 'cherry pick' only NVQ units they see as relevant to their job, whilst others will not accept NVQs that have been partially completed at a previous employer (SERTUC 2004a). Further, the construction and use of these occupational qualifications have been criticised as being functionalist and reductionalist in nature, written by employers to reinforce a multi-functional but low discretion work environment, and enabling horizontal skill acquisition rather than vertical. Learning in this context is likely to be 'conservative' in outcome (Taylor 1993), with the 'teacher' again acting as 'banker' (Freire 1972), training to a predetermined institutional agenda. Thus, rather than liberate, such qualification-based training may constrain worker development, contribute to over-qualification and be potentially discriminatory (Stewart and Hamblin 1992; Ainley 1999; Grugulis 2003b; Grugulis *et al.* 2004).

In embracing learning as consumption through vocational qualifications, the risk for trade unions is that they will perpetuate the skill and knowledge divide, reinforce a separation of learning delivery from control and further stigmatise those at the bottom end of the qualification structure, thus risking colluding with capital. This collusion is exacerbated by a third tension surrounding union involvement in vocational learning, with trade union learning structures playing the game of private sector capitalism by competing for and winning contracts, using the language of customers, within a context of a contractual state (Clarke and Newman 1997) that has increasing presence. In so far as state-funding through ULF provision is aimed at basic skill needs across a variety of subjects, this could be seen as adding to and being in keeping with the traditional trade union education role. However, caution must be exercised here and trade unions might question the extent to which ULF initiatives offer anything substantially 'useful' as in new or additional learning rather than a re-channelling of public funding for existing learning activities and organisational training. In addition, funding can be for relatively short timescales and over-dependency on the ULF can bring uncertainty about the long term provision (Calveley *et al.* 2003).

Overall, there is a danger here that trade union learning is providing a channel for public funding for training to replace that which should be provided by employers. Seen from a radical perspective, this is training on employers' functionalist agendas, likely to have limited outcomes for individual development and even more limited wider collective or class outcomes. As such, trade unions risk being complicit in employers' agendas here and risk losing credibility in terms of their independence.

Radical Learning

The radical interpretations of learning discussed here derive from collective and class perspectives on the employment relationship in a structuralist and Marxist sense (Fox 1974; Ainley 1994). In such a 'radical' frame of reference 'useful' learning enables outcomes in terms of political and class activity that lead to revolutionary over-throw. The direct focus is on transforming society through collective as well as individual action (Elsey 1986). Such learning will be through explicit approaches to content and method of learning that reveal oppression and through which learners are able to challenge existing organisational and societal norms (Freire 1972). A key feature is ownership, with Elsey (1986) seeing participant involvement and self determination as important and Ainley (1994) suggesting that learning takes place through practical work and where the control of the whole learning process is by workers rather than by experts, in order to overcome the division between ruling and working class. Such a radical analysis of pedagogy (Taylor 1993), has the teacher operating as a learner, learning with other learners (Freire 1972). In this way, collective self-realisation and transformation occurs as knowledge is actively discovered by learners and teachers together (Ainley 1994). Returning to the initial aim of this chapter, the question is whether this radical interpretation offers an appropriate analysis of the 'reality', distinctiveness and usefulness of union learning. On initial inspection it could well be that the full quote from the Union of Shop Distributive and Allied Workers (USDAW), introduced in brief at the beginning of this chapter, can be interpreted as having such a radical meaning:

> We have our own interest in skills training and acquiring knowledge ... [where] no-one else should presume to know what's in our best interest. This is about real learning, learning from and guided by each other, not just by experts; learning what we want to learn, not just what we're meant to know; learning about what we're interested in and what's useful to us, not what passes for being clever in someone else's world (USDAW 1999, 21).

However, it is here that there is a lack of direct evidence in union learning (although perhaps there is more in the union education and training discussed in section four of this book). In respect of radical outcomes from union learning however, it is necessary to interpret the extant reports of such learning, which are of a prevailing mainstream liberal humanist and vocational nature, more deeply. However, it must also be acknowledged firstly that more empirical research is needed in order to draw concrete conclusions and also that there may be scope for redefining 'radical' notions of 'usefulness' in contemporary employment relations. These points are returned to at the end of the chapter. In the meantime, some radical interpretations can be explored through recognition of the complexity of the outcomes of union learning in two respects.

Firstly, recognition that the outcomes of learning can be not only individual but also collective. Secondly, that direct humanistic and vocational learning outcomes such as skill acquisition can be differentiated from outcomes that can be interpreted in other ways. Further, these dimensions are not mutually exclusive but may exist together. Thus direct outcomes of learning for an individual may be employer and task-specific, but indirect outcomes may be collective ones of attitude and ownership (Shelley 2005) and of union organising and renewal (Calveley *et al.* 2003).

Ownership is an important part of a worker-controlled agenda (Freire 1972; Elsey 1986; Ainley 1994). Ownership can be individual and collective, and in the design of the learning as well as its delivery and receipt. Granted, employers are involved in the physical provision of many examples, and exert control over qualification structures, currently through Sector Skills Councils (SSCs). Nevertheless, learners show a willingness to undertake shared learning, with a collective spirit, 'doing something for ourselves' (SERTUC 2004a).

The independent status of trade unions, and the fact that access to learning and learning advice is via a source other than representatives of management, often through Union Learning Representatives, gives two obvious benefits. Firstly, openness and equality of opportunity in raising awareness of learning opportunities and for accessing learning itself (CIPD 2004). Secondly, the proximity to those who are union and political activists. The role of the ULR would seem key here, as the first contact for many employee-learners and the person to direct learners to specific courses and learning environments. Twenty six per cent of ULRs report an increased interest in union membership as a result of their activity (York Consulting 2003), whilst 22 per cent of ULRs are new to union activities and these new activists are more likely to be women, from black and ethnic minorities and younger than other activists (Moore and Wood 2005).

Physical location and ownership arrangements would also appear to be important here. There is a range of physical locations for union learning, from situations where premises, computers and other equipment are provided by the employer, together with some time off for learning; through to those where learning takes place out of the workplace, including trade union-owned premises, and in the learners' own time. Examples of work-based learning centres, jointly-funded by employer and trade union include LG Philips, Durham (Amicus); Hydro Aluminium Motorcast, Leeds (Amicus); Merseytravel (Amicus, GMB, TGWU, UCATT, Unison); Royal Mail (CWU); Pittards (TGWU); South West Trains (RUL); and Metroline Buses (TGWU) (The Learning Rep 2004a and 2004b; SERTUC 2004b; RUL 2005). Further examples of jointly-run employer and union initiatives are Employee Development Funds to finance courses, in which employees can apply to a joint union/company committee for grants to fund learning of various work and non-work-related subjects (SERTUC 2002).

Examples of non-workplace-based learning centres/programmes include that which was run by the union Unifi in its own regional offices, although the union did persuade some employers to allow staff to pursue their own learning programmes using company training facilities (The Learning Rep 2004a). In 2004 a multi-union learning centre was opened in a trades union hall (see Chapter 11). There are also partnerships with other training and education providers. USDAW (North Yorkshire) runs programmes with colleges, a university and the Workers' Education Association (WEA) (The Learning Rep 2004a); and a 'Return to Learning' programme is run by Unison also with the WEA (Unison 2005). The association with the broader educational aims of the WEA (which provides courses as diverse as cultural studies, art history, architecture, music and science) (WEA 2004), clearly should stimulate learning for personal interest and fulfilment, although the extent to which this enhances worker discretion and control over work as opposed to being purely recreational, requires further analysis.

There are a number of examples where access extends beyond employees and beyond the physical confines of workplaces. Retired workers can use the learning centre jointly run by the company Pittards and the Transport and General Workers' Union (TGWU) (The Learning Rep 2004 and 2004b); there is twenty four hour and seven day access for employees to the Rail Unions Learning (RUL)/South West Trains centre at Waterloo station (RUL 2005); and in the Metroline Buses/TGWU example, Metroline own the mobile learning centre, a double-deck bus, equipped with Personal Computers, that provides mobile access to all garage depots, and for different shifts (SERTUC 2004a). The GMB union (Grantham Community Branch) take mobile learning centres to shopping centres and libraries (TUC 2004b).

It can be argued that such initiatives provide an ownership context that is separate from employers' agendas. The location of ULF learning initiatives next to continuing trade union education policy on broader issues about the labour movement, may also provide opportunities to develop generalised knowledge and understanding of societal and political issues. In this context there are examples of ULRs directing workers to courses at Trade Union learning centres based in colleges (TU Studies Centre, Sheffield College; College of North East London; Trade Union Education Unit, Stockport College; TU Education Department, Derby College; TU Studies Centre, Lewisham College) (TUC 2004b). Further, two workplace union learning centres report that they anticipate running 'tutor-led courses' as well as PC-based ones, and one of these plans to base the training in the room used for training union representatives, next door to the PC-fitted union learning centre (Shelley 2005).

The attitude with which learners become involved in union learning also resonates with the ownership theme. Overwhelmingly, learners become involved in trade union learning initiatives in order to better themselves (O'Grady 2006). The benefit of outcomes to individuals in terms of their attitude to life and access to increased life opportunities would appear to hold great potential for workers. Thus increased confidence, a frequently quoted benefit previously discussed in a liberal humanist context can be related to the immediate work situation, but may provide opportunities to progress out of disadvantage. In such ways, self confidence and commitment to action correlate strongly with Elsey's (1986) radical views on education.

However, undoubtedly it is often difficult to differentiate outcomes for learners from the same event – for many there will be a multiplicity of outcomes. An example of complexity of interpretation is through consideration of the numerous cases of ESOL (English for Speakers of Other Languages) training provided by union learning for migrant workers. Examples include programmes for non-European Union asylum-seekers and refugees in Lincolnshire agricultural and food and industry jobs (TUC 2004b), for Eastern European construction workers in a learning centre run by the construction union UCATT at Canary Wharf, London (TUC 2004c) and for TGWU's United Workers Association training of migrant hospitality and domestic workers from the Philippines, Sri Lanka, Africa, India and Malaysia (The Learning Rep 2004b). Although such activities may be interpreted as vocational as well as humanistic in that they directly benefit employers and economic growth, they may also have potential for outcomes that enable trade unions to meet explicit aims to promote the growth of the international trade union movement (see for example CWU 2005) by engendering international solidarity and cooperation.

Conclusion

This chapter has sought to interpret the usefulness and distinctiveness of outcomes from union learning initiatives through notions of liberal humanist, vocational and radical learning. Overall, examples, evidence and policy rhetoric suggest a prevailing task and employer vocational orientation, with some evidence of liberal humanist but little of radical learning input and outcomes. However, interpretations of union learning using these categorisations is far from straightforward and there is a multiplicity of outcomes for learners which may be deemed 'useful' in differing ways. It is this complexity in interpretation that enables some alternative conclusions to be drawn.

In terms of the mainstream learning and skills policy agenda, there is potential for trade union learning to find useful ground in raising demand and expectations from workers of high skill work, and high-discretion work, which may go some way towards eroding the UK's prevailing employer-controlled low-skill equilibrium (Ashton and Felstead 2001; Nolan 2001; Taylor 2003). This potential for union influence on skills demand is discussed by Lloyd and Payne in Chapter 4 of this book.

However, stretching analysis beyond this reading of skills and topics to consider the broader context in which the learning takes place and the purposes for which it might be used, offers insight into the part that attitude and ownership play in the learning process and, it can be argued, also a redefinition of radical learning. Recognising that education and learning is never neutral (Taylor 1993), union learning that is explicitly liberal humanist and vocational in appearance can also be distinctive and useful as a means of individual and societal change.

This redefinition has to be understood in the contemporary context of employment relations, where a unitarist neo-liberal orthodoxy makes recognition of the radical as defined a century ago, and its differentiation from social democracy, somewhat problematic, and where accommodative forms of business unionism are manifest (Maheu 1995; Pimlott and Cook 1991; Spencer 2002). It may be argued that theoretical analysis of the usefulness of learning and its radical nature requires a move beyond original structuralist and class-based interpretations to an acknowledgement of social realism (Berger and Luckmann 1971). Whilst learning may be 'useful' in a radical Marxist sense if it leads to recognition of structural inequality in the class relationship between capital and labour, an acknowledgement of worker agency (Thompson 1989) leaves the door open to argue that learning which leads to incremental change rather than revolutionary overthrow may be just as 'radical' in this context. Indeed, it is suggested here that the attitude with which the topic is approached, drawing upon the collective nature of the unionised learning process, is at least as relevant as the topic itself. In this sense, learning which places emphasis on building self-confidence primarily, as a basis for critical analysis and a commitment to action, radical characteristics identified by Elsey (1986), suggests scope for radical outcomes out of what may otherwise be seen as liberal humanist and vocational learning.

Clearly, there are practical limitations for many of the union learning initiatives at present. Unions and workers will be aware of the risk of becoming subsumed in an all-embracing mainstream rhetoric that emphasises tripartite consensus on this matter and, in particular, will be wary of supporting employers' training and of an over-dependence on vocational qualifications to the extent that it may be seen to jeopardise the independence of trade unions. There are also practical limitations on union learning, including limited statutory rights on training, and practical difficulties in gaining time off for learning. A major restriction is the lack of provision in the Employment Relations Act (2002) for paid time off for employees to take part in learning. Conference delegates have told of problems in this respect, with resultant issues of lack of access and lack of support for carers of dependents, when learning is forced outside of working hours (SERTUC 2002), therefore often blocking access to those most in need. In addition, of course, there are also limitations for learning centres and ULRs due to statutory support being limited only to workplaces where trade unions are recognised, and there being no legal right to bargaining on learning and skills matters (Moore and Wood 2005).

Nevertheless, in terms of wider societal outcomes, trade union learning can raise political and class awareness, trade union activism, community awareness and activism, family and individual outcomes (such as confidence and assertiveness). Such characteristics hark back to earlier understandings of the purpose of trade union education and worker emancipation in seeking to readjust the balance of power between labour and capital. Despite the constraints already outlined, the challenge for those involved in the practice of trade union learning is to further explore the potential for worker emancipation. On the basis of the evidence examined here, in order to do this it will be important to strengthen delivery through student and tutor-led discussion, operate in physical environments that are controlled by the union and workers, and emphasise broader educational provision both in physical location and in defining learning aims. This strengthening should aim, in Elsey's (1986) terms, to incorporate critical analysis as well as continue building self-confidence and commitment to action. The ability of the new Unionlearn organisation to embrace this agenda would seem to be key here. As Forrester (2004) suggested, there is also potential to develop community-based work with other local learning fora, community agencies and voluntary organisations. Union learning can increasingly include non-workers and workers other than direct employees, with the potential to extend the power of an 'attitude' associated with the labour movement to the more diverse range of groups in society (Maheu 1995; Urry 1995). A key agenda for unions will be to diversify funding sources away from limited qualification-based public funding and from employer-subsidised learning centres.

Finally, the challenge for those researching in the field is largely methodological. Firstly, to recognise the cross-disciplinary nature of the field, where more recent areas of interest in IT-based distance learning, geography and community unionism can be combined with the more traditional interests in industrial relations, training skills and education. Secondly, what is required is to get behind the façade of unproblematic reporting of topics and frequencies of learning activities that typifies so many of the reports and accounts produced by and for government and trade unions, and in doing so to better understand the nature of union learning, much of which does have multiple interpretations. This means engaging with learners and other actors involved in the delivery of union learning on the ground.

Note

For a fuller report of the range of union learning activities, see Shelley (2005).

References

Ainley, P. (1994), *Degrees of Difference. Higher Education in the 1990s.* (London: Lawrence and Wishart).

Ainley, P. (1999), *Learning Policy. Towards the Certified Society.* (London: Macmillan).

Ashton, D. and Felstead, A. (2001), 'From Training to Lifelong Learning: The Birth of the Knowledge Society?', in Storey (ed.).

Barber, B. (2004), 'Address to the 2004 Union Learning Fund Conference by Brendan Barber TUC General Secretary', *The Learning Rep*, Autumn 2004, (London: TUC Learning Services).

Berger, P. and Luckmann, T. (1971), *The Social Construction of Reality.* (Harmondsworth: Penguin).

Blyton, P. and Turnbull, P. (2004), *The Dynamics of Employee Relations.* 3rd Edition. (Basingstoke: Macmillan).

Booth, A. and Snower, D. (eds.) (1996), *Acquiring Skills. Market Failures, their Symptoms and Policy Responses.* (Cambridge: Cambridge University Press).

Burawoy, M. (1979), *Manufacturing Consent: Changes in the Labour Process under Monopoly Capitalism.* (Chicago: University of Chicago Press).

Calveley, M., Healy, G., Shelley, S., Stirling, J. and Wray, D. (2003), 'Union Learning Representatives: a force for renewal or "partnership"?' University of Hertfordshire Business School Working Paper. Employment Studies Paper 48. (Hatfield: University of Hertfordshire).

CIPD (2004), *Trade Union Learning Representatives: The Change Agenda.* (London: Chartered Institute of Personnel and Development).

Clarke, J. and Newman, J. (1997), *The Managerial State.* (London: Sage).

Clarke, C. (2004), 'Address to the 2004 Union Learning Fund conference by Charles Clarke, Secretary of State', *The Learning Rep*, Autumn 2004. (London: TUC Learning Services).

Communication Workers' Union (CWU), (2005) 'Education and Training', <http://www.cwu.org.uk/default.asp?step+2&id.16>, accessed 9 November 2005.

DfES (2003a), *21st Century Skills: Realising our Potential.* (London: Department for Education and Skills).

——, (2003b), *Skills for Life: Improving Literacy and Numeracy at Work.* (London: Department for Education and Skills).

——, (2005), *Skills: Getting on in Business, Getting on in Work.* Cm 6483. (London: Department for Education and Skills).

Elsey, B. (1986), *Social Theory Perspectives on Adult Education.* (Nottingham: University of Nottingham).

Forrester, K. (2004), 'The Quiet Revolution? Trade Union Learning and Renewal Strategies', *Work, Employment and Society* 18: 2, 413–420.

Fox, A. (1974), *Beyond Contract: Work, Power and Trust Relations.* (London: Faber and Faber).

Freire, P. (1972), *Pedagogy of the Oppressed.* (Penguin: Harmondsworth).

Grugulis, I. (2003a), 'Putting Skills to Work: Learning and Employment at the Start of the Century', *Human Resource Management Journal* 13: 2, 3–12.

——, (2003b), 'The Contribution of National Vocational Qualifications to the Growth of Skills in the UK', *British Journal of Industrial Relations* 41: 3, 457–475.

Grugulis, I., Warhurst, C. and Keep, E. (2004), 'What's Happening to Skill?', in Warhurst, C., Grugulis, I. and Keep, E. (eds.).

Heyes, J. and Stuart, M. (1998), 'Bargaining for Skills: Trade Unions and Training at the Workplace', *British Journal of Industrial Relations* 36: 3, 459–467.

Karabel, J. and Halsey, A. (eds.) (1977), *Power and Ideology in Education.* (Oxford: Oxford University Press).

Keep, E. and Mayhew, K. (1999), 'The Assessment: Knowledge, Skills and Competitiveness', *Oxford Review of Economic Policy* 15: 1, 1–15.

The Learning Rep, (2004a), Autumn 2004. (London: TUC Learning Services).

——, (2004b), Summer 2004. (London: TUC Learning Services).

Lloyd, C. and Payne, J. (2002), 'Developing a Political Economy of Skill', *Journal of Education and Work* 15: 4, 365–390.

Maheu, L. (ed.) (1995), *Social Movements and Social Classes. The Future of Collective Action.* (London: Sage).

Moore, S. and Wood, H. (2005), *An Evaluation of the UK Union Learning Fund – its Impact on Unions and Employers.* (London: TUC).

Nolan, P. (2001), 'Shaping things to come', *People Management*, 27 December, 30–31.

O'Grady, F. (2006), 'Speech at the 'Union Learning – Making a difference, changing lives' Union Learning Fund conference', The Congress Centre, 11th Ocober 2006.

Pimlott, B. and Cook, C. (1991), *Trade Unions in British Politics. The First 250 Years.* 2nd edition. (London: Longman).

Rainbird, H. (ed.) (2000), *Training in the Workplace: Critical Perspectives on Learning at Work.* (London: Macmillan).

Ranson, S. and Stewart, J. (1994), *Management for the Public Domain. Enabling the Learning Society.* (London: Macmillan).

RUL (Rail Unions Learning) (2005), 'RUL in England', <http://www.rul.org.uk/learning_country>, accessed 25 October 2005.

SERTUC (2002), Delegate discussion in the 'Learning with the Unions' presentation, South East Regional Trades Union Congress, 2nd Union Learning Representatives conference, 8th November 2002, Congress House, London.

——, (2004a), 'Union Organising' seminar, South East Regional Trades Union Congress, 4th Union Learning Representatives conference, 5th November 2004, Bloomsbury, London.

——, (2004b), *Learning with the Unions. Case Studies.* (London: South East Regional Trades Union Congress, Learning Services).

Shelley, S. (2005), 'Useful Outcomes for Workers in Trade Union Learning Activities. The Significance of Attitude and Ownership'. University of Hertfordshire Business School Working Paper. (Hatfield: University of Hertfordshire).

Simon, B. (1965), *Education and the Labour Movement 1870–1920.* (London: Lawrence and Wishart).

Spencer, B. (ed.) (2002), *Unions and Learning in a Global Economy. International and Comparative Perspectives.* (Toronto: Thompson Educational Publishing).

Stevens, M. (1996), 'Transferable Training and Poaching Externalities', in Booth and Snower (eds.).

Stewart, J. and Hamblin, B. (1992), 'Competence-based Qualifications: The Case against Change', *Journal of European Industrial Training* 16: 7, 21–32.

Storey, J. (ed.) (2001), *Human Resource Management: A Critical Text.* (London: Thomson).

Taylor, P. (1993), *The Texts of Paulo Freire.* (Buckingham: Open University Press).

Taylor, R. (2003), *Skills and Innovation in Modern Workplaces.* ESRC Future of Work Programme seminar series. (Swindon: ESRC).

Thompson, P. (1989), *The Nature of Work: An Introduction to the Debates on the Labour Process,* 2nd edition. (London: Macmillan).

Trades Union Congress (2002), *The Quiet Revolution: the Rise of the Union Learning Representative in the East of England.* (London: TUC).

——, (2004a), *Only One in Four Non-union Members get Regular Training.* TUC press release, 18th May 2004.

——, (2004b), *Right Directions: Quality IAG in Union Learning Projects.* (London: TUC).

——, (2004c), *Union Learning Reps Train 25,000 in their First Year.* TUC press release, 26th April 2004.

Unionlearn (2007) *Unionlearn Annual Report 2007.* (London: TUC).

Unison (2005), 'Lifelong Learning', Learning and Organising Services (LAOS), <http://www.unison.org.uk/learningandorganising>, accessed 25 October 2005.

Urry, J. (1995), 'Rethinking Class', in Maheu, L. (ed.).

USDAW (1999), *Lifelong Learning.* Executive Council statement to the 1999 Annual Delegate Meeting. (Manchester: Union of Shop Distributive and Allied Workers).

Warhurst, C., Grugulis, I. and Keep, E. (ed.) (2004), *The Skills that Matter.* (London: Palgrave Macmillan).

Workers' Education Association (WEA), (2004) Home page. <http://www.wea.org.uk>, accessed 9 November 2005.

York Consulting (2003), *Union Learning Rep Survey*, for TUC Learning Services. (Leeds: York Consulting Group).

——, (2006), *Evaluation of the Union Learning Fund, 2001–2005.* DfES Research Brief RB789. (London: Department for Education and Skills).

Chapter 8

Becoming Visible?
Notes on Work, Union
Learning and Education

Keith Forrester

Stuart's Story: Commodified Learning in a Differentiating Context

Stuart works as an administrator in a local union office for a major British insurance and financial company. He was interviewed as part of an evaluation exercise for his union on completion of a government funded, two-year union project designed to promote workplace learning amongst employees (1). The company strongly promoted the project and recently had created a Learning Centre in the workplace. The interview was structured around the progress achieved by the trade union during the project. The following quotes are taken from his interview. The discussion with Stuart was unusual in that learning was situated within a strongly perceived differentiated and differentiating context. In contrast to the strong local, sector and government policy pressures that viewed workplace learning as a joint employer-union 'partnership' designed to benefit all 'stakeholders', Stuart's experience and understanding of learning resulted in a number of distinctive perceptions.

First, while agreeing with the national union that 'learning and education is probably the best way of moving trade union issues forward', he saw this learning and education as a means of challenging or questioning:

> some of the things that they [the members] have been told ... Education is about getting people to think for themselves.

The strong emphasis on locating learning within issues of control within the labour process resulted in Stuart repeatedly rejecting the dominant rationale underpinning workplace learning. As he said:

> getting more people training and you therefore get a better job and could earn more money ... is meaningless really ... I would like to earn more money but it's not the be all and end all.

Secondly, Stuart's experience as a union representative led him to distinguish between different types of learning. Training was a task-orientated exercise with little developmental potential. 'You can train in how to put things in a box but are you actually learning anything?' he asks. When the questions were broadened to include lifelong learning and the workplace as a site of learning, Stuart was adamant about these distinctions. 'What people are talking about is training. Training to do a job is not necessarily education'. Instead of a depolitised and universal conception of education, Stuart's experiences suggested that education was about:

> getting people to think about why things happen ... It's political with a small 'p'. You can't sit on the fence. You would have to come down on one side or another.

In contrast to the employers providing employees only with the training necessary to do the job, Stuart uses the notion of 'development' to situate his understanding of learning:

> The union is not here purely to service people. [Instead it is about developing people], about opening up people's minds to what is out there.

Involvement and participation are integral to this notion of 'development'. 'The confidence these people get, it's unbelievable,' he says. By contrast, the company's new Learning Centre with its library facilities is accorded little importance. 'It is geared towards what [the company] does and anything that [the company] might be interested in'. These distinctions that Stuart is making over the nature and objectives of learning in the company are rooted in his understanding of the employment relationships:

> We all know that the only reason why [the company] want people to have this training and these skills is so that they are there to be employed by somebody who makes a barrel load of money and that's it [he says]. It's to make profits for somebody ... It's not for the individuals at all.

Situating learning within this 'profits' framework pervades Stuart's entire discussion of workplace learning. It shapes his apprehensive views about the local union getting too involved in company initiatives; it fuels his suspicions of union-employer 'partnerships' as 'they will only do the bare minimum. It will always do that'.

Although Stuart is unlikely to publicly voice his opposition to union policy due to his strong political commitment to unionism, there is a strong ambivalence towards his union's campaign for workplace learning:

> I don't know if we should or not [he says]. Currently, I can't see a company, whose only reason for existing is to make money, is going to invest more than it has to in training or educating its workforce.

Introduction

Stuart's views on workplace learning are not only unusual but also raise awkward issues for those interested in employee learning. They raise a number of questions that are rarely addressed by the research or professional community. In contrast to the assumptions and perspectives shaping Stuart's views, the emergence of human capital theory as an integral aspect of economically and educationally engaging in a 'post-Fordist' environment has encouraged views of workplace learning as an apolitical, adaptive and individualistic process (Baptiste 2001). Envisaging employees as 'human resources' has emerged as a powerful ideological discourse both within international agencies such as the Organisation for Economic Co-operation and Development (OECD) and in scholarly areas such as organisational and management studies. The alleged moves in late capitalist economies towards post-Taylorist strategies of flexibility as the dominant pathway towards remaining competitive within the global economy, has stimulated academic and policy interest in employee know-how in particular and workplace knowledgeability in general.

Stuart's company has superficially at least, adopted this 'human-resources-are-our-most-valuable-assets' route with the accompanying rhetoric of 'stakeholders' and 'partnerships'. However, the situating of this 'knowing' within the exploitative social relations characterising the financial sector led Stuart to question this rhetoric framework and to pose alternative formulations and understandings.

In all likelihood, Stuart's company is representative of a more generalised trend towards situating 'workplace knowledge' and 'knowing' within a need for employees to move from an *ability* to perform towards a *willingness* to perform, with its emphasis on employee motivation, commitment and identification to the company. While such developments have increased scholarly and policy interest in employee learning, they have done so within a deficit discourse. Employee learning and, more generally, working class learning is couched in connotations of inadequacy, failure and shortcomings. The periodic policy declarations of this or that 'skills crisis' together with a financial and policy focus on remedying 'basic skills' contribute to this picture of negativity and despondency regarding the capabilities and abilities of employees. International league tables 'benchmark' the host county's acquisition of qualifications and skills against the economic competition. Annual numerical and literacy rates fuel new policy and funding arrangements for the adult education sector resulting in for example, either the closure or drastic curtailment of local authority or voluntary sector adult educational agencies in Britain. As employer organisations increasingly influence the agenda of educational reform and bemoan the lack of 'relevant' vocational know-how in school leavers and within higher education, the push for a 'learning workforce' within 'the knowledge economy' and, it seems in Stuart's company, drives policy development.

This chapter has been informed to a significant extent by the issues raised by Stuart in his discussion of education and training. The overall concern is to examine worker or employee learning within the workplace. The first section of the chapter briefly summarises understandings of union education – an important vehicle for Stuart of 'getting members to think for themselves', as he puts it. It is suggested that in the main, curriculum and pedagogic concerns have dominated analysis of union education. While such approaches have stressed the distinctive 'union' or 'labour' nature of the provision, commentaries have tended to leave unexamined the conceptions of learning implicit in the provision or in the links between work and everyday life. As a result, much of the complexity, richness and sources of union learning remain as 'taken-for-granted' phenomena. This section of the chapter briefly reviews these approaches to union education as well as outlining the wider cultural setting within which such education is situated. The second section of the chapter highlights a number of theoretical issues that characterise union learning. Although rarely discussed or explored in an educational context, these issues, it is suggested, help to frame understandings of the complexity and contradictory nature of 'union knowing'.

The third section of the chapter argues that an increased socio-cultural dimension to understanding workplace learning in recent years has contributed to more generous and critical perspectives on the nature of learning and which directly or indirectly challenges the dominance of human capital theory. Stressing the 'everyday' social and participative nature of learning, these alternative understandings provide an opportunity to begin grasping the complexities and richness of human development that extends beyond the 'instrumental rationality' of the dominant paradigm (Beckett and Hager 2001). Whilst recognising the influence of cultural factors, the emphasis on the situated contextual nature of learning identifies the learner as part of the environment rather than as a detached spectator (Hager 2004).

The argument informing this chapter is located within this 'learner-environment' relationship which is seen to be at the centre of emerging understandings of learning as a social activity. The immediate focus is on the employees' environment, namely the workplace; which is a distinctive and particular type of environment. Ignoring or minimising the particularities of this environment result in ahistorical, partial and ideologically driven views of learning. It is suggested that while no single view of social learning can adequately capture the extent and complexity of this learning, particular perspectives usefully highlight particular aspects of the developments resulting from employees' engagement in and with this environment. It will be argued that there has been a strong tendency in many studies to insufficiently explore the particular characteristics of the working environment in late capitalist economies. As a result of this neglect, there has been an inclination to misconstrue the character and contradictory nature of this learning at work as well as to underestimate the contribution of 'everyday', non-workplace learning for employees. While the emphasis on the ubiquitous nature of learning as an essential aspect of 'growing' and 'coming to understand' the world weakens the dominant 'deficit' perspectives of employee or worker learning mentioned above, this emphasis fails to explain and illustrate sufficiently strongly the differentiated and differentiating nature of knowing, in and out of the workplace. An underdeveloped analysis of the particular character of 'work' and of 'everyday life' in advanced capitalist society risks over-generalised understandings of employee learning which may be portrayed as 'totalising' (as, for example, in Casey 1995). Uncritically accepting the alleged widespread nature of new management controls based on employee incorporation and 'colonisation' of the subjectivity and of the 'shock-and-awe' version of the 'globalisation' thesis has provided the basis for the resistance-free 'new worker' in the 'new workplaces'. For the 'post-structuralists' as Thompson and Ackroyd (1995) argue, power is everywhere and nowhere and has dropped off the research agenda. However, recognising that significant but uneven and contradictory changes have been, and are occurring, in people's lives increases the importance of a discriminating and critical analysis in making sense of these changes and continuities. In contrast to these dominant discourses, this chapter will argue that insufficiently recognising the materiality of learning has important consequences for understandings of social learning as well as for practitioner practices.

The issues that shape the immediate focus of this chapter then revolve around the differentiated and differentiating nature of workplace learning. Given the historically strong association between learning and social class, how does employee learning challenge or contribute to this association? In what ways does the material inequality of 'being a worker' shape what is learned and how learning occurs? How does union education contribute towards contesting or affirming dominant conceptions of 'coming to know'? How do particular understandings of learning marginalise or contribute towards illustrating the nature and processes of workplace learning and do these understandings provide space for other inequalities such as gender, ethnicity, disability and sexual orientation? How do particular management strategies enhance, ignore or hinder employee learning? While this chapter does not seek to answer such 'big' questions, it raises a number of issues that point towards approaches to employee learning that do encompass such concerns.

Situating Union Education

As was indicated in the opening section to this chapter, Stuart is a strong advocate of union education as opposed to joint union-employer initiatives:

> Union education [he says] is about getting people to think about why things happen ... it's about developing people ... The confidence these people get, it's unbelievable.

For many employees in Britain and elsewhere, the education provided by their trade union has remained an important and often, the only source of 'knowing' and discussion of changes within the workplace. Definitions of trade union education or more broadly, worker education within the general literature however, are often characterised by a marked display of circumspection. Hopkins (1985, 8) in his international survey of workers' education for example, warns of the historical variety and culturally contested understandings of 'education', 'workers' and 'trade unions', saying that 'there are grave dangers of over-simplification and confusion'. Newman (1993, 11) agrees and notes that:

> the world of union affairs, of workplaces, of industrial relations is a complicated and confusing one. No two unions, no two workplaces are the same. No issues are identical.

The International Labour Organisation (ILO 1976, 10) recognises the complexities and offers a broad understanding:

> Worker's education [it suggests] is designed to develop the workers' understanding of 'labour problems' in the broadest sense of these words.

It continues however with an important caveat which begins to differentiate workers' education with other types of education. It:

> should always be regarded as a means to useful action. In many cases the education will make clear both the need for action and the best forms the action can take (ILO 1976, 10).

Spencer (2002) in his collection on 'labour education' provided by trade unions, goes further when distinguishing between 'tools' or 'role' courses (those preparing members for active roles in the union), 'issues' or 'awareness' courses (linking workplace to societal issues such as racism, union campaigns or new management techniques) and 'labour studies' courses (examining union contexts through historical, economic and political perspectives). Such a taxonomy, common in the Anglo-Saxon literature, approximates to Hopkins' longer five-fold classification of the 'major components of the curricula of workers' education'. These he sees as basic general skills, role skills, economic, social and political background studies, technical and vocational training and finally, cultural, scientific and general education (Hopkins 1985). In contrast to the classificatory approach, Burke and her Canadian union educators (Burke *et al.* 2002, 3) identify a number of 'threads' which:

> hold together the fabric of our work: community, democracy, equity, class-consciousness, organisation-building, and the greater good.

The situating of 'trade union education' or 'workers' education' within perspectives that focus on curricula, programme design and ('worker-centred') pedagogy has contributed towards framing important discussions about the particularities of this type of learning. Implicit within many of the discussions, however, are a number of broader societal features that shape not only the content but also the language, values, pedagogy, relationships, objectives and nature of the learning provided through the courses. Although not always made explicit in the written learning materials, the examination and linkages between union experience, reflection, knowing and action in courses occur within a number of characteristics that powerfully shape the culture and the nature of the union learning. Identifying these characteristics will not only influence the choice of theoretical formulations when seeking to understand 'trade union learning' but will also direct attention to the sources and nature of empirical data. The organisations claiming the allegiance, commitment, effort, and 'learning' of members for example, are contradictory mediating agencies. As the historical result of the relationship between wage labour and capital, trade unions make possible resistance and opposition to capitalism while simultaneously making such opposition more manageable, confinable and predictable. Representing the economic and working interests of workers under capitalism while maintaining the interest in abolishing wage labour is seen by Sommer and his colleagues (1996, 143) as a 'categorical contradiction' of unions. In their discussion around their large-scale survey of union education amongst Danish unions in the early 1990s, they argue that unions have little choice other than to pursue interests and activities 'which are in conflict with each other'.

The dynamic resulting from this contradiction provides an enduring tension in the earlier mentioned ILO's 'best forms of action', in the practice of unionism and in union learning. Conflict is central to waged labour (seen as 'employment') in the capacity to work and in the translating of this capacity to work into productive activity. Trade union education acknowledges often strongly, these conflictual relationships, usually seen as 'management'. Burke and her colleagues (Burke *et al.* 2002, 15) go further. One of the objectives of union education they suggest is to gauge the weight of our opponents, the employing class.

Developing workplace health and safety audits, understanding and using procedural agreements, involving members and embedding anti-discriminatory practices are examples from courses of 'everyday' workplace issues of contestation. Pressures on the wage-bargain relationship through a dizzying array of expanded systems of monitoring and surveillance provides a given sub-text for the classroom discussion and also, for empirical studies (Warhurst and Thompson 1998; Danford *et al.* 2003).

Closely related to this conflictual context of trade union education is 'the remarkably persuasive relationship between work and inequality', as Hyman (1989, 15) puts it. The depth and nature of this inequality, operating at different levels and in different forms has been extensively documented and includes consideration of for example, remuneration systems, authority relations and patterns of industrial accidents and ill-health.

The cultural, ideological and material structures of inequality and domination experienced by workers within the workplace on a daily basis provides an informal curriculum on union education courses that informs discussion of the more formal procedural and substantive issues. Underpinning such discussions is the exploration and uncovering of 'being a worker' or being a 'female trade unionist' (Weber 1996); namely, the marginalisation and often negation of the knowing and experiences of employees. Although rarely explored outside adult learning literature, the questions of what is recognised, relevant or legitimate knowledge in the workplace and elsewhere and for whom, are and have been major concerns in any discussion of learning and education. Significant exceptions who have addressed such issues include Livingstone and Sawchuk (2001) and Salling Olesen (2001). Hart for example has explored critically the ideological assumptions underpinning dominant understandings of work-related knowledge and skills. As she points out:

> Work is a basic issue, not only in terms of survival but also of representing a particular dense web of cultural notions of competence, ability, skills, knowledge and ways of knowing or coming to know .... It is a web that can be unravelled into all its many strands of oppression, division, exploitation, degradation and destruction *and* into a however muted alternative economic, cultural and ecological orientation (Hart 1995, 101).

The 'unravelling' of this 'dense web of cultural notions' that underpins the dominant discourse of for example, the knowledge economy, flexibility, skills and lifelong learning, begins to reveal a systematic portrayal of worker knowledge and skills that is deficit-driven. However, working people within circumstances characterised by job insecurity and the uneven distribution of jobs, have always been learning and developing new skills and competencies. What is novel however is the increasingly dominant human capital perspective that is currently shaping and legitimating what counts as workplace knowledge and skills and rhetorically at least, the emergence of this tacit knowledge as an important feature of new regimes of accumulation. The suppression of worker knowledge, participation and responsibility within Taylorist work regimes is to be replaced, suggest human capital advocates, by regimes that use and depend upon worker knowing, identification, motivation and loyalty in the development of the high commitment workplace. Making capital out of what workers know of course has been an integral and historical aspect in the development of capitalism. Current strategies that intensify attempts to appropriate workers' knowledgeability can be seen as a major reason behind the explosion of 'workplace learning' at both a policy and funding level.

Trade unions, who too have been historically dependent on members' knowledge, strategies for knowing and on member confidence, have not been immune from the structural and ideological forces that have encouraged the fracturing of collectivism and a more individualised agenda (Ackers *et al.* 1996). Union educational opportunities not only provide a collective vehicle for situating particular workplace strategies within these wider managerial changes but also more importantly, affirm and encourage the use of the experiences, knowledge and skills amongst course participants. Although rarely made explicit within the learning materials, these contexts can be understood as an expression of 'practical sense' that is rooted within a particular, historically situated socio-economic world characterised by a differentiated and differentiating sense of power, respect, well-being, equity and of knowing. Ultimately perhaps, union education can be understood as a contributing vehicle for both understanding the characteristics of inequality, discrimination and domination that pervades 'being a worker' and secondly, for challenging the constraints and potentialities traditionally associated with this everyday practical sense.

Union Learning, Culture and Experience

The section above, however, has also hinted at a wider, more complex conception of the educational experience. Not only do a variety of societal and increasingly, global issues interrelate with the immediate learning tasks within the course, it has also implied that the union course is but only one part in learning to become a trade unionist. Newman's (1993, 16) use of 'a general union culture' which he suggests 'becomes discernible when union activists from a number of different unions or sectors gather together for training', points towards some of the complexity involved in the learning. A sense of ownership by members towards 'their' union, the sense of unity or solidarity with others, of being 'us' against 'them' in a continual struggle to guard and promote the interests of 'ordinary' people like 'oneself' and of feeling that the unions and their activities are important to people's lives', are seen by Newman (1993) as some of the cultural attributes within courses. Union education from such a perspective is more than an understanding of roles; instead it has to do with coming to inhabit a certain socio-economic realm defined by a particular objective hierarchy of relationships within which individual sensibilities take shape (Charlesworth 2000). Sensibilities or intelligibilities (or simply, learning) are developed within differentiated social experiences. The sense of 'union culture' understood by Newman is echoed to some extent by Hopkins' (1985, 163) emphasis on the importance in workers' education of the participant's experience when discussing 'making use of the student's personal experience'. The Canadian union educators Burke *et al.* (2002, 65), suggest that people's knowledge and experience helps members recognise that they have something to say about their own experience.

Legitimating and encouraging this knowledge and experience remains a key dimension in union education. The notion of 'personal experience' however is fraught with difficulties. The 'experience' within the classroom is rooted in people's subjectivity. As Salling Olsen (1989) puts it:

> experience is thus a *subjective* process as it is seen from the point of view of the person experiencing. It is also a collective process ... and it is finally, an *active, critical* and *creative* process where we both see and adapt. However the production and extent of this subjectivity is encouraged [however minimally] and constrained by the experience of wage labour. Experience is socially constituted and constructed in historically particular forms. Capital is a social relation through which all people who live in a capitalist society *act subjectively in certain ways* (Salling Olesen 1989, 41; italics in original).

Individual experiences and hence subjectivity, arise within a particular societal framework and correspond to the contradictory experiences of those dependent on wages.

Understandings of 'these common experiences ... and identity of interests ... against other men (sic) whose interests are different from (and usually opposed to) theirs' (Thompson 1968, 10–11), suggests the fruitfulness of social class as a means of understanding worker experience within the incessant social and spatial restructuring of capitalist development. The significance and value of social class in the interpretation of socio-economic life remains the subject of much sociological debate. Despite the challenges to its relevance by some postmodernists and many politicians, class formulations remain at the centre of social theory concerns. Reay (1998) for example, argues that we need greater ethnographic examinations of how class is 'lived' in gendered and raced ways to compliment the macro versions that have monopolised our ways of envisaging social class. Focusing on the way 'class is lived' has the advantage of moving analysis away from dry social classification schemas to a focus on the experiential dimension and to situating differentially gendered and racial differences in 'life chances'. Recent studies on the subjective experience of class illustrates recognition is about more than identity (Skeggs 1997). An understanding of the everyday materiality of class (and of gender, ethnicity, disability) moves beyond representation, text, discourse and symbolisation and returns attention to 'outdated' concerns such as the labyrinth of inequality, alienation and domination. This attention to the 'curriculum of everyday life' – or 'class as it is lived' – focuses critical theoretical and empirical attention on the reproduction of power, domination and legitimacy, its perpetuation and its 'normality'.

Union education too has this focus on the often contradictory and partial subjectivity of course participants (and usually, union members and workplace employees). Encouraging active participation and discussion within the course encourages confidence in and the sharing of, 'everyday life' knowledge and experience. Again, the formal aspects of the 'course' depend upon 'hidden' experiences developed outside of the classroom. From this perspective, much union education can be seen as the 'production of experience' (Salling Olsen 1989), i.e. as the means for articulating the experiences within the group, for critically reviewing the compartmentalisation and fragmentation of these experiences and for encouraging the identification of possible alternatives to particular 'problems' which contribute towards emancipatory directions.

If union education is to be seen as promoting and developing the union presence and purposes to advance the union collectively (Spencer and Taylor 2006), it can only do so within identified parameters of societal possibilities; namely, within possibilities shaped by considerations of agency and structures. The emphasis on exploring how people understand their own position in society is a long-standing issue of contention within social and educational theory. The analytical and empirical distinction and debates around the relationship between human agency and social structure today frames discussions around possibilities and nature of societal and individual change. Recent approaches that seek to resolve the thorny theoretical interrelationship between agentic activity within the structures they inhabit include formulations such as the 'social construction of reality' (Berger and Luckmann), 'structuration theory' (Giddens), 'habitus' (Bourdieu) and 'communicative action and the lifeworld' (Habermas), suggests Hubbard (2000). They all can be seen as sharing a broad perspective that sees human experience and activity not as the mechanical outcome of objective structures but on the other hand, as not 'completely untouched by structural relations in society' (Hubbard 2000, 2).

As was indicated in the introductory remarks to this chapter, while the importance of agency is strongly emphasised, it is seen as heavily constrained especially at the macro-level. Rather than seeing agency as increasingly free floating reflexive agents (as in Lash and Urry 1994) the emphasis in this chapter is on 'the interplay of structural forces and individuals' attempts to control their lives' (Evans 2002, 265). Although obviously not articulated within such concerns and perspectives, 'advancing the union collectively' requires considerations and decisions of such theoretical dilemmas.

Sociocultural Learning

Stuart grasps this interplay between structural forces and agency. In the discussion of education and training experiences in his insurance and financial workplace, the company's 'profits framework' strongly shapes his analysis of what is possible and worthwhile from a union educational and learning perspective. Workplace education, learning and training exist and are shaped by exploitative relationships characterising the making of 'a barrel load of money', he suggests. As was mentioned earlier in the chapter, the recent explosion of theoretical and empirical interest in workplace learning has to a large extent been driven by the interest of employers in the 'new' knowledge and skills of workers seen necessary to underpin the strategic concerns of capital. Appropriating the hidden or tacit 'know-how' of employees ('the company's most valuable assets') is seen as necessary it is alleged, to survive in the more competitive neo-Fordist business environment. For the purposes of this chapter, two important theoretical interests have flowed from this at least, rhetorical turn towards a post-Taylorist agenda. First there has been growing attention in the understanding and practice of 'informal learning' (Colley *et al.* 2003; Straka 2004) and secondly, in learning at work (Beckett and Hagger 2002). It is now widely acknowledged that learning is a great deal more complex and problematic than has traditionally been recognised. Furthermore understanding learning is the subject of much dispute. The dominant 'common-sense' picture of learning – and much in evidence with employer's views and prescriptions – is of skills and knowledge as discrete, decontextualised 'blocks' that are acquired and transferred. Students and employees 'consume' educational commodities or 'products' (Hagger 2004). In contrast to 'learning as a product', the newer emerging view sees 'learning as a process'; that is, as the human capacity to grow and readjust constantly to the environment (Hagger, 2004). Learning from this perspective is an everyday, 'normal' activity shaped by the context as well as cultural and social factors. Problem solving, reflection, making judgements and decisions on what to do are illustrative of this learning and involve the 'whole' person rather than just part (the mind) of being human. Instead of seeing the learner or worker as 'inexperienced', 'incompetent' or being 'deficit' in particular decontextualised skills and knowledge, the emerging learning framework sees the human capacity to grow or to work, as necessarily involving capacities, skills, abilities and knowing. As Schoenfeld (1999) puts it, learning is best understood as 'coming to understand things and developing increased capacities to do what one wants to do or needs to do' (as quoted in Hagger 2004, 13).

Sfard's (1998) use of the two metaphors – learning as *acquisition* and as *participation* – is commonly used to contrast the approaches and differences to learning. Learning as participation emphasises the social and context-driven nature of developing as human beings through participation in societal-organised practices (such as work, the family, the trade union, leisure activities). Within particular class experiences, people act and in turn, are acted upon by a variety of different experiences in their everyday lives; we learn individually as well as collectively. As Hodkinson and Hodkinson (2006) point out, no single person is entirely synonymous with their working context, even though they are part of it. The differentiated social class-based nature of this 'social participation' and differentiated structural characteristics of 'societal practices' does not in other words entail a mechanistic or reductionist view of learning.

Being a worker and learning to become a trade unionist then constitutes participation in particular differentiating and differentiated material and cultural processes. It results in a distinctive and often contradictory sense of knowing; knowing about 'work', knowing about self and knowing about and with others. Whether as a bus driver, a care-worker, a retail worker or a 'professional worker', being a worker constitutes a particular experience that is 'learnt' within relationships that affirms their usual, devalued status. Empirically exploring the detailed micro-nature and patterns of workplace relationships, tasks, division of labour and current employment 'rules' begins to unpack the multi-layered dimensions through which, as Gaventa (1980) puts it:

> power influences, shapes or determines conceptions of the necessities, possibilities and strategies of challenging in situations of latent conflict (as quoted in Welton 2005, 130).

The invisibility of this decision making and of existing worker knowledge and skills methodologically requires attention being given to the use, shaping and manipulation of language, symbols and representations as well as the structural barriers, argues Welton (2005). Learning while in work then entails critically unravelling 'roles'. As Charlesworth (2000, 65) puts it, it is:

> coming to inhabit the world in a certain way through powerfully internalising senses based in an objective hierarchy of relations within which individual sensibilities take place.

There is of course a rich tradition of educational inquiry that has recognised the differences in 'coming to inhabit the world in a certain way'. Social justice and radical change themes have influenced strongly adult education inquiry and practice in the community (Lovett 1988) and in the workplace (Simon 1990). Freire's notion of 'conscientisation' is an explicit recognition of the importance of understanding learning as a racialised, gendered and classed experience. As argued in the introductory sections to this chapter, these 'pre-modernity' traditions are not reflected strongly in the recent workplace learning literature. However the growing influence of participatory approaches to learning has introduced the likelihood of greater theoretical and empirical detail being focused on the unequal processes of knowledge development within the field. The situated 'communities of practice' (Lave and Wenger 1991) literature for example, with its emphasis on context, doing, collaboration and tools, encourages a focus on the constraints as well as creation of knowledge by participants. Workplace relationships and tasks are crucial aspects influencing learning affordances and constraints. However, for some commentators these issues are ignored by many situated studies resulting:

> in the apolitical position of situated cognition. Relations and practices related to dimensions of race, class, gender and other cultural and personal complexities ... determine flows of power, which in turn determine different individuals ability to participate meaningfully in particular practice systems (Fenwick 2000, 250).

Other studies informed by the classed, gendered or racialised inequalities governing schooling, workplace or community learning have increasingly used Bourdieu's ideas of habitus and forms of capital (for example, economic, social and cultural) within and across different fields as a means of addressing these issues. Central to Bourdieu's (1984) concerns is the re/production of educational inequalities resulting from the uneven distribution and use of forms of capital between different groups resulting in unequal encounters between working class and middle class habituses. Educational inequalities are produced and maintained when more powerful groups are able to secure access to scarce and valued resources. The value of Bourdieu's conceptions is often legitimated within perspectives that react against the more economistic determinist conceptions of class.

Although not as influential as Bourdieu within the field of workplace learning, Habermas's notion of communicative action and defence of the lifeworld similarly situates learning within the differentiated structures of late capitalism. Although perhaps empirically less useful than Bourdieu, Habermas's formulations and concerns are informed by a stronger focus on adult learning as an emancipatory project in rescuing the lifeworld from the incessant commodification and damage of late capitalism (Welton 1995). The extensive studies and outputs by Bourdieu and Habermas can be seen as a lifelong sympathetic but critical dialogue with Marx and amount to a trenchant critique of contemporary capitalism.

It was suggested earlier that it is not useful to conceive of different understandings of learning as correct or incorrect; different approaches stress or minimise, ignore or acknowledge, illustrate or confuse aspects of what is to be understood as learning. For those interested in worker or working class learning, context specific participatory-based approaches to learning provide an opportunity for beginning to address these concerns. From varying perspectives, Bourdieu, Habermas and Lave and Wenger understand learning as a differentiating process as well as acknowledging to some extent the economic dimension influencing learning possibilities. Recent studies within the cultural historical activity tradition (henceforth referred to as activity theory) share these concerns and in some instances are situated within an historical materialist framework. Tracing its origins back to the works of Vygotsky in the 1920s in post-1917 Russia and later, Leontiev and Luria also from Russia, the tradition of activity theory is marked by considerable diversity over emphasis, direction, conceptions and context (Chaiklin 2001).

For the purposes of this chapter, activity theory is to be understood simply as the study of the development of learning through materially and culturally mediated participation in societal-organised practices. Learning is through historically, culturally and materially mediated participation. The distinctive notion of 'activity' (with the associated sub-notions of subject, object, actions, operations, relations, tools, goals) is seen as the basic unit of analysis. Learning is intrinsic to the activities of the human individual situated within a system of historical lived relationships. As Ehammoumi (2006) has persuasively argued, a strong historical materialist perspective informed the work of the Russian psychologists which, in recent Western studies, has been 'lost or domesticated'. It is the contradictory relationship between the forces of production with the social relations of production that accounts for the dynamic of both change and struggle in socially organised practices. Expansive learning as contrasted with constrained learning, argues Engestrom (1987), is that learning that emerges from the resolution of the contradictions characterising activity systems. It is these social relations of production that mediate and influence human forms of thought through historically organised human activity. Shared meanings and understandings, semiotic processes, human cognition or co-operative activity are situated within the concrete practical activity of labour. Socially organised practices such as work, the school or the family are neutered when divorced from the practices of ownership, production and distribution of wealth and resources.

From an activity theory perspective it is not the case that workers or subordinated groups learn less, are incapable of learning, are uninterested or are passive, reactive learners. Instead the emphasis is on identifying how subordinate groups learn different things in different ways or how this learning is embodied in ongoing cultural material life. Labour market survival requires the acquisition of various 'skills and knowledges' demanded by employers but it also involves learning 'to survive' together with learning that creatively and imaginatively challenges these requirements through identifying alternative possibilities and courses of action. Livingstone and

Sawchuk's (2003) empirical studies into working knowledge and learning practices across five occupational sites, illustrates the insights and explanatory value resulting from theoretical formulations informed by activity theory (see also Sawchuk 2003). Similarly although from a slightly different perspective, the studies on union and working class knowing from the Adult Education Research Group at Roskilde University, Denmark demonstrate the benefits of this wider societal analysis.

How learning is to be understood and theoretically situated then, greatly affect what is known about worker and more specifically, union learning. The recent emergence of more sophisticated frameworks has begun to reveal not only the extensive nature of worker knowledge but also the complexities of this 'knowing'. It is within these wider societal frameworks that union education courses need to be situated in order to begin appreciating their value.

Conclusions

Stuart's experiences of working in the financial and insurance sector resulted in views of learning that were not shared by most other union colleagues from the sector. This is not surprising given the almost hegemonic nature of human capital formulations that situate understandings and practices of workplace education, training and learning in most countries around the world. In contrast to the dominant perspectives, Stuart's views were shaped and strongly influenced by wider societal considerations based on the centrality of wage labour:

> I would question the subject of 'employability' because I regard it as a fallacy (he remarks). Employers 'get rid' of their most experienced skilled employees as it is cheaper to get someone in who is fresh from school, give them the training, offer them a cheap wage and carry on that way.

Although views such as these are not commonly reflected in the educational professional and research literature, it has been argued in this chapter that there are theoretical frameworks that elucidate and make sense of such views. More recent 'participative' based formulations on the nature of learning moreover have stressed the significance of context in any analysis of learning and so given greater prominence and focus to analysis and understandings of 'work'. Empirical studies of the workplace, informed by activity theory it was suggested, engage with this materiality and so provide an understanding of learning that overcomes the dominant ahistorical, politically and socially undifferentiated analysis of learning. Above all, by situating 'workplace learning' within wider societal relationships, studies informed by activity theory begin to make visible the previously hidden ways and forms of knowing and of becoming a trade unionist that are not always recognised nor valued by employers and government policy makers.

Note

I would like to acknowledge my colleague, Dr. Cilla Ross' work in undertaking the interviews.

References

Ackers, P., Smith, C. and Smith, P. (eds.) (1996), *The New Workplace and Trade Unions: Critical Perspectives on Work and Organisation.* (London: Routledge).

Baptiste, I. (2001), 'Educating Lone Wolves: Pedagogical Implications of Human Capital Theory', *Adult Education Quarterly* 51:3, 184–201.

Beckett, D. and Hager, P. (2002), *Life, Work and Learning: Practice in Postmodernity.* (London: Routledge).

Bourdieu, P. (1984), *Distinction.* (London: Routledge and Kegan Paul).

Broncano, M., Salling Olesen, H. and Cisneros, A. (eds.) (2001), *Adult Education and the Labour Market V1.* (Denmark: University of Roskilde).

Burke, B., Geronumo, J., Martin, D., Thomas, B. and Wall, C. (2002), *Education for Changing Unions.* (Toronto: Between the Lines).

Casey, C. (1995), *Work, Self and Society.* (London: Routledge).

Chaiklin, S. (ed) (2001), *The Theory and Practice of Cultural-Historical Psychology.* (Denmark: Aarhus University Press).

Charlesworth, S. (2000), *A Phenomenology of Working-class Experience.* (Cambridge: Cambridge University Press).

Colley, H., Hodkinson, P. and Malerlow, J. (2003), *Informality and Formality in Learning: A Report for the Learning and Skills Research Centre.* (London: Learning and Skills Research Centre).

Danford, A., Richardson, M. and Upchurch, M. (2003), *New Unions, New Workplaces: A Study of Union Resilience in the Restructured Workplace.* (London: Routledge).

Elhammoumi, M. (2006), 'Is There a Marxist Psychology?', in Sawchuk *et al.* (eds.).

Engestrom, Y. (1987), *Learning by expanding: An activity-theoretical approach to developmental research.* (Helsinki: Orienta-Konsultit).

Fenwick, T., Nesbit, T. and Spencer, B. (eds.) (2006), *Contexts of Adult Education. Canadian Perspectives.* (Toronto: Thompson Educational Publishing).

Foley, G. (1999), *Learning in Social Action: A Contribution to Understanding Informal Education.* (London: Zed Books).

Hager, P. (2004), 'Conceptions of Learning and Understanding Learning at Work', *Studies in Continuing Education*, 26:1, 3–17.

Hart, M. (1995), 'Motherwork: A Radical Proposal to Rethink Work and Education', in Welton (ed.).

Hopkins, P. (1985), *Workers' Education: An International Perspective.* (Milton Keynes: Open University Press).

Hubbard, G. (2000), 'The Usefulness of Indepth Life History Interviews for Exploring the Role of Social Structure and Human Agency and Youth Transitions', *Sociological Research Online*, 4:4, 1–16.

Hyman R. (1989), *The Political Economy of Industrial Relations: Theory and Practice in a Cold Climate.* (London: Macmillan Press).

International Labour Office (1976), *Workers' Education and its Techniques.* (Geneva: International Labour Office).

Lash, S. and Urry, J. (1987), *The End of Organised Capitalism.* (Cambridge: Polity Press).

Lave, J. and Wenger, E. (1991), *Situated Learning. Legitimate Peripheral Participation.* (Cambridge: Cambridge University Press).

Livingstone, D. and Sawchuk, P. (2003), *Hidden Knowledge: Organized Labour in the Information Age.* (Toronto: Garamond Press).

Lovett, T. (ed.) (1988), *Radical Approaches to Adult Education.* (London: Routledge).

Newman, M. (1993), *The Third Contract: Theory and Practice in Trade Union Training.* (Sydney: Stewart Victor Publishing).

Reay, D. (1998), 'Rethinking Social Class: Qualitative Perspectives on Class and Gender', *Sociology*, 32:2, 259–275.

Salling Olesen, H. (1989), *Adult Education and Everyday Life.* (Roskilde, Denmark: University of Roskilde).

——, (ed.) (1996), *Adult Education and Labour Market 11.* (Denmark: University of Roskilde).

——, (2001), 'Experience and Learning: Theorising the Subjective Side of Work', in Broncano *et al.* (eds.).

Sawchuk, P. (2003), *Adult Learning and Technology in Working-Class Life.* (Cambridge: Cambridge University Press).

Sawchuk, P., Duarte, N. and Elhammoumi, M. (eds.) (2006), *Critical Perspectives on Activity. Explorations Across Education, Work and Everyday Life.* (Cambridge: Cambridge University Press).

Sfard, A (1998), 'On Two Metaphors for Learning and the Dangers of Choosing First One', *Educational Research,* 27:2, 4–13.

Shoenfeld, A. (1999), 'Looking Towards the 21st Century: Challenges of Educational Theory and Practice', *Educational Research*, 28:7, 4–14.

Simon, B. (ed.) (1990), *The Search for Enlightenment. The Working Class and Adult Education in the Twentieth Century.* (London: Lawrence and Wishart).

Skeggs, B. (1997), *Formations of Class and Gender.* (London: Sage).

Sommer, F., Anderson, A. and Salling Olesen, H. (1996), 'Organization Legionaries or Life Artists? The Shop Steward; Past and Future', in Salling Olesen (ed.).

Spencer, B. (ed.) (2002), *Unions and Learning in a Global Economy: International and Comparative Perspectives.* (Toronto: Thompson Educational Publishing).

Spencer, B. and Taylor, J. (2006), 'Labour Education', in Fenwick *et al.* (eds.).

Straka, G. (2004), *Informal Learning: Genealogy, Concepts, Antagonisms and Questions.* (Bremen, Universitat Bremen).

Thompson, C. (1968), *Education and Experience.* Fifth Mansbridge Memorial Lecture. (Leeds: Leeds University Press).

Thompson, E. (1968), *The Making of the English Working Class.* (London: Penguin).

Thompson, P. and Ackroyd, S. (1995), 'All Quiet on the Workplace Front? A Critique of Recent Trends in British Industrial Sociology', *Sociology*, 29:4, 615–633.

Thompson, P. and Warhurst, C. (eds.) (1998) *Workplaces of the Future*. (London: Macmillan Press).

Warhurst, C. and Thompson, P. (1998), 'Hands, Hearts and Minds: Changing Work and Workers at the end of the century', in Thompson, P. and Warhurst, C. (eds.).

Weber, K. (1996), 'Learning Processes in Trade Union Education. What do Unskilled Women Actually Learn?', in Salling Olesen (ed.).

Welton, M. (ed.) (1995), *In Defence Of The Lifeworld. Critical Perspectives on Adult Education.* (New York: State University of New York Press).

——, (2005), *Designing the Just Society: A Critical Study.* (Leicester, National Institute of Adult Continuing Education).

SECTION III

UNION LEARNING AND UNION RENEWAL

Chapter 9

Integrating Learning into Workplace Bargaining: Case Studies of Evolving Trade Union Learning Agreements

Mark Stuart and Emma Wallis

Introduction

The key purpose of this chapter is to explore the processes by which union engagement in learning at the workplace develop and how these connect with, and evolve in relation to, broader, and typically more established, structures of workplace industrial relations. As numerous chapters in this collection detail, union involvement in the learning agenda has increased substantially in recent years. This can be seen partly in terms of a longer-term campaign by trade unions to engage with employers around more productivist concerns and 'occupational interests' (Leisink 1993), and, more contemporaneously, an increasingly positive set of supports from the state (Forrester 2004). Soon after its election in 1997 the Labour government declared that it regarded learning 'as a natural issue for partnership in the workplace between employers, employees and their trade union' (DfEE 1998, 35). It has backed this position with a dedicated fund, the Union Learning Fund (ULF), for union-initiated projects around learning, and regulatory support for Union Learning Representatives (ULRs) (Wallis *et al.* 2005). The significance of these developments is a matter of some debate. For Hoque and Bacon (2006), trade union involvement in workplace training decisions is, in quantitative terms, limited, with little significance for employee outcomes. Others argue that union-initiated learning partnerships are contributing in qualitative terms to a process of new institution-building that can deliver potential benefits for both employees and employers (see Munro and Rainbird 2004).

In purely empirical terms, data from the 2004 Workplace Employment Relations Survey (WERS) (Kersley *et al.* 2006) reveal that the joint regulation of workplace learning is indeed limited. Across all workplaces, unionised and non-unionised, training is the issue least likely to be subject to negotiation (along with staff selection and staffing plans). The situation within unionised firms themselves appears little different – only staffing plans are less commonly an issue for negotiation – with negotiation over training taking place in only 9 per cent of cases, consultation in 31 per cent of cases and no-involvement at all in 36 per cent of cases (see Kersley *et al.* 2006). In longitudinal terms, the extent of negotiation appears to have increased significantly between 1998 and 2004 and levels are also higher where ULRs are present (Stuart and Robinson 2006), but in itself such aggregation tells us very little about how trade unions have been looking to develop the learning agenda or the processes by which they have sought to engage with employers over learning matters.

It is clear from specialised surveys of ULRs commissioned by the Trades Union Congress (TUC) that union impact in the workplace, particularly in terms of encouraging and helping individuals towards learning, has been increasing year on year (TUC 2006). One of the most striking findings has been the degree of institutionalisation that appears to have taken place. Survey evidence suggests that six out of ten ULRs have a learning agreement at their place of work and that in nearly eight out of ten cases these agreements are considered 'formal' (TUC 2006). What this means exactly is far from clear. Just because a learning agreement is formal does not mean that in practice it forms the basis for on-going, or effective, negotiation over learning – in many cases they could be simple framework agreements – or that it is connected more explicitly to broader structures of collective bargaining. Such concerns have been under-researched to date, but we would argue that understanding these issues is most likely to be uncovered by qualitative rather than quantitative analysis (Forrester 2004). It is necessary to situate the evolution and practice of learning agreements, and the institutions, procedures and processes that develop around them, within the context of the workplace and the contested terrain that operates therein (Stuart 1996). In the context of this chapter, such approach allows us to investigate the 'spill over' effects that result from union involvement in the learning agenda to the broader workplace terrain of industrial relations, and to explore the way that industrial relations context shapes developments around the learning agenda. Empirically, the chapter presents a case study analysis of two high profile examples of workplace learning agreements. It seeks to identify the processes by which union-led learning can become embedded at the workplace, and the conditions most likely to foster sustainability and generate mutual gains outcomes. The chapter is organised into three further sections. First, we consider the potential position of learning within partnership relations and bargaining structures at the workplace and set-out a framework to situate our empirical data. Second, we present two detailed cases studies of union-management learning arrangements, the first of BusCo and the second of Citytravel. In both cases, we draw our data from lengthy semi-structured interviews with union officials (at various levels), union learning representatives and management representatives, relevant company documentation and workplace visits. In conclusion, we draw out the key explanatory factors that may shape the evolving trajectory of workplace learning arrangements, how they link with broader industrial relations machinery and the potential gains that may (or may not) accrue for trade unions. This provides some important insights into the contexts where union learning agreements are most likely to work and union-led learning is likely to flourish.

Learning and the 'New' Bargaining Agenda

Trade union concerns with training and learning matters intensified from the late 1980s onwards. Faced with a declining membership and the potential challenge of new managerial strategies around human resource management, training was taken-up as a new and innovative issue around which trade unions could mobilise to demonstrate their value to both potential and existing members and, crucially, employers. This was epitomised by the TUC's reassessment of bargaining priorities for the 1990s, which called for a move away from the 'traditional, often adversarial' bargaining approach, towards a more 'constructive ... developmental emphasis' (TUC 1992). The substantive aims of this new agenda focused on equal opportunities, payment for skills and a minimum of five days training for all employees. This was to be achieved procedurally through the negotiation of specific training agreements, augmented by workplace training committees (see Stuart 1996 for a detailed account). Whilst training was positioned as an issue that could be sold to employers on productivist grounds, engagement with matters of employee development were also seen as a way of inscribing unions within the broader strategic decision-making processes of employers. For example, the negotiation of training agreements with set training targets would require some knowledge of the wider business plan.

Analysis at the time by Claydon and Green (1994) suggested that the 'new bargaining agenda' had little impact. Their study of 944 company and sector collective agreements signed between January 1991 and June 1993 found that just 40 made specific reference to training issues and only 11 contained a procedural clause outlining specific trade union participation. One reading of the recent findings from WERS 2004 suggests that little headway has been made in the intervening years. As we noted in the introduction, such a reading does not adequately capture the full extent to which trade union involvement in the area has developed. Three further points are worth noting. First, there has been a linguistic turn, away from training and development to learning. Whilst the significance of this could be debated, it has raised important questions about the nature, focus and mode of delivery of skills acquisition (either at or beyond the workplace) and in whose interests such learning best serves (Forrester 2004; Shelley 2005). Second, in ideological and conceptual terms, it is clear that the TUC's call for the new bargaining agenda to move beyond 'adversarial' interests has become, to some extent, ingrained in contemporary employment relations discourse. Key here is the perceived need for trade unions to move beyond narrow distributive concerns (around pay and conditions) towards an agenda more likely to foster co-operative relationships. In this regard, the pursuit of strategies of integrative bargaining, around learning, competence and skilling are seen as more credible in the pursuit of building employment relations where both parties stand to gain (Mathews 1993). Indeed, the notion of 'mutual gains' bargaining (Kochan and Osterman 1994) has become central to debates not only around the furtherance of the learning agenda but trade union renewal and social partnership at the British workplace more generally (see Ackers and Payne 1998; Martinez Lucio and Stuart 2004; Stuart and Martinez Lucio 2005). That the potential of the 'mutual gains' bargaining approach has received extensive examination and critical commentary (see Stuart 1996; Kelly 2004; Danford *et al.* 2005; Stuart and Martinez Lucio 2005) is unquestionable: the point here is that flawed though it may be the discourse has become near hegemonic and in relation to learning matters has remained almost constant. Third, and relatedly, it has been suggested that union strategies for advancing the learning agenda (as an integrative concern) at the workplace, and the forms this takes, should be separated from traditional (focused on distributive issues) trade union channels of collective bargaining (Munro and Rainbird 2004). Understanding what this means in practice requires further empirical research.

In order to understand how unions may look to develop the learning agenda at the workplace and build institutions around this, the work of Munro and Rainbird (2004) on Unison/employer learning partnerships is particularly instructive. They assert that partnerships around learning, in the Unison case at least, can be seen as distinct from more 'general' partnership arrangements: first because they focus on a 'single-issue' rather than 'broader industrial relations concerns'; second, because they 'tend to be informal and are outside of normal industrial relations structures'; and, third, because they are 'union-initiated' and have the benefits of members as core. Extrapolating from these empirical findings of how a union-learning role may develop Munro and Rainbird identify a number of potential gains for unions that may derive from such an approach. First, single issue, informal learning partnerships can contribute to union organisation through increased membership enthusiasm. By separating learning from general industrial relations matters there is also less risk of undermining workplace organisation. This makes it possible for unions to cooperate around learning, whilst at the same time taking a stronger, more adversarial stance on other industrial relations concerns. Second, to be credible they must deliver benefits that have clear membership utility. In other words, the learning must be 'useful' to members, rather than the specific interests of employers (see also Shelley 2005; Wallis *et al.* 2005). Third, where learning partnerships are initiated from a proactive rather than defensive union position, they can contribute to a 'process of establishing new worker entitlements and workplace institutions' (Munro and Rainbird 2004, 421; see also Wallis and Stuart 2004). Finally, to the extent that such learning partnerships generate increased communication, and ultimately trust, between unions and employers, they have the potential to 'spill-over' into more traditional industrial relations machinery and lead to the formation of more 'robust', rather than 'shallow' general partnerships (Oxenbridge and Brown 2004; Munro and Rainbird 2004).

It is possible, however, that any 'spill-over' from a partnership approach, based around consensus decision-making, could lead to the denigration of traditional negotiating structures based more around adversarialism. Conversely, as Roche and Geary (2005) note, it is also possible that where a separation exists between a partnership approach and pre-existing industrial relations institutions the latter may influence the former, and partnership-based decisions and developments may lack legitimacy and stall. As Munro and Rainbird (2004) argue, the extent to which union learning interests are embedded in the structures of (strong) union branches is important here (see also Wallis *et al.* 2005). Their research found examples of positive relations between union-learning roles and union branches and more general spill-over effects. The key point is the degree of support and commitment afforded to the learning agenda by key union representatives. Where leading workplace trade unionists regard learning as of secondary interest or importance to more traditional union concerns, then union-led learning developments are likely to remain marginal. Munro and Rainbird (2004) focus their analysis on Unison, a union with a very specific history of innovation and engagement around the learning agenda. Yet, beyond this, we have a very limited knowledge of the processes by which unions are advancing learning at the workplace, the institutions that are evolving in relation to this and the potential gains that may accrue.

It is against this backdrop that our case studies are situated. Following the discussion above we examine how union-learning initiatives, principally learning agreements, evolve at the workplace and the various forms they take, and consider the types of gains that can be deduced from such initiatives. First, where do such initiatives lie in terms of evolving as single issue, informal partnerships that focus on a union-defined agenda? Second, what are the potential impacts of such initiatives, and their various evolving forms on: learning interests (employee or employer-related); new entitlements and institutions; and spill-over effects in terms of broader industrial relations institutions and interests. Third, what are the conditions most conductive for effective union intervention in the learning agenda?

The Bus Transport Case: Developing Union-led Learning in a Hostile Climate

Our first case, TransportCo, is a British owned passenger transport company with operations in the UK, Ireland, and north America. In the UK, the company currently operates bus, rail and tram services, and also has interests in rail freight and airport management. The bus division of TransportCo comprised twenty-four subsidiary companies, which together formed the largest bus operating company in the UK. Our research focused on a subsidiary in the north of England, what we refer to as BusCo. Subsidiaries had considerable autonomy, despite increased corporatisation in recent years, and independent industrial relations arrangements. BusCo employed some 2,100 staff based at four depots at the time of the research. The development of the learning agenda took place against a history of poor industrial relations and a recent, bitterly contested, pay dispute.

According to management and trade union representatives, the promotion of the lifelong learning agenda within BusCo had its genesis at corporate level. In common with other employers in the sector, TransportCo had experienced difficulties in recruiting and retaining staff. A significant proportion of employees in many subsidiaries were migrant workers for whom English was a second language. Additionally, many employees had basic skills needs. The promotion and provision of learning opportunities to address these needs consequently came to be regarded both as a major component of the company's strategy for recruitment and retention, and as a route to improving customer service and business performance. The Transport and General Workers Union (TGWU), which represented the majority of organised employees, linked lifelong learning to broader issues relating to employability and developmental opportunities for staff. Discussions between corporate level managers and representatives of the union within both formal and informal arenas led to a recognition that the learning agenda had the potential both to deliver mutual gains and act as a central plank for the development of a partnership-based approach to human resource management issues. Several TGWU officials nevertheless indicated that the union experienced significant initial difficulties in convincing management of the need for initiatives that would operationalise such an approach. The main catalyst proved to be the availability of funding under the Union Learning Fund (ULF). A successful application for funding in 2002 enabled the company and the TGWU to pilot three projects at bus subsidiaries in Essex, Leeds and Glasgow. Each initiative involved promoting the value of lifelong learning, and sought to facilitate increased learning opportunities through the creation of local learning partnerships (involving management, TGWU representatives, local Learning and Skills Councils and educational providers) and the establishment of workplace learning facilities. The projects also provided for the recruitment and training of Union Learning Representatives (ULRs) and Learning Co-ordinators, who would act as senior ULRs. The legislation governing ULRs was identified by BusCo management as a specific stimulus for developments at the subsidiary.

Alongside these developments, the TGWU sought to negotiate a company-wide agreement around learning, but this had not yet materialised. Following the conclusion of the pilot projects a joint union-management seminar was convened to look at ways of progressing a partnership-based approach to learning in the company. At this event the union was presented with a document entitled the Standard Operating Procedure (SOP), which detailed how practice in relation to lifelong learning was to be standardised across the bus division. A number of TGWU learning co-ordinators suggested this could potentially act as a 'precursor' to a formal corporate level learning agreement. However, both the process and content of the SOP can be seen as problematic. First, it was presented and developed unilaterally by corporate level management representatives. Second, the document sought to prescribe not only the roles and responsibilities of ULRs but also the criteria and process that should be utilised to select ULRs. This, as we detail below, was to prove a particularly sensitive issue within the union. Thus, despite TrasnportCo's rhetorical commitment to partnership, the company's initial intentions seemed to suggest a strategy designed to delimit and control the activities of the TGWU in relation to learning. This had not gone unnoticed in union quarters:

> It's [the Standard Operating Procedure] very much a management document. Management are controlling the agenda. That's something we don't like (TGWU Learning Co-ordinator).

Whilst it would have been possible for the union to have sought a subsidiary level learning agreement, this had also not happened. Rather, a more explicit partnership-based approach to learning had evolved that resulted in a number of informal agreements. These agreements were concluded, however, within the framework of existing bargaining machinery. First, was an agreement around the funding of a series of learning centres within the subsidiary. These had been rolled out at all depots following the pilot project. Second, an informal substantive agreement negotiated within the Joint Functional Council (JFC)[1] established that each of the

---

1   The JFC is comprised of nine trade union representatives representing occupational groups rather than the unions that operate within the subsidiary (5 drivers, 2 engineers and 2 from the administrative function), the Managing Director, the HR Director and other managers on an ad hoc basis as appropriate.

subsidiary's depots would have two ULRs, each of whom would be able to spend half a day per week on union activities without loss of pay. A Learning Co-ordinator was also appointed, and funded, by BusCo to organise learning activities and support the work of the ULRs. Even though the salary was paid for by the company, the Learning Co-ordinator was to be engaged on a full-time basis as a TGWU official (in a similar manner to that of a convenor steward), reporting directly to the JFC. The TGWU was largely supportive of this appointment, although concerns were also expressed about the relationship to management:

> I don't see him [the Learning Co-ordinator] as a trade union rep. He answers to the Human Resource Manager (TGWU representative).

It was agreed that the Learning Co-ordinator would take responsibility for the administration of a long-established Learning Fund – that provided grants of up to £250 for non-vocational learning – that had previously been management controlled. Third, negotiations within the JFC led to the conclusion of an informal procedural agreement to establish a JFC sub-committee, the Learning Steering Group (LSG). The LSG included an array of management and union representatives (including the Learning co-ordinator) and was designed to formalise union involvement in developing the learning agenda within the company.

Somewhat curiously, the first meeting of the LSG moved that ULRs would be excluded from the forum, except when their presence was specifically required. The reasons for this were far from clear. One explanation centred on ensuring that learning issues were integrated rather than separated from the framework of existing bargaining machinery. More simply may have been the related fact that key actors within management and the TGWU did not wish to disturb existing relationships with the introduction of new personnel. This was particularly pertinent given a recent history of relatively turbulent industrial relations within the company and at the subsidiary.

There had been a history of poor industrial relations in TransportCo, with management taking a robust approach towards trade unions that largely excluded their influence on the corporate policy formation process. Against this backdrop, it was noted that the more consensual agenda of learning had led to a thawing of management-union relations to some extent:

> The learning initiative broke the ice in the negotiating arena. Relations were crap. On every other issue we were struggling. It was all doom and gloom until we got to learning (TGWU representative).

This had arisen due to the lead role that the TGWU had played in leading debates around learning, and the expertise they had accrued in the area served to increase their credibility within the company. This had spill-over effects in relation to the broader bargaining agenda, and recent corporate level agreements had been concluded on pensions and alcohol and driver assault policies. These corporate gains aside, however, the most significant influence on industrial relations at BusCo had been a three-week strike as part of an industrial dispute around pay in 2004. The strike forced management to make financial concessions, but they responded with a counter-offensive designed to weaken the long-term position of the union: they sought to withdraw TGWU facilities and check-off arrangements. These proposals were only withdrawn following the threat of further strike action, and an agreement from the TGWU to restructure the composition and operating arrangements of the Central Negotiating Committee (CNC). The CNC had been criticised by management because its impenetrable structure[2] made bargaining protracted and bureaucratic. The slimmed down CNC now meets with management representatives on a regular basis, an arrangement welcomed by the TGWU. The increased dialogue that resulted from this arrangement was attributed by TGWU representatives to the adoption of a confrontational approach towards the employer, with one stating 'we've earned a bit of respect [as a result of the strike]. If they didn't have to, they wouldn't talk to us'.

For management representatives, the strike forced both the subsidiary and TGWU to reconsider industrial relations strategies. 'Since the strike, we knew we had to do things differently, but the unions have had to change too', said one management representative. This included new management practices that have emphasised direct channels of communication with employees. Nonetheless, the recent emphasis placed upon the learning agenda within BusCo remained largely unaffected by developments within the broader industrial relation arena. That this was so resulted from the fact that both management and TGWU representatives presented learning as an issue around which they could work to potentially deliver mutual gains. For example, ULRs in the subsidiary were trained to deliver basic skills training to new starters as part of a revised induction programme. Also, whilst discussions around learning were procedurally inserted within existing industrial relations machinery, learning was nonetheless regarded as an issue that should be separated from broader bargaining agendas:

> We want a situation where we can talk about the industrial relations issues, but where this doesn't affect what goes on in there [the learning centre]. The learning must be unaffected; therefore it has to be separate (TGWU Learning Co-ordinator).

This was epitomised by the LSG, which created a distinct space for the development of a partnership-based approach to the learning agenda, whilst simultaneously embedding this agenda within the framework of existing bargaining structures.

The TGWU was the largest union at the subsidiary and, accordingly, dominated the development of the learning agenda. The original ULF project was developed solely by the TGWU, with no reference to other unions[3][4]. The numerical dominance

---

2   The CNC is a sub-committee of the JFC. It represents drivers (the largest occupational group within BusCo) and was formerly comprised of 12 representatives, 6 of which would be involved in negotiations with management. Agreements reached in negotiations then had to be discussed by the full CNC, and were not infrequently voted down by the committee's non-negotiating members. Following the 2004 strike, the CNC was reduced to 8 members, all of whom would be involved in negotiations.

3   Amicus has a small presence amongst mechanics and engineers, whilst some white collar staff are members of Unison.

4   Members of the other unions, and employees not in any union, are nevertheless welcome to use the on-site learning facilities.

of the TGWU seemed to limit inter-union frictions over the direction of the learning agenda: the other unions appeared happy to be led on this. Nonetheless, a number of internal political issues were apparent. For example, it was TGWU policy (specified in the rule book) that all ULRs should be elected rather than selected. A policy that was questioned by many officials at the subsidiary, as it allowed for committed ULRs to be removed if their members disagreed with the direction in which the learning agenda was being driven. This was seen as a particularly pertinent issue given the desire of the union to use learning as an issue to organise and support the numbers of ethnic minority and migrant workers working for the company:

> There are 230 Asian workers at xxxx garage. Not one of them has got any chance whatsoever of progressing within this company. We used ULF money to develop courses for these workers, but there's been a horrendous backlash from the white lads. I have to be very, very careful. If I run anything for the Asian lads, the white lads start saying you're not doing anything for them. The racism is horrendous. I have to be very careful. I could get de-selected over these sorts of issues (TGWU Learning Co-ordinator).

The issue was also thrown into sharp relief by the recruitment process of the subsidiary's Learning Co-ordinator. As noted, whilst this was ostensibly a trade union role, it was paid for by management, but more significantly the position was advertised as an internal vacancy and there was no opportunity for candidates to stand for election. The bypassing of the union rulebook was questioned by the TGWU, as was the appropriateness of management influencing the selection of a trade union official. There was also some suspicion that the individual appointed had colluded with management to facilitate this:

> This didn't sit well with the other ULRs who were elected. The Learning Co-ordinator definitely came by a different route … (TGWU Regional official).

Finally, concerns were also expressed over the extent to which ULRs, and the interests they stood for, were fully incorporated into local branch structures:

> ULRs are not part of the union committee. The branch is not all that interested. The Secretary doesn't give a buggery, they've got enough troubles of their own (TGWU Learning Co-ordinator).

There was also a debate within the TGWU over the balance to be struck around the type of learning on offer at the learning centres. Such tensions were indicative of wider debates around where the balance of responsibility for funding training and development lies. Management was looking to utilise the learning centres to provide job related training, in line with proposals outlined within the SOP. This was opposed by some factions of the TGWU, who stressed that learning centres should focus on union-led learning and non-vocational activities. For this camp there was some suspicion that the company had used ULF monies to subsidise its own investments in training facilities. Others within the union were more pragmatic. They pointed to the learning centres as important examples of a partnership-based approach to learning and stressed that job-related training could be seen as an acceptable solution to an initial under-utilisation of the learning centres, which, because they were wholly supported by the company, may be threatened with closure as a consequence.

The learning centres were, nonetheless, at an early stage of development. They were greatly under utilised and there appeared to be widespread ignorance amongst the workforce both of the learning opportunities available to employees, and of the potential value of learning, despite on-going publicity by BusCo and the TGWU. At the time of the research around 50 employees were using the centres each week, with 26 of those currently on courses. Drivers were proving particularly difficult to engage. Management representatives conceded that this may have been due to employee suspicions of motives and that this may have influenced perceptions of the developing learning agenda:

> If it's got a BusCo logo on the top you know what's going to happen. It will be screwed up and thrown in the bin (management representative).

Engaging employee interest in learning was seen by management representatives as the key priority for the emerging learning partnership. It was also understood as the main reason why the union had yet to attempt to link learning matters to broader distributive concerns. Nonetheless, not all aspects of the learning agenda were seen as consensual, and management representatives recognised that conflict could arise in the future as employee engagement in learning increased and the union sought to support their developing aspirations:

> I don't think we've reached that point yet because we haven't switched a lot of people on to learning yet ... I can see that there is a potential for conflict, and you're going to get more and more of that as people get better educated (management representative).

Key actors within the TGWU branch acknowledged that their understanding of the learning agenda, and the way it could connect with both broader trade union agendas and the wider industrial relations environment needed finessing, as the latter does not necessarily guarantee the former:

> It's [learning] not my area. It's never been the top of my list of priorities, but I realise this is an area where we need to make progress (TGWU representative).

This factor explains, in part, why the branch had not sought to link learning and skills formation with broader distributive issues or engage management in discussions about time off for learning. Both parties, nonetheless, were of the view that the learning partnership had delivered mutual gains. The union had increased its role in the policy formation process around learning. The learning partnership had also generated positive publicity for the company and had enabled it to present itself as a good employer. Indeed, it was the view of some within the TGWU that such publicity was the primary reason for continued management support for the partnership-based approach to learning:

> I've been told by our Regional Director that whilst ever the company look good, they'll keep on with the initiative (TGWU Learning Co-ordinator).

In summary, a number of union-led learning initiatives had been established at BusCo and a formal apparatus for the joint regulation of training was starting to evolve. But, the history of conflict at the case had engendered uncertainty over motives for engagement, there was some evidence of management control of the agenda and the union branch did not see learning as a priority issue. Whilst it was the case that the learning agenda played a role in generating more open relationships between management and union, it was also the case that a history of conflictual industrial relations cut deep and that 'spill-over' effects from established industrial relations structures had a delimiting effect on progressing learning matters (eg. in terms of supporting the role of ULRs).

The Citytravel Case: Building Learning Institutions for Mutual Gains

Citytravel is a public sector organisation that provides public transport in a conurbation in northern England. It employed around 1,000 employees located across three areas, ferries, road tunnels (including tolls and maintenance) and the Passenger Transport Executive (PTE – responsible for a bus network and administration). Historically, these areas operated very much as discrete entities, with their own locally determined terms and conditions. Five unions were recognised across the sites: Amicus, GMB, TGWU, UCATT and Unison. There was no coherent policy towards training and development. The annual training budget was targeted exclusively at job specific training and was allocated on a first come first served basis that was highly dependent on the extent to which individual managers were supportive of training activities or not. As a result, the majority of employees, and particularly those in manual occupations, had little access historically to training and development opportunities.

The need to adopt a more systematic approach to employee development had been recognised by local unions since the late 1990s, but the fragmented structure of the company, and the opportunities this afforded management to play unions off against each other, militated against a co-ordinated approach. Two key factors were to act as catalysts for change in 2002. First, in response to a critical District Auditor's Report, a new Learning and Development Manager was appointed, charged with developing a more effective human resource development strategy. Second, was the increased availability of public funds for learning-related projects (primarily through the Union Learning Fund) that either involved or that were led by trade unions. There had been an early Bargaining for Skills project in the Tunnels section, but, as a management representative observed, the Union Learning Fund, proved particularly attractive:

> I suppose when we sat down and looked at it [and saw that we could get hold of half a million pounds] we saw that there were advantages to working in partnership with the trade unions (management representative).

Such developments, along with statutory recognition for ULRs, paved the way for the establishment of a partnership-based approach to learning. The most immediate result was the Citylearn project, funded under the ULF, which led to the establishment of three learning centres and an increased variety of learning opportunities for staff. Representatives of both management and unions took up posts as Citylearn project workers, albeit whilst continuing in their customary roles.

Following this, a learning agreement was concluded in 2003. The agreement is a broad framework document that, whilst not detailed, formalises the role of ULRs at the company and commits management and unions to a partnership-based approach to learning. Management initially favoured a more substantive agreement, but unions were opposed to this, fearing that such an agreement, given the structure of the company and the complexity of different working conditions, would result in lengthy (and potentially debilitating) negotiations that would divert attention from the principles of partnership working that they were looking to formalise:

> We wanted to gain a general consensus rather than being bogged down in the detail. Some trade unionists would have argued about a single word (trade union official).

The learning agreement was designed to operate alongside extant bargaining machinery, rather than be formally integrated into it. It had a crucial procedural element that led to the formation of a Joint Learning Forum (JLF), responsible for the development, and delivery, of learning policies and opportunities within Citytravel. The JLF and its sub committees comprised an equal number of management and union representatives and equal representation from the company's three operational areas. Regular ULR meetings were also organised alongside the JLF. These procedural forums were considered to have far greater significance than the learning agreement itself, as they acted as important conduits for the improvement of communication within the company and the building of relations of trust not only between management and unions but the different unions themselves.

Nonetheless, the learning agreement paved the way for a number of subsequent ad hoc substantive agreements, mostly concerned with time-off and support for learning. For example, employees directed towards courses as a result of the company's Performance Review and Development (PRD) process were entitled to full-time off or time in lieu. Also, the company agreed to offer interest free loans (of up to £1,000) to purchase a computer for any employee undertaking any course. Management saw these advances as 'stand alone' arrangements that are separate from the learning agreement itself. But, all have subsequently been ratified by the JLF, thereby according them a degree of formality.

There is some evidence that the management-union partnership around learning had a broader industrial relations impact. Both management and union respondents suggested that the partnership-approach led to increased channels of communication that engendered improved levels of trust between management and unions. This meant that relatively trivial issues that would previously have led to resentment and conflict could now be diffused more amicably and efficiently. More significant was the influence on the broader industrial relations environment. Discussions over less consensual issues were also considered to be less problematic and improved management perceptions of the productive role that trade unions could play resulted in increased union influence within the organisation. This was evident in union inclusion on a number of key company strategy groups, for example around

Dignity at Work, and also formal union involvement in preparations for Investors in People (IiP) assessment. As part of this, a ULR was trained by Citytravel to act as an IiP advisor. The successful operation of the JLF also resulted in an agreement to establish a Joint Negotiating Forum (JNF), operating on the same basis, but with a remit to consider broader industrial relations issues. According to a management representative, the formation of the JNF was only possible 'because of the mutual trust generated by learning'. Where previously management held separate negotiations with unions in each service, the JNF established the principle of single-table bargaining. This development was also welcomed by unions, as it limited the capacity of management to play one union off against the other and reduced the transaction costs of negotiations:

> It's an advantage from the trade union perspective because we all see things at the same time. It should speed things up too because there will be only one set of negotiations instead of three (trade union official).

Yet despite evidence of increased union influence across the organisation, not least in terms of human resource development policies, their influence over workplace practices was still open to debate. Notably, line management support remained variable, something that is widely recognised as problematic (Thompson *et al.* 2007), and, as a consequence, employee access to learning opportunities unequal:

> Line managers are very variable in their approach to learning. Some are really up for it, but others see it as a threat. The culture here is top down. There is more support for learning amongst the top managers (ULR).

Union involvement in the learning agenda not only led to improved relations with management, it also acted as a fulcrum for improved relations between the different unions themselves. Whilst all five unions signed up to the learning agreement, there was some initial opposition amongst a minority of shop floor union representatives. Such opposition turned on recognised trade union concerns about working in partnership with management. There were also suspicions that management might look to use the learning agenda as a way to facilitate company restructuring. Such views were prevalent within the ferry section, where unions had past experience of this. But more broadly, staff employed in ferries and tunnels, in particular, initially regarded the learning opportunities provided by the Citylearn project as a management initiative, and believed that associated learning opportunities were mandatory. A certain degree of employee resistance to participating in available learning activities was thus observable at the outset, although such fears were largely allayed with the passage of time. Likewise, initial union opposition to the establishment of a partnership-based approach to learning dissipated over time. It was recognised that the structures created from the learning agreement had led to a number of key benefits for the unions in Citytravel, most notably improved levels of inter-union communication and co-operation and with it a more co-ordinated union approach to the learning agenda.

The relationship between the learning partnership and wider bargaining structures was relatively fluid. At the outset both management and unions agreed to 'firewall' learning from the traditional bargaining agenda. In essence, learning was to be advanced through a 'single purpose' agreement underpinned by 'mutual gains' bargaining that operated alongside existing bargaining machinery. The situation in reality proved more complex. Thus, even though ULRs had responsibility for approaching management with regard to learning issues, some aspects of learning were subject to the provisions of pre-existing bargaining arrangements. For example, the pursuit of formal grievances around access to learning agreed under the PRD process fell within the remit of shop stewards and branch officials rather than the ULRs. In some cases, of course, ULRs were also stewards, but a significant number were new to trade union activism, and were attracted to the post because they saw learning as a non-adversarial issue. Accordingly, it was argued that the more non-consensual aspects of the learning agenda should be handled by trade unionists with a more traditional role:

> The ULRs are not stewards. We need different people. Stewards have to be confrontational. A lot of the ULRs wouldn't be happy in that role and wouldn't have the skills (trade union official).

One concern expressed by management representatives was that unions would use the learning agreement to make demands for linking skills acquisition to rewards. This did not happen. Whilst learning was linked to employee performance within the PRD process, any attempt to link this to performance-related pay was resisted by unions on traditional equity grounds. Nonetheless, aspects of the learning agenda started to creep into the terrain of informal distributive bargaining. Most notably, a new equal opportunities clause was agreed in relation to staff recruitment to ensure that internal staff were not disadvantaged. In practical terms internal applicants were offered pre-application courses, run jointly by ULRs and the HR Department. There was also evidence of 'spill-overs' from the more conflictual terrain of industrial relations to the more consensual sphere of the learning agenda. For example, some employees withdrew their support for learning activities when a minor dispute occurred over an unrelated non-learning issue:

> They had some dispute in ferries or tunnels over tea breaks or something and people refused to come in and do their courses. They said it was because they were in dispute, but the two had absolutely nothing to do with each other (project worker).

The adoption of a partnership based-approach to learning was, to a large extent driven by the objective of effecting cultural change and transforming Citytravel into a learning organisation. Both management and trade unions viewed this positively. Around one third of employees had accessed Citylearn facilities and it was argued that improvements in management-union communication and trust had impacted more broadly on employee attitudes. According to one management representative, staff regarded Citytravel as a better employer:

> We were always accused – probably fairly – that the manual and general workers didn't have access to training. The project has meant that staff now think we are a good employer. This may help us to recruit and retain the staff we need (management representative).

Such views were echoed by union representatives and ULRs, who suggested that staff morale and motivation had improved across the organisation as a result of the developmental opportunities afforded by increased access to learning. This was most apparent in an increased willingness for employees to apply for jobs in other parts of the organisation.

In contrast to the BusCo case a wide range of mutual gains appeared to have been generated by the learning agreement at Citytravel and this had impacted positively on the broader industrial relations environment. Relationships between management and unions appeared to have improved and levels of trust were higher than in the previous case. The relationship between the learning and collective bargaining agendas was more explicitly separated than in BusCo, but this not only provided space for the union role to grow it helped to establish clear boundaries between different union roles, around for example the ULR role and how they could be supported.

Discussion and Conclusions

Our empirical analysis offers a dynamic, case-study based approach to understanding the evolution of union-learning arrangements at the workplace. In structuring our analysis we have been guided by Munro and Rainbird's (2004) study of Unison. Their work suggested that significant union gains were possible where workplace learning partnerships were organised around the single issue of learning, were informal and distinct from traditional structures of industrial relations and were clearly union initiated and defined. Our cases provide some support for their assertions (see Table 9.1). In both cases the learning arrangements evolved as single-issue concerns and attempts were made to separate developments in relation to learning from more traditional industrial relations machinery. This was most explicit in the case of Citytravel where the learning partnership arrangements were considered to be 'firewalled' from broader distributive concerns. In the case of BusCo, the arrangements were distinct, but at the same time inserted within existing bargaining machinery. Positive outcomes were observable in both cases.

There was no evidence to suggest that the evolving partnerships had any detrimental impact on union organisation. But, equally there was no real indication that, in generating new membership enthusiasm, this had impacted significantly on the strengthening of branch organisation. New institutional arrangements, through procedural committee structures, had emerged in both cases, there were new mechanisms for learning delivery through workplace learning centres and, in the case of Citytravel, new entitlements around time-off for learning had been concluded. In terms of the learning itself there were clear benefits for employees. Access was raised, equal opportunities improved and the take-up of learning was high in Citytravel, whilst in BusCo ULRs were now leading learning initiatives around basic skills. Whilst it is certainly the case that such learning does not meet the 'radical' or broader societal objectives stressed by Shelley (2005) and Forrester (2004), the opportunities for many workers to access learning and the individual confidence this can instil is a valuable trade union goal in itself (Munro and Rainbird 2004).

Table 9.1   Summary of processes and outcomes of learning agreements

Nature of union-learning arrangements	Citytravel	BusCo
Extent union-initiated and defined	ULF and ULR recognition as key drivers Early union project New HR Manager	ULF and ULR recognition TGWU commitment to learning Clearly defined management problems for learning
Focus of issues	Sole focus on learning through development of new initiatives, processes and procedures	Sole focus on learning through development of new initiatives, processes and procedures
Relationship to existing bargaining structures	High degree of formality through agreement and forums Separate and alongside IR structures – 'firewalled'	Informal, no agreement; procedural forum Inserted within IR structures, but as single issue
Outcomes		
Workplace organisation	increased inter-union communication and co-ordination	little impact, but did not undermine
Learning interests	employee and employer need increasing joint regulation high employee interest	employee and employer need employer control little employee interest
New entitlements and institutions	New Procedural arrangements New entitlements	New procedural arrangements Limited new entitlements
Spill-over effects	Strong in terms of management-union relations and inter-union relations	Moderate in terms of management-union relations

Nonetheless, the learning initiatives put in place also met employer needs as well. In the case of Citytravel, the use of ULRs in the IiP accreditation process could be seen as possible cooption to managerial goals. More positively it could be seen as the extension of union influence into the 'joint regulation' of learning (Munro and Rainbird 2004). In BusCo, the balance between employer and employee need seemed more firmly tilted in favour of the former, as management sought to utilise union-learning centres specifically for company-related training and control the process of appointing so called union learning co-ordinators. Given the uneasy tension that can exist between employee and employer need and the motives for management support of union-led learning initiatives, it is perhaps unsurprising that employees were suspicious of new learning initiatives in both cases, although the impact on outcomes was most noticeable with the lack of take-up in the BusCo case. Yet, despite these complexities, there was evidence of positive spill-over effects in both cases, with rolling initiatives and a recognised improvement in communications and relations between management and unions.

In crude terms, the learning arrangements evolving at Citytravel appear to be generating more significant and sustainable mutual gains than at BusCo. There are clearly a number of factors at play in explaining this, but we would argue that there is a clear relationship between the evolving institutional architecture around union-led learning and sustainable mutual gains. In both cases the unions were the key instigators of learning partnerships, but equally there were strong management motives for engaging in learning. The potential of financial support from the ULF was seen as a key inducement, as was the need to respond to the ULR initiative. But, clearly, these factors can only exist as drivers. As Caverley *et al.* (2006) explain, often the intervention itself is not as important as the process surrounding the intervention in understanding how partnership relations evolve. In this regard, three factors stand out. First, is the legacy and context of industrial relations: 'previous experiences that illustrated honest intentions' (Caverley *et al.* 2006, 65) help shape and condition the likely outcomes of evolving and future partnership relations. Whilst both cases had problematic histories of industrial relations, this had been more profound in the case of BusCo. And whilst attempts had been made to insulate the learning partnership from this, the strategies and activities of management in terms of the Standard Operating Procedure and their attempts to control the learning agenda clearly acted as an impediment to the fostering of, what some commentators refer to as, 'genuine' partnership (Wray 2005).

Second, the relationship between the evolving learning partnerships and extant bargaining machinery was complex and fluid. To some extent the more explicit integration of the learning agenda at BusCo led to its being downgraded as a central issue of consideration by the branch. Yet, whilst the differentiation between the learning partnership and traditional industrial relations structures at Citytravel were more clearly defined, there was also a high degree of formality and codification of learning and its procedural elements, and there was also a more 'positional' (Caverley *et al.* 2006) inclusion of learning matters within traditional structures in relation to grievances over access to learning. Thus, whilst Munro and Rainbird's (2004, 420) study of Unison found strong support for learning partnerships that were informal and 'outside traditional industrial relations structures', since integrative and distributive interests are best kept apart, this may take different forms in different situations depending on the history and experience of union engagement with learning initiatives and the overall context of industrial relations. It is also the case that the relationship between learning arrangements and broader bargaining machinery is likely to evolve over time.

Finally, whilst evidence suggests that the integration or not of union-learning initiatives within branch structures is an important variable in shaping outcomes

(Munro and Rainbird 2004; Wallis *et al.* 2005; Thompson *et al.* 2007), broader intra and inter-union factors are also worth further investigation. In the case of Citytravel we found that one of the gains of the learning partnership was increased inter-union communication and coordination – in other cases this could be a subject of friction (Wallis and Stuart 2007) – whilst in the BusCo case there were intra-union differences over whether ULRs should be elected or selected.

Pulling this together, it is clear that the context into which learning agreements are situated shapes their development and effectiveness. A recent history of conflict and turbulent industrial relations, such as at BusCo, can engender uncertainty about motives, which in this particular case meant a limited take-up of new learning activities. At Citytravel initial scepticism around union-led learning initiatives was overcome as relations of trust between management and unions improved and gains became discernable. The manner in which such learning was institutionalised proved significant. Where partnerships around learning are separated from the broader bargaining agenda they have more space to flourish. They are accordingly less prone to 'capture' by disputes exercising broader industrial relations machinery and the possibility of learning concerns (and ULRs) being marginalised as a consequence is mitigated. Nonetheless, the formal codification of such learning procedures is necessary if their separation from broader industrial relations machinery is to be reinforced. Such codification, to the extent that it legitimises the learning agenda and union-learning roles and underpins more robust partnership arrangements, also forms the springboard by which 'spill overs' to the broader industrial relations agenda can be effected. Such boundaries can also help to delineate the respective responsibilities of different union actors, in relation to learning and bargaining and the priorities accorded to each. That said it is self-evident that the advancement of the union-led learning agenda at the workplace needs accord between different union bodies and support, mentoring and signalling from experienced union representatives and union branches.

In conclusion, our case studies provide some insights into how union-learning initiatives are being advanced at the workplace level. They reveal some of the gains that are being derived from such initiatives and point to the challenges that may lie ahead.

Acknowledgments

Thanks to Miguel Martinez Lucio, Ian Greer and Ian Greenwood for comments on a previous draft of this chapter. Our research was part funded by the Trades Union Congress.

References

Ackers, P. and Payne, J. (1998), 'British Trade Unions and Social Partnership: Rhetoric, Reality and Strategy', *International Journal of Human Resource Management* 9:3, 529–50.

Caverley, N., Cunningham, B. and Mitchell, L. (2006), 'Reflections on Public Sector-based Integrative Collective Bargaining: Conditions Affecting Cooperation within the Negotiation Process', *Employee Relations* 28:1, 62–75.

Claydon, T. and Green, F. (1994), 'Can Trade Unions Improve Training in Britain?', *Personnel Review* 23:2.

Danford, A., Richardson, M., Stewart, P., Tailby, S. and Upchurch, M. (2005), *Partnership in the High Performance Workplace: Work and Employment Relations in the Aerospace Industry.* (Basingstoke: Palgrave Macmillan).

Department for Education and Employment (1998), *The Learning Age: A Renaissance for a New Britain.* Cm3790. The Stationary Office.

Forrester, K. (2004), '"The Quiet Revolution"? Trade Union Learning and Renewal Strategies', *Work, Employment and Society* 18:2, 413–420.

Healy, G., Heery, E., Taylor, P. and Brown, W. (eds.) (2004), *The Future of Worker Representation.* (London: Palgrave/MacMillan).

Hoque, K. and Bacon, N. (2006), 'Trade Union Recognition, Union Learning Representatives and Training Incidence in Britain', paper presented at *British Universities Industrial Relations Association (BUIRA) 56th Annual Conference.* University of Galway, 28th–30th June.

Kelly, J. (2004), 'Social Partnership Agreements in Britain: Labour Cooperation and Compliance', *Industrial Relations* 43:1, 267–92.

Kersley, B., Alpin, C., Forth, J., Bryson, A., Bewley, H., Dix, G. and Oxenbridge, S. (2006), *Inside the Workplace: Findings from the 2004 Workplace Employment Relations Series.* (Abingdon: Routledge).

Kochan, T. and Osterman, P. (1994), *The Mutual Gains Enterprise: Forging a Winning Partnership among Labor, Management and Government,* (Boston, MA: Harvard Business School Press).

Leisink, P. (1993), 'Is Innovation a Management Prerogative? Changing Employment Relationships, Innovative Unions', Leverhulme Public Lecture, University of Warwick, May.

Martinez Lucio, M. and Stuart, M. (2004), 'Swimming Against the Tide: Social Partnership, Mutual Gains and the Revival of 'Tired' HRM', *International Journal of Human Resource Management* 15:2, 410–424.

Mathews, J. (1993), 'The Industrial Relations of Skill Formation', *International Journal of Human Resource Management* 4:3, 591–609.

Munro, A. and Rainbird, H. (2004), 'Opening Doors as well as Banging on Tables: Unison/employer Partnerships on Learning in the UK Public Sector', *Industrial Relations Journal* 35:5, 419–433.

Oxenbridge, S. and Brown, W. (2004), 'A Poisoned Chalice? Trade Union Representation in Partnership and Cooperative Employer-union Relationships', in Healy *et al.* (eds.).

Roche, W.K. and Geary, J.F. (2006), *Partnership at Work: The Quest for Radical Organizational Change.* (Abingdon: Routledge).

Shelley, S. (2005), '"Useful" Outcomes for Workers in Trade Union Learning Initiatives: The Significance of Attitude and Ownership', Working Paper Series, 2005: 5. University of Hertfordshire Business School.

Stuart, M. (1996), 'The Industrial Relations of Training: A Reconsideration of Training Arrangements', *Industrial Relations Journal* 27:3, 253–265.

Stuart, M. and Martinez Lucio, M. (eds.) (2005), *Partnership and Modernisation in Employment Relations*. (Abingdon: Routledge).

Stuart, M. and Robinson, A. (2006), 'Getting Training onto the Workplace Bargaining Agenda: Opportunities and Constraints', Midlands Regional TUC Unionlearn seminar, June.

Trade Union Congress (1992), *Bargaining for Skills: A Call to Action. A TUC Initiative to Deliver the National Education and Training Targets*. (London: TUC).

——, (2006), *Making a Real Difference: Union Learning Reps: A Survey*. (London: TUC Unionlearn).

Thompson, P., Warhurst, C. and Findlay, P. (2007), *'Organising to Learn and Learning to Organise: Three Case Studies on the Effects of Union-led Workplace Learning'*, Unionlearn Research Paper No.2. (London: TUC Unionlearn).

Wallis, E., Stuart, M. and Greenwood, I. (2005), '"Learners of the Workplace Unite!" An Empirical Examination of the Trade Union Learning Representative Initiative', *Work, Employment and Society* 19:2, 283–304.

Wallis, E. and Stuart, M. (2004), 'Partnership-based Approaches to Learning in the Context of Restructuring: Case Studies from the Steel and Metal Sectors', *Career Development International* 9:1, 45–57.

——, (2007), *A Collective Learning Culture. A Qualitative Study of Workplace Learning Agreements*. Unionlearn Research Paper No.3. (London: TUC).

Wray, D. (2005), 'Management and Union Motives in the Negotiation of Partnership: A Case Study of Process and Outcome at an Engineering Company', in Stuart and Martinez Lucio (eds.).

Chapter 10

The Longer-term Influence of Women-only Trade Union Schools

Gill Kirton

Introduction

Trade union education constitutes a significant expense and investment for trade unions and is believed to be one resource through which unions might revitalise themselves (Holford 1993; Bridgford and Stirling 2000; Munro and Rainbird 2000). With women such an important source of members for British trade unions, it is thought that union education, especially women-only schools, can help to foster their participation (Greene and Kirton 2002; Munro and Rainbird 2000a; McBride 2001; Parker 2003). Kirton and Healy (2004) explore the relationship between women's experiences of women-only courses and social identities, arguing that such courses provide the conditions for women to question, reinforce or transform their social identities and that this can lead to greater union identification and participation. Cunnison and Stageman's (1995) and Parker's (2003) case studies also demonstrate that participants find women's schools personally valuable and believe them to be critical to the development of female union activism. It is clear that it is highly useful for British trade unions to garner a deeper understanding of the role that union education might play in revitalising the movement.

However, studies designed specifically to evaluate the longer-term effects of union education generally are almost unknown, at least in the more recently published literature, although there are two studies of more than a decade ago that provide useful insights. Miller and Stirling (1992) surveyed (male and female) British trade unionists who had attended union courses in the previous year, asking respondents to indicate what developments had taken place in their participation and what they felt they had achieved since the course(s). They concluded that the courses engendered increased confidence and encouraged members to become more involved in both workplace trade unionism and the wider labour movement and they called for further studies following up on students to provide a 'proper assessment' of the utility of trade union education. Catlett's (1986) survey of women's summer school participants in the US attempted to measure and quantify post-course changes over an 18-month period in women's union activity and to investigate their lasting perceptions of the school. An overwhelming majority of respondents indicated that the school had encouraged them to become more active in their unions and perceptions of the school remained overwhelmingly positive with most students believing it to be beneficial.

Women-only Courses, Separate Organising and Empowerment

For historical and cultural reasons, the main emphasis of British trade union education is on meeting the educational requirements of representatives, not least because legal rights to paid release for union courses are restricted to 'properly appointed officers' of recognised trade unions (McBride and Miller 2000:310). Women-only courses, usually made available to 'ordinary' members, are one exception to this general orientation. Women-only courses are now widely established as a form of separate organising and offered by the Trades Union Congress (TUC), most large TUC unions and many small unions. They are believed to have three main purposes: induction of inexperienced activists; exposing members to female role models; and acting as pressure groups for equality (Greene and Kirton 2002; Cook *et al.* 1992), which together render them pivotal in the development of female activism.

In order to understand why women-only courses serve these purposes, it is useful to position them as a form of separate organising. Briskin's (1993) work has been particularly influential in developing conceptual approaches to understanding women's separate organising and its transformational potential. She (Briskin 1993) considers three possible claims: (i) that separate organising is a form of 'ghettoisation', (ii) that it is necessary to correct the 'deficits' in women, and (iii) that it is a proactive positive appropriation of women's experiences. The main debates in the contemporary period centre on the latter two claims. The deficit model recognises the salience of gender and the need for separate organising, but the emphasis is on women changing or on correcting women's inability to function in a male dominated environment. The proactive model is informed by recognition of the gender-specific character of experience in employment, the home and wider society.

Many authors, including Briskin (1993), clearly believe that the proactive, more politicised, model of separate organising offers the greatest potential for transformation because by organising collectively women bring their gender-specific knowledge to the mainstream (e.g. Colgan and Ledwith 2002). In practice, Parker's (2002) study finds that the objectives of women's groups (including women's courses) reflect a pragmatic and gradual pursuit of change shaped by the constraints of the existing union framework. Therefore women's separate organising has more of an evolutionary than revolutionary effect, where it is possible to identify a place for both deficit and proactive models. In other words, trade union women have to learn to function within the existing male-dominated context, but it is necessary for them to move beyond simply coping with that environment if they are to contribute to a transformational equality agenda.

Within her model, Briskin (1993) positions some women's courses as having a deficit character, arguing that there is often a focus on changing women by developing their confidence and assertiveness. Such courses, she argues, lack the politicised content of the proactive model of women's separate organising. While there is no disagreement with this conceptual distinction, it should not be assumed that 'deficit type' courses result in women becoming integrated into the male norms and co-opted to the masculine agenda, rather than being politicised into critically challenging the status quo, through the learning processes of the courses. Indeed, as McBride's (2001) study indicates, it is possible that through women-only courses women learn to 'run the union' because the skills learnt in the women-only environment can provide the means to challenge wider union bureaucracy. Thus talking about experiences of gender oppression in the women-only environment can strengthen gendered trade union identities as well as increase confidence (Kirton and Healy 2004). From this perspective, in the longer term, even deficit type courses can empower women and might contribute towards gendered transformation.

Colgan and Ledwith's (2002) continuum of strategies of social creativity and social change offers a conceptual alternative to positioning women-only courses either within a deficit or proactive model of separate organising. Broadly, women-only courses can be regarded as a strategy of social creativity, whereby group identity and group consciousness are built and strengthened (resonating with Kirton and Healy 2004). This strategy is necessary to move oppressed groups towards the collective action contained within strategies for social change, so that in the longer term women-only courses could influence or even contribute to transforming the mainstream union. What is clear is that if women-only courses are to contribute to gendered transformation it is necessary for them to influence the form and substance of subsequent participation of women. It is not sufficient for women to find the courses enjoyable and personally valuable.

If, for the reasons discussed, we accept that it is possible for women's courses to contribute to gendered transformation, how and why does this happen? Traditional trade union pedagogy in Britain emphasises student-centred learning and learning as a collective activity; but there are competing pressures to communicate information and develop skills (Bridgford and Stirling 2000) that can limit the extent to which course content can be negotiated with participants. The pedagogic underpinning of women's courses more closely approximates the 'active learning methods' approach outlined by Croucher (2004): (i) there is a course outline, but this can be negotiated with participants; (ii) the tutor is a facilitator/resource; (iii) group work is central and interactive lectures are used sparingly (see for example, Greene and Kirton 2002; Kirton 2006). In addition, it is believed that women-only courses empower women to participate because the environment represents a 'safe space' where 'women's issues' can be privileged. Further, in the women-only space gender identities are not questioned, but are reinforced; consequently the learning that takes place has greater transformational potential (Cunnison and Stageman 1995; Greene and Kirton 2002; McBride 2001; Parker 2003; Kirton and Healy 2004).

However, it must be acknowledged that empowerment is a slippery concept used in a variety of different ways. Young (1997) offers a more precise definition, usefully distinguishing between two types of empowerment. She states that empowerment can be defined either as the 'development of individual autonomy, self-control and confidence' or as the 'development of a sense of collective influence over the social conditions of one's life' (Young 1997, 89). In the former, an empowered woman might take action to change her individual life, but in ways that do not directly affect gendered social conditions. The latter is described as a process in which relatively powerless individuals engage in dialogue with each other, with each person undergoing some personal transformation so that they come to understand their powerlessness and see the possibility of acting collectively to change conditions.

The collective orientation of Young's (1997) latter definition is clearly resonant with the aims and purposes of trade union education and trade unionism generally.

Regarding women's post-women-only-course union participation several inter-related research questions arise out of this discussion. Does the form and substance of women's participation change? Do participants develop a sense of collective influence? What strategies do they use in their union roles post-course? In essence, is the nature of the influence of the courses on women's participation such that women-only courses could be said to contribute towards gendered transformation of unions? This chapter evaluates the longer term influence of women-only schools in two large British male-dominated trade unions.

Research Methods

The research is situated in two large British trade unions, MSF (Manufacturing, Science and Finance) and TGWU (Transport and General Workers Union). It is important to state that the study was not about evaluating women-only courses *per se*; rather it was concerned with evaluating the impact participants perceived the courses had had on their participation. One methodological issue that arises in any attempt to evaluate the impact of an intervention such as a training course is the near impossibility of isolating other variables, as noted by Catlett (1986) and Miller and Stirling (1992), not least the impact of the context of participation (enabling or constraining) and other significant events that might have had an influence. However, this is not to say that courses have no influence nor does it mean that it is futile to investigate people's perceptions of their influence on subsequent development. To emphasise, this study explores the longer term influence of the courses from the perspective of the participants themselves. To achieve this, the study took a multi-method approach.

The research began with participant and non-participant observation of the two unions' national, residential women-only schools in late 1999 and mid 2000 in order that the subsequently gathered interview and survey data could be interpreted against the researcher's own observations. In the five months after the schools in-depth, semi-structured interviews were carried out with a sample of course participants (14 from MSF and 15 from TGWU). Biographical information on the complete group of interviewees is presented in Table 10.1. The aim of these first in-depth interviews was to seek an understanding of the women's 'life-worlds' by allowing them to talk openly (Stroh 2000) about the contexts and circumstances surrounding their trade union participation. Interviews addressed broad questions such as why women joined unions in the first place; their routes to participation; the context and nature of participation; their perceptions and experiences of women-only union courses. This stage of the research is reported in Kirton (2005) and Kirton and Healy (2004).

Second interviews were held in 2001 and 2002 approximately two years after the schools with 24 (11 MSF, 13 TGWU) of the original sample of 29 women and the research focus turned to the perceived longer-term influence of women-only courses. Interview questions and probes were framed so as to avoid leading interviewees to particular answers or issues and all interviews were tape-recorded

Table 10.1   Biographical Information on survey respondents and interviewees

	MSF survey respondents (N= 105)	MSF Interviewees (N = 14)	TGWU Interviewees (N = 15)	All interviewees (N = 29)
Age				
30 or below	10%	2	1	3
31–40	25%	7	8	15
41–50	34%	4	5	9
51 and over	31%	1	1	2
Ethnicity				
White	79%	10	13	23
Black	13%	4	2	6
'Marital' Status				
Married/partnered	59%	5	9	14
Partner free	38%	9	6	15
Family				
Children < 16	22%	6	6	12

and fully transcribed. It is also important to note that some interviewees had a long history of prior union involvement and that the majority (6 MSF, 11 TGWU) of the 24 interviewees participating in the second interviews had prior experience of trade union courses and a minority of women-only courses (4 MSF, 5 TGWU). Repeated periods of observation at the women's schools were also undertaken.

In 2002, in order to capture the experiences and perceptions of a larger group of women's school participants, a postal survey was conducted of all women who had attended MSF Women's Week in the past three years. 105 completed surveys were returned, representing a response rate of 29 per cent. Table 10.1 provides a profile of survey respondents. It is also important to note that most of the survey respondents (75 per cent) and interviewees (25 of 29) worked in unionised organisations where there was usually relatively generous time-off for union duties and a relatively active branch life. The vast majority of respondents (83 per cent) had previously attended a trade union course, while 30 per cent had attended Women's Week more than once. Therefore, in reflecting on the longer-term influence of women's schools, many interview and survey participants were drawing on broad experiences over the previous few years, rather than evaluating the impact of a single course. The research also included interviews with directors of education and course tutors about how they saw the role of women-only courses. Finally, there was analysis of course packs and course monitoring data supplied by the unions (from which Tables 10.2 and 10.3 were constructed). Analysis of this data allowed women-only courses to be placed within the context of each union's overall education provision (see also Kirton (2006) for more detailed information).

Before turning to the research findings it is necessary to define how the term participation is used in the discussion. There is an ongoing debate about what counts as union activism (for example, Fosh 1993; Klandermans 1992), but this chapter makes a distinction between informal and formal participation. Here the former means active engagement with the democratic processes and structures of the union, for example, interacting with union representatives, actively seeking information, voting in elections, attending union meetings. In short, taking an active interest in the union, rather than simply paying membership dues for 'insurance' purposes. The latter involves participating in the union's committee structures or holding a workplace union position.

The Union Context of the Research

MSF and TGWU are heavily male-dominated, but have achieved or exceeded women's proportional representation in two senior lay structures – the executive council and TUC delegation – whereas women are under-represented among national and regional paid officers. There is little concrete information about the gender composition of workplace representatives and branch officials, although women's under-representation is thought to be an issue in need of tackling.

Table 10.2   Gender composition of selected mixed-sex MSF national courses 1999–2000

Course	Female %	Male %
Introductory Courses		
New Representatives	39%	61%
Health and Safety	41%	59%
Skills for Organising	45%	55%
NHS Representatives	68%	32%
Intermediate Courses		
Representing Members at Work	22%	78%
Improving Negotiating Skills	25%	75%
Tackling Bullying and Stress	17%	83%
Advanced Courses		
Contemporary IR	15%	85%
Economics	31%	69%
Pensions	0%	100%
Other Courses		
Lifelong Learning	69%	31%
Family Learning Week	57%	43%

With regard to education, both unions provide a range of general courses, largely aimed at representatives. Although overall women are proportionally represented in these, there are gendered patterns of attendance, as shown in Table 10.2 and Table 10.3. Of particular note is the fact that in both unions higher level courses, that are critical to the sustenance and development of participation, are extremely male-dominated. These patterns also have profound implications for the student educational experience, particularly when in some instances women are in a tiny minority among course participants. Both unions have established a raft of gender equality strategies, aimed at increasing women's participation, including various forms of women's separate organising, among which are women-only courses, which are believed to provide a 'safe space' where women can develop their union skills in a supportive and encouraging environment (see also Greene and Kirton 2002; McBride 2001; Parker 2003). Both unions provide women-only courses at regional and national levels. The research focuses on national level courses. In MSF this is a biannual five-day residential event – Women's Week – where in 2000–2002 courses in Developing Women's Leadership, Negotiating Skills for Women, Assertiveness for Women, and Organising Skills for Women were offered. In TGWU the event is a biennial five-day residential school – National Women Members' School – offering in 1999–2001 courses including Women at Work, Women Beyond the Workplace, Women in Europe, Recruitment and Organization for Women, Understanding the Union and Maximising Women's Involvement.

Table 10.3   Gender composition of selected mixed-sex TGWU region one courses (2000)

Course	Female %	Male %
Introductory Courses		
Shop Stewards	24%	76%
Safety Reps	19%	81%
Voluntary Sector Reps	57%	43%
Pensions	21%	79%
Intermediate Courses		
Shop Stewards Part 2	22%	78%
Safety Reps Part 2	12%	88%
Advanced Courses		
Branch Secretaries	13%	87%
Shop Stewards Part 3	22%	78%
Safety Reps Part 3	13%	87%
Other Courses		
Bargaining for Equality	56%	44%
Race Equality	16%	84%
Law at the Workplace	10%	90%

Interviews with the directors of education established that the aim of women-only courses in both unions is to empower women to participate, which includes developing women's skills and confidence to participate and promoting women's networking in order to combat the isolation many union women report experiencing (Kirton 1999). Outcomes the unions hope for include an increase in the number of women involved and developing the range of forums and activities in which women participate. For example, the TGWU explicitly uses women's courses as an opportunity to identify women felt to have the ability to go further in the union, perhaps onto the national executive council. The MSF courses focus more on developing in women the skills and confidence to sustain participation in the male-dominated context. Therefore, while it is clear from observation and interviews with officials that the unions accept that not all women will sustain activism in the longer term, they expect that attending women-only courses will help nourish the development of female activism in both qualitative and measurable ways.

To pursue these objectives, the women-only courses in both unions employ the active learning methods approach outlined earlier, where students define their own problems in relation to the course topics and bring their own experiences. Tutor input is minimised and the role of the tutor is more one of facilitator than expert or lecturer (Croucher 2004). The titles and outlines of the MSF courses appear to emphasise skills building, making them appear more reflective of Briskin's (1993) deficit model of women's separate organising outlined earlier. In contrast the titles and outlines of the TGWU courses seem to emphasise an understanding of women's position in society, making them seem more reflective of the proactive model. However, the active learning approach in both unions means that the content of courses is fairly flexible and adaptable to the needs and wishes of different groups of students. This was apparent from interviews with tutors and observation of the courses. Therefore it is not possible to characterise the women-only courses of either union as falling clearly within a deficit or proactive model. Using Colgan and Ledwith's (2000:178) terms, the courses can be regarded as a strategy of social creativity as they constitute an opportunity for women 'to build up a sense of identity, political consciousness, confidence, and solidarity, and to develop and practice activist skills' (Kirton and Healy 2004). These increased personal resources might later encourage participants to pursue strategies of social change in the context of the workplace and union.

Longer-term Influence of Women's Schools

The chapter now discusses the evidence from the study of the longer term influence of women's schools on the form and substance of women's participation. First, it is worth stating that women in both unions approved strongly of the women's schools. Eighty-eight per cent of the MSF survey respondents and all of the MSF/TGWU interviewees said that they would attend a women-only course again. However, as stated above, if women-only courses are to contribute to gendered transformation, it is not sufficient for women to enjoy the courses and find them personally valuable. Therefore, in addition, the MSF survey respondents were asked what they thought women-only courses achieve and there was a strong level of support for the range of statements presented in Table 10.4. These positive evaluations were also reflected in the interview data from both unions (see Kirton and Healy 2004).

Table 10.4   What do women-only courses achieve?

	N = 101
Provide a space for 'women's issues' to be discussed	73%
Build solidarity among women	71%
Work towards changing union culture	51%
Encourage women to become activists	55%
Provide an opportunity to meet other women activists	61%
Deal with mainstream union issues in a safe environment	54%
Develop skills in a safe environment	68%

Influence on Forms of Women's Participation

There was evidence in both unions of increased formal and informal participation following the women's schools. 55 per cent of the MSF survey respondents held union positions and just over half (53 per cent) said that their involvement in the union had increased since first attending Women's Week. Some had since become formally involved by becoming a workplace representative (19 per cent), a learning representative (6 per cent), a women's representative (8 per cent) or a women's committee delegate (17 per cent). Others had become informally involved by attending meetings (27 per cent), going on other courses (32 per cent), voting in union elections (25 per cent). In addition, the majority of MSF and TGWU interviewees (15 out of 24) had increased their participation during the two-year period between the first and second interviews. Some had taken on new roles and responsibilities often beyond the workplace union in the union's broader committee structures. For example, three women joined their union's national women's committee, another three joined industry/regional committees, while others became members of their branch negotiating committees. One TGWU woman had become a paid official with another union. Others had started regularly attending union meetings and were generally paying more attention to union affairs.

   Further, a substantial proportion (43 per cent) of the MSF survey respondents also had plans or aspirations to deepen their participation by going further in the union, as did a number of interviewees. Of the former, 27 per cent (of non-office holders) aspired to become a workplace representative, 40 per cent to join a women's committee, 11 per cent to join the union's national executive committee and 24 per cent to become a paid official. Whether or not these aims would ever be realised cannot of course be established by a survey undertaken at one point in time. However, to the extent that a future union career is envisaged and desired, this does indicate a strengthening attachment to union participation, which was also borne out in many of the interviews, with a small minority of interviewees aspiring to become paid officials and others to become involved in wider committee structures.

Influence on Substance of Women's Participation

Of course it is not possible to state categorically that any of the objective changes in union participation described were a direct result of attending women-only courses. However, the survey and interviews both revealed a very strong perception that the courses had a lasting influence, largely centred on the belief that they empowered women. Indeed, many survey respondents and interviewees explicitly used the word 'empowered' to describe how they felt after the women's schools. Earlier the discussion positioned women-only courses as a form of separate organising, the ultimate objective of which is to achieve gender democracy within unions. It is critical that women, as a relatively powerless group of people, develop a sense of collective influence over social conditions within the workplace and union if women's separate organising is to achieve the strategic aim of contributing to gender democracy. Drawing on Young's (1997) definition of collective empowerment, this section discusses how the women's sense of empowerment impacted on the substance of their participation.

Dismantling Gendered Barriers to Participation

There was evidence from the study that many women were seeking to challenge the gender regimes in work and unions, which disadvantage them and marginalise their concerns (McBride 2001; Munro 2001). MSF survey respondents identified various ways in which they felt that Women's Week had made a difference to the way they carried out their union duties, as shown in Table 10.5, which resonate with Young's (1997) notion of collective empowerment. As can be seen, the highest level of support was for items 9–11 which related specifically to the content focus on 'women's issues', and for the confidence building capacity of the courses, underscoring the women-only environment as a 'safe space' for developing women's union skills (Kirton and Healy 2004). For example, there were many comments from MSF survey respondents and from interviewees in both unions, such as:

> it's improved my confidence level and negotiation skills; I'm now a more confident and informed activist; it's given me more confidence and I've used ideas learned from other women; I'm more confident in dealing with management in an assertive manner.

The evidence suggests that women-only courses are a vehicle for women to come to understand the social sources of their powerlessness and combined with the enhanced union skills (indicated by a substantial minority's support for items 2–8 in Table 10.5), to see the possibility of acting collectively to change their social environment, thus fitting with Young's (1997) notion of collective empowerment.

From the interviews it was clear that over time the women had begun to use a range of gender conscious strategies in order to make the union more attractive to other women and to build a critical mass of active women prepared to voice their needs. Many explicitly stated that they sought to identify individual women whom they thought might be interested in the union and to develop initiatives to encourage them to participate. There were examples of women leading recruitment and

Table 10.5   Main purpose MSF women's week served for you

Purpose	N= 105
1. Built my confidence	69%
2. Developed my negotiation skills	48%
3. Gave me a better understanding of how the union works	42%
4. Improved my decision-making ability	39%
5. Developed my skills as a representative	35%
6. Improved my understanding of bargaining	33%
7. Developed my organising ability	28%
8. Gave me a better understanding of my role in the union	32%
9. Gave me an opportunity to share experiences with other women	84%
10. Gave me practical suggestions to improve things for women at work	51%
11. Deepened my understanding of women's position in society	48%

organising campaigns aimed at women workers, women persuading other women to go to women-only courses or to put themselves forward as representatives. One TGWU woman recruited two cleaners as 'women's reps' because she was concerned that women in manual jobs had never been represented among the stewards and she felt the branch had made little effort to try to involve them. Another TGWU woman instigated monthly women's meetings in her male-dominated branch because she felt that women members were isolated and reluctant to voice their concerns at the general branch meetings. Two MSF women from the same workplace established some union roles, such as health and safety representative, as job share posts in order to appeal to women who were afraid of the time commitment involved.

There was also evidence that some women interviewees had become more politically astute during the two-year period of the study, developing the resources to break down the gender hierarchy in their branches. For example, some were 'women's reps' in their branches or workplaces, which meant that they had special responsibility for representing women's concerns. Most of those who had started out as 'women's reps' had done so because they were interested in improving women's conditions of employment and some felt that women lacked voice in the union branch. Most soon found that the role was marginal and marginalised within the local structure and they had found it necessary to operate in ways which were more sensitive to the gender politics of branch life. A couple of women seized opportunities to become 'ordinary' workplace representatives in order to have more power and influence in the branch. One TGWU woman, for example, reported how she had quickly recognised the limitations of being a 'women's rep' and found that once she became a shop steward, she had more influence in the workplace negotiating committee. However, she also retained her 'women's rep' position as a vehicle for advancing women's concerns when her position as non-senior shop steward otherwise excluded her within the branch structure, as she explains:

> With all this change [in management and work organisation] a lot of the men felt it was their responsibility – there were no women involved in the negotiations at all and I felt that was really bad. We're hoping to organise union visits to other airports, so I will suggest that I go as the women's rep so that I can put womens' view forward because I feel that's important. Otherwise it will be just the [all male] senior stewards.

The possibility for women's voices to be marginalised within the branch was evident from the discussions observed on the women-only courses and from interviews with women tutors and course participants and is consistent with other research (McBride 2001; Munro 1999). This in part at least explains why many interviewees felt a need to participate in some form of women's separate organisation, often regularly returning to women's schools for repeated 'doses' or 'fixes' (as they said) of the women-only space, which seemed to renew the resources necessary to challenge. However, research has established that not all union women are wholly supportive of women's separate organising (e.g. Munro 1999) and this was found in the study. Nevertheless, some interviewees reflected on how their ideas about union practices and objectives had altered after being exposed to the more gender conscious discourse of women's courses. For example, one TGWU woman, an extremely experienced and successful trade unionist, had in the first interview been very sceptical about the principle of women's separate organising. In the second interview she expressed unequivocal support for women-only courses:

> I think having seen women coming through that route [women's schools] and then actually taking part, I think I've changed my mind. I think what disturbed me and still disturbs me is that they can become too dependent on women and not try to work with their male colleagues. But, over these last two years, watching new women come through from the women's schools, I think they're very valuable.

Gendered Bargaining

It is clear from the evidence presented above that many women felt it was important for the unions to become more representative of women. Seventy six per cent of the MSF survey respondents agreed that women bring special qualities and abilities to trade unions. Most of the qualitative comments made by respondents concerned the 'different perspectives' or 'points of view' that women bring, especially 'understanding of women's lives', 'the importance of family issues for women' and women's commitment to 'giving a voice to women and women's issues'. Further, in interviews with women from both unions it often seemed a taken for granted assumption that it was necessary to have women at the negotiating table if their concerns were to be properly represented (echoing Colling and Dickens 1989). Many interviewees gave examples of how they used their union roles to identify gender dimensions to management policy and practice and gender-specific issues as their priorities for the union agenda. For example:

One of my main things [priorities] is the women here – how they're treated. I mean recruitment and selection for example – all that [good practice] seems to have fallen by the wayside – we've got people coming in and they seem to be friends of friends and they only seem interested in promoting male graduates, instead of promoting women up from the floor. There are a lot of issues for women. The bus drivers have problems with their blouses because they're see-through and they're refusing to wear them, so I'm dealing with that at the moment (TGWU woman).

Some women indicated that this gender conscious approach to bargaining had evolved over time and sharing experiences with other women at women-only schools had been part of the ongoing process of gendering the union agenda. This was particularly evident for women who worked in male-dominated contexts, as in the case of the following TGWU woman:

You don't think you're discriminated against any more. Until it hits you, you don't realise it's there, but it is and we're not aware of the issues until they're put forward to us.

One MSF woman had instigated a job evaluation exercise for predominantly female secretaries in her organisation because she believed that there was significant under-evaluation of the role when compared with jobs in predominantly male areas of the organisation. Revealing her tenacity she explained that negotiations had lasted for two years, but had resulted in an upgrading of most secretaries. This woman was quite clear that her view of job evaluation as a gendered social practice, rather than an objective, scientific one, had evolved after one of the women's courses where it had featured as a discussion topic. Another MSF woman explained how she had led an organising campaign in the factory where she worked where until recently the women office workers had not been unionised. Now that the union was established, and she had attended Women's Week twice, low pay and working time had become the main bargaining issues and she commented:

We're so much better off since we started the union. There was never anything there for the admin people [all women]. We've benefited tremendously from having a union. It's from collective bargaining, from looking at things as a group.

The ability and willingness to identify pro-actively women's concerns and to bring these to the union agenda is highly significant. Research has shown that union agendas typically emphasise 'bread and butter' issues over what might be classified as 'women's issues' (Parker 2003) and that even membership-led agendas are problematic because of the generally low levels of (female) attendance at union meetings (Sinclair 1995; Sinclair 1996). The space on women-only courses for issues of particular concern to women to be discussed is highly important because it enables women to share and develop ideas for gendering the union agenda that often do not get discussed at workplace or branch level. Thus, women's union participation can then begin to influence women's collective employment conditions at workplace level.

Developing Individual Autonomy, Self-control and Confidence

Although the survey and interview data indicate that women-only courses strengthen both the form and substance of women's participation, it also suggests that this is not the case for a substantial minority of women participants. It is therefore worth saying something about this group. There is some evidence from the study, echoing Munro and Rainbird (2000), which suggests that women-only courses can have a lasting influence even on those who do not develop or sustain union participation in the longer term. Using Young's (1997) framework of empowerment outlined earlier, some women's school participants were empowered in the sense that they developed a greater sense of individual autonomy and then sought greater control over their own lives. Some women described very private and personal meanings the women's school had had for them empowering them to escape situations such as domestic violence, or simply to stand up to a bullying boss. In addition, after the women's schools, feeling more confident of their own abilities some women sought upward job mobility. A small number moved into non-unionised work environments where they perceived (rightly or wrongly) few opportunities to exercise collective influence. The point was that the work and union contexts of these women were or became such that there was little opportunity to develop a sense of collective empowerment. These individual outcomes are of course paradoxical, in view of the fact that the aim of women-only trade union courses is essentially to empower women as a collective group, but are a reminder that unions can serve broader purposes in people's lives extending their reach beyond the immediate concerns of workplace bargaining. It was clear from interviews with the directors of education that it is an accepted risk that union courses will not draw in all those who participate in them.

Conclusion

Women-only trade union schools have become an established form of women's separate organising, widely used in British trade unions as one strategy in the effort to foster female participation and work towards gender democracy. This chapter has explored the longer-term influence of women-only union courses on female trade unionists in two large British male-dominated trade unions. The women's post-course reporting of their experiences indicated that they had found the schools extremely valuable (see also Kirton and Healy 2004; Kirton 2006; Kirton 2006a) and this chapter has attempted to unpack how the courses subsequently influenced the form and substance of women's trade union participation.

The chapter's findings were largely structured around Young's (1997) dual definition of empowerment since empowerment is both an aim of women's schools (according to the unions themselves and to theories of women's separate organising) and a necessary outcome if women's participation is to make any substantive difference in the union and the workplace. According to Young (1997), individuals can be empowered in the sense of developing individual autonomy, self-control and confidence, or in the sense of developing a feeling of collective influence over the social conditions of one's life. The study found that most women talked of having undergone the kind of personal transformation Young (1997) believes to be necessary if people are to arrive at a sense of empowerment. For some women this translated in the longer term as developing individual autonomy and their seeking to take greater control of their own lives at the individual level. However, it was clear that the majority developed a greater sense of collective empowerment with trade union participation being the vehicle through which influence over gendered social conditions could be achieved.

With regard to the form of women's participation many women in the study had increased the range of union activities they were involved in such that attendance at the women-only schools had the effect of strengthening the pro-union orientation and actual participation of many course participants (see also Kirton and Healy 2004).

Turning to the substance of women's participation, within a deficit model of women's separate organising (Briskin 1993), the aim of women-only courses is to equip women to function more effectively in the male-dominated environment, specifically by increasing their confidence and assertiveness. This approach is clearly reflected in the MSF, and to a lesser extent some of the TGWU, course titles and outlines. However, as discussed the courses employ the 'active learning methods' approach (Croucher 2004) meaning that the content is flexible according to the needs and wishes of different groups of students. It is clear from the survey and interview data that the women participants gained a deeper understanding of the gender specific character of women's employment experiences that is more resonant with the proactive model. The courses seemed to influence how women subsequently operated in the workplace union context, specifically in the ways that they adopted gender conscious practices and strategies, this reflecting the more transformational outcomes expected of a proactive approach. There was, for example, evidence of women using the skills they had gained to challenge the gender hierarchy in the unions (see also McBride 2001; Parker 2002). Therefore, whether the courses are evaluated within the deficit or proactive model, they can be regarded as successful as women felt empowered to participate and to influence gendered social conditions. Using Colgan and Ledwith's terms (2002), the women's schools constitute a strategy of social creativity whereby group identity and group consciousness are built and strengthened, the longer term influence of which is that many women develop strategies for incremental gendered social change.

One caveat when evaluating this potential is that it is clear from the literature that there are a number of significant barriers in the work, union and family contexts that stand in the way of women's union participation (Colgan and Ledwith 1996; Cunnison and Stageman 1995; Munro 1999). Therefore, whether or not women's union participation after courses increases is not simply a function of 'choice', but also of context. This was reflected in the fact that the active women in the interview sample reported relatively enabling work, union and family contexts.

This study has focused on the perceptions of participants of the longer term influence of women's trade union schools. It is important to remember that experiences and perceptions do not equal 'truth', but in voicing their perceptions, the message was very clear that the women in the study did believe that their experiences of women-only trade union courses had a significant and lasting influence on them, echoing Munro and Rainbird (2000). Thus the study suggests that women-only union education could contribute to the incremental gendered transformation of unions. Finally the words of one TGWU woman capture the views of many who participated in the study:

> I think it's brilliant [referring to the women's school]. I think you get a hell of a lot from it. I wouldn't be where I am now if I hadn't been on them courses. I'd recommend it to anybody.

References

Bradley, H. (1999), *Gender and Power in the Workplace*. (Basingstoke: Macmillan).

Bridgford, J. and Stirling, J (2000), *Trade Union Education in Europe*. (Brussels: European Trade Union College).

Briskin, L. (1993), 'Union Women and Separate Organising', in Briskin and McDermott (eds.).

Briskin, L. and McDermott, P. (eds.) (1993), *Women Challenging Unions*. (Toronto: University of Toronto Press).

Burton, D. (ed.) (2000), *Research Training for Social Scientists*. (London: Sage).

Catlett, J. (1986), 'After the Goodbyes: a Long-Term Look at the Southern School for Union Women', *Labor Studies Journal* Winter: 300–311.

Cockburn, C. (1994), 'Play of Power: Women, men and equality initiatives in a trade union', in Wright (ed.).

——, (1995), *Strategies for Gender Democracy*. (Luxembourg: European Commission).

Colgan, F. and S. Ledwith (1996), 'Sisters Organising – Women and their Trade Unions', in Ledwith and Colgan (eds.).

——, (2000), 'Diversity, Identities and Strategies of Women Trade Union Activists', *Gender, Work and Organisation* 7:4, 242–257.

——, (eds.) (2002), *Gender, Diversity and Trade Unions*. (London: Routledge).

——, (2002), 'Gender, Diversity and Mobilisation in UK Trade Unions', in Colgan and Ledwith (eds.).

Colling, T and L. Dickens (1989), *Equality bargaining – Why Not?* (Manchester: EOC).

Cook, A., V. Lorwin, *et al.* (1992), *The Most Difficult Revolution: Women and Trade Unions*. (Ithaca: Cornell University Press).

Croucher, R (2004), 'The Impact of Trade Union Education: A Study in Three Countries in Eastern Europe', *European Journal of Industrial Relations* 10:1, 90–109.

Cunnison, S. and J. Stageman (1995), *Feminising the Unions*. (Aldershot: Avebury).

Fosh, P. (1993), 'Membership Participation in Workplace Trade Unionism: The Possibility of Union Renewal', *British Journal of Industrial Relations* 31:4, 577–592.

Greene, A. M. and Kirton, G. (2002), 'Advancing Gender Equality: The Role of Women-only Trade Union Education', *Gender, Work and Organisation* 9:1, 39–59.

Hartley, J. and Stephenson, G. (eds.) (1992), *Employment Relations: The Psychology of Influence and Control at Work*. (London: Blackwell).

Healy, G. and Kirton, G. (2000), 'Women, Power and Trade Union Government in the UK', *British Journal of Industrial Relations* 38:3, 343–360.

Holford, J. (1993), Union Education in Britain: a TUC Activity. (Nottingham, University of Nottingham).

Kirton, G. (1999), 'Sustaining and Developing Women's Trade Union Activism – a Gendered Project?', *Gender, Work and Organization* 6:4, 213–223.

——, (2006), *The Making of Women Trade Unionists*. (Aldershot: Ashgate).

——, (2006a), 'Alternative or Parallel Careers for Women: The Case of Trade Union Participation', *Work, Employment and Society*, 20:1, 47–66

Kirton, G. and Healy, G. (1999), 'Transforming Union Women: the Role of Women Trade Union Officials in Union Renewal', *Industrial Relations Journal* 30:1, 31–45.

Kirton, G. and Greene, A. M. (2002), 'The Dynamics of Positive Action in UK Trade Unions: The Case of Women and Black Members', *Industrial Relations Journal* 33:2, 157–172.

Klandermans, B. (1992), 'Trade Union Participation', in Hartley and Stephenson (eds.).

Labour Research (2004), 'Women's Rise in Union Patchy', March, pp10–12, Labour Research Department.

Layder, D (1993), *New Strategies in Social Research*. (London: Polity Press).

Lawrence, E. (1994), *Gender and Trade Unions*. (London: Taylor and Francis).

Ledwith, S. and Colgan, F. (eds.) (1996), *Women in Organisations*. (Basingstoke: Macmillan).

McBride, A. (2001), *Gender Democracy in Trade Unions*. (Aldershot: Ashgate).

McBride, J. and Miller, D (2000), 'United Kingdom', in Bridgford and Stirling (eds.).

Miller, D. and Stirling, J. (1992), 'Evaluating Trade Union Education', *The Industrial Tutor* 5:5, 15–26.

Munro, A. (1999), *Women, Work and Trade Unions*. (London: Mansell).

Munro, A. (2001), 'A Feminist Trade Union Agenda? The Continued Significance of Class, Gender and Race', *Gender, Work and Organisation* 8:4, 454–471.

Munro, A. and Rainbird, H (2000), 'The New Unionism and the New Bargaining Agenda: Unison – Employer Partnerships on Workplace Learning in Britain', *British Journal of Industrial Relations* 38:2, 223–240.

– (2000), 'Unison's 'Approach to Lifelong Learning', in Terry (ed.).

Parker, J. (2002), 'Women's Groups in British Unions', *British Journal of Industrial Relations* 40:1, 23–48.

Parker, J (2003), *Women's Groups and Equality in British Trade Unions*. (New York: Edwin Mellen Press).

Sinclair, D. (1995), 'The Importance of Sex for the Propensity to Unionise', *British Journal of Industrial Relations* 33:2, 239–252.

——, (1996), 'The Importance of Gender for Participation in and Attitudes to Trade Unionism', *Industrial Relations Journal* 27:3, 239–252.

Stroh, M. (2000), 'Qualitative Interviewing', in Burton (ed.).

Terry, M. (ed.) (2000), *Redefining Public Sector Unionism: Unison and the Future of Trade Unions*. (London: Routledge).

Wright, S (1994), *Anthropology of Organisations*. (London: Routledge).

Young, I. M. (1997), *Intersecting Voices. Dilemmas of Gender, Political Philosophy and Policy*. (Princeton, New Jersey: Princeton University Press).

Chapter 11

Multiple Partnerships in Trade Union Learning

Steve Shelley

Introduction

As Tailby and Winchester (2005) comment, the idea of partnership formed part of the 'new' Labour government's election manifesto in 1997, aiming to find the 'third way' in redefined relations between state, trade unions and business. In this vein, a number of new individual and collective employment rights were introduced in the first few years of the Labour government, particularly the national minimum wage and trade union recognition procedures. At more micro levels, a partnership fund encouraged new workplace involvement procedures whilst in the public sector framework agreements have been intended to force partnership at local levels. Much commentary suggests that partnership is a working relationship between the three main stakeholders of the state, employers and employees (Sutherland and Rainbird 2000), with a focus on pay and representation (Tailby and Winchester 2005) and on a 'new bargaining agenda' including equal opportunities, working hours and workers' rights (Heyes 2000).

This chapter focuses on a specific example of partnership in the learning and skills agenda, adding to the analysis provided in other studies in this book and to previous papers (see for example, Sutherland and Rainbird 2000; CIPD 2004; Forrester 2004; Shelley 2005) which have tended to focus on workplace partnerships between employer and trade unions, and on outcomes of workforce skills and union organising.

Through analysis of a case study of one union learning project, the chapter identifies a complex set of multiple partnerships with a variety of stakeholders. These partnerships are explored through the organisational arrangements of this learning project and are organized here into four types; partnership amongst unions, partnership between unions and employers, partnerships between unions and education providers and also with community bodies. The multi-union and community links are particularly new developments, although the nature of relationships with employer and with government funding agencies also indicate the existence of forms of partnership that have been more frequently identified in previous studies.

From the wider literature on skill, there is a strong perception of a 'lifelong learning' approach commonly shared by government, trades unions and employers (Rainbird 2000), with a unitarist impression that all learning outcomes are inherently 'good', and to the benefit of all. But questions remain about whether trade unions should be collaborating with employers to deliver work-based training and becoming entangled with mainstream learning and skills policy, and the extent to which they are able to retain independence in a partnership arrangement (Sutherland and Rainbird 2000). This chapter provides a deeper understanding of the various agendas that are involved through the union learning project described here.

The Case Study

The case study is of a Trade Union Learning Centre (subsequently referred to as The Learning Centre), a multi-union facility and a two-year Union Learning Fund (ULF) project (2004–2006). Over the two-year duration, interviews, participant research and access to databases and other documents were used to identify four forms of partnership.

The project consists of a main learning centre in a large town in the 'home counties' of the south-east of England, together with various satellite centres. At the outset, the project aim was to provide a facility for developing links with trade unions, training and supporting union activists and engaging individuals into life-long learning. The project aimed to train and work directly with Union Learning Representatives to train, plan, support and implement strategies for engaging employers in learning and to raise awareness and uptake of Information and Communication Technology (ICT) and Skills for Life (SfL) learning opportunities. Thus, the project was to deliver learning programmes directly itself, and to support the establishment of other learning centres, outreach and learning representative activities in workplaces (and other locations) in the county. The project was explicitly aimed at including learners who were non-union members as well as members, to have a community role with which to interact, provide learning services and accept referrals from other community groups (particularly the Local Learning Partnership) and even to welcome learners who may walk in off the street.

The centre is in a dedicated room equipped with 12 flat screen computers linked to the internet. In addition, there are meeting rooms and quiet areas for one-to-one advice. Full access and facilities are provided for disabled users. The centre opened its doors in the summer of 2004, with an official opening by Brendan Barber the TUC General Secretary, the local (Labour) MP and the Regional Director of the Learning and Skills Council.

During the two years of the project, over 1,000 course enrolments were made, with over 100 learners a month using the learning centre. A variety of courses were undertaken, mainly IT courses (including Using a Computer, Wordprocessing, Databases, Spreadsheets, Desk Top Publishing, Photoshop, Surf Direct, Web Design, and the European Computer Driving Licence), Skills for Life, Literacy and Numeracy. The enrolment figures include initial assessments and national tests, and also multiple enrolments per learner (with the average being 3.3 enrolments per learner).

Multi-union Partnership

The first form of partnership identified is that between a number of unions. The Learning Centre was unique in being the first in the UK not to be based at a workplace or college, and the first to be wholly owned and run by trade unions (TUC 2004). The base was in the Trades Union Halls, not on employers' premises. This may be seen as symbolic of a union-owned agenda – this is a new hall, opened in 2003, but on the site of the original Trades Union Hall built entirely by voluntary trade union labour during the 1920s and opened in 1931 by Ramsay McDonald. The project as a whole was run by joint unions: Amicus, Amicus/GPMU, Amicus/Unifi, CWU, ASLEF/RMT/TSSA (The Rail Union Partnership) and NUT. The joint unions were represented on a Steering Group and committee structure, to which the appointed Project/Centre Manager was accountable.

Nearly ninety per cent of learners were union members. The union membership of learners involved in the project extended to 13 unions: Amicus (including former GPMU), ASLEF, ATL, CWU, GMB, PCS, Police Federation, RCN, RMT, TGWU, TSSA, Unison and USDAW – a list that is notable for illustrating a broad reach of the project across the union movement, and for having a different composition than the original joint union project (both including learners from a wider range of unions, and for non-representation of some project unions). Numbers of users ranged from single figures for some unions, to several hundreds of the largest union represented, the TGWU. The TGWU represent the learners employed by the local bus company included in the project once it was extended to include a satellite centre at the bus garages in neighbouring towns. The fact that a number of learners are not union members is an indication of wider partnership with the community discussed later in the chapter.

In addition to the obvious aim of the project to develop multi-union partnership, there are also aims of union membership and renewal. One of the explicit ULF themes is to develop systems to support the training and development of Learning Representatives in the workplace and an aim of the project is to 'develop links with trade unions, training and supporting union activists'. Two features of the project may enable this to happen.

Firstly, although the learning centre physically consists of 12 PCs in a single small room, this is next door to a room used for the education of trade union representatives, where training on representation, organizing, employment law, and occupational health and safety is provided by a local college. Development of this relationship between trade union education and the learning centre, and the training of ULRs themselves, indicates potential for the union organising agenda through the use of the centre as representatives enroll on other learning courses and potentially learners enroll on courses for representatives. As one example, the centre hosted an Amicus project workers event. In addition, the learning centre is adjacent to a larger education/conference hall which is hired out for various conferences, and to unions to run events such as information sessions and 'taster courses' offered by the learning centre to specific unions, such as stress management, language courses and other 'tasters' offered to members of the rail unions. Also the learning centre is upstairs from the main Trades Union Hall, used for a variety of functions from rallies to ballroom dancing and private functions. The close physical relationship of these activities suggests the potential for synergy and union renewal, through interaction between the people involved and through referred activities, albeit evidence on this is scarce.

Union Learning Representatives (ULRs) are trained through the project and themselves gain related qualifications including Adult Learner Support Level 2 and Information Advice and Guidance (IAG) at Level 3. It is intended that these ULRs make a significant contribution to raising the profile of unions back in their workplaces. However, although an accurate assessment is not possible, indications are that the number of ULRs trained has not reached the target set; nor is it clear how many continue to be active once they leave the centre. There is suggestion that ULRs and other organizers of specific unions do not find it easy or convenient to use The Learning Centre itself because it is away from their workplace. Users are limited to short bursts of learning at work and need access to materials in their workplace. The centre has attempted to overcome this barrier by setting up regular support visits to the link centres, although these do not reach all workplaces and ULRs. In addition, each union has its own learning materials and policy. In this respect the very strength of the multi-union-owned centre may also be its weakness. For a final comment on this matter, the conclusion to this chapter updates the case after the end of the initial two-year ULF project, describing how a new single union project has now taken over the centre.

Partnership Between Trade Unions and Employers

The project aimed to develop an engagement strategy in partnership with employers, particularly working with union learning representatives to engage employers (as well as union members) in learning. An explicit aim was to further develop employer/union partnerships in the workplace and engage new employers in 'Lifelong Learning' and 'Workforce Development' (both following government policy terminology) by promoting awareness of learning and training opportunities through union learning representative activity.

Six employers were named as partners in the ULF bid. In fact, one of these, a leading telecommunications organisation, provided free internet connections to the centre. Outside The Learning Centre itself, the project developed two satellite centres in the garages of the local bus company, involving the ULRs of the TGWU; and also included a longer standing facility at a printing and publishing company.

At the level of ownership and logistics, this dimension of partnership is clear in that the relationship with these employers was crucial in order for the satellite centres to operate. It was strongly felt by project staff that much of this partnership has enabled 'new' learning to take place, involving employees who had not previously been enrolled on courses. However, there is no evidence here that the unions are able to influence the wider workplace context of training, in terms of placing training on a bargaining agenda and stimulating demand for higher skills by employers.

In addition, it is unclear how effective such union learning projects can be in involving 'new' employers in the partnership arrangements. This raises the question about how far such learning projects can break out of established union-recognised workplaces. It is significant that the two key partnerships, with the bus and print companies, were long-standing and may be viewed as working with employers who are already happy to promote such learning activities. As further evidence of their support, these employers were able to give paid time off for ULR activities, as required by law, although time for learners to access training does seem to be more problematic.

By way of illustration, one explicit aim of the project was to develop a Small and Medium-sized Enterprises (SME) engagement strategy (a target of 150 SMEs was initially identified). In fact, according to the ULF bid, this was to be a pilot for SME engagement and would be monitored and written up as a case study. In learning and skills policy, engagement with SMEs is important due to lack of employer training in this sector (Ashton and Felstead 2001). From the union renewal perspective, an extension of influence here would be significant because of the relatively poor union organising in small enterprises (Kersley *et al.* 2005). However, evidence suggests this activity did not take place in this case study, and the limited extent of union influence here probably explains why this was so.

The types of courses offered by the project were outlined earlier, and some background about learning and the nature of the learners who participate is given in discussion about community involvement later in the chapter. Whilst the outcomes of the courses can be considered to have personal outcomes that are not directly work-related, the majority of the courses provided here can be seen to have direct work-related outcomes from which employers as well as the learners and unions will benefit. It is here that unions have to exercise care in ensuring that embracing of the learning and skills policy agenda does not lead simply to unions' provision of employers' training.

Finally in this section, it is worth noting another of the aims of this ULF project which was to increase learner volume in the Learndirect Business and Management portfolio, with 'Learndirect' being the national training provider. Indeed, written into the ULF bid was the 'need for the centre to become self financing and operate as a business', which included marketing a chargeable Learndirect/UfI (University for Industry, a government web-based training provider) business portfolio to companies.

There are clearly mixed messages here. To quote the TUC General Secretary Brendan Barber's comments about the opening of The Learning Centre (TUC, 2004), 'a better educated workforce is fundamental in the drive for a more tolerant society'. However, although the project places an emphasis on individual learners, 'the new learning centre offers all local employees the chance to improve their skills and enhance their lives' (TUC, 2004), it also emphasises the economic business outcomes 'opening up learning to a whole generation of workers is crucial to the success of business at both local and national level' (TUC, 2004). In entering into partnerships with employers, trade unions must be acutely aware of providing learning that is meeting specific job training needs of employers and that thus risks compromising trade union independence.

Partnership with other Education and Training Providers

This third dimension of partnership has been based on relationships with the local Further Education (FE) Colleges, Learndirect, community groups and with an IAG (information and guidance) organisation. A further unique feature is how the project has been independent of colleges and has its own qualified training and learning support staff. It was in the referral process that partnership operated, with The Learning Centre not only referring learners to colleges, but also receiving learners referred to it from the colleges.

However, the operation of such a partnership has been far from straightforward. An aim of the project was to become self-sustaining in the way described above, an emphasis that has become stronger in the new project of extended funding from 2006 onwards. Implicit in this was the establishment both of collaboration and of competition with colleges and other local training providers. There is an acknowledgement by project workers that The Learning Centre was increasingly seen as strong locally in its provision of basic skills training, and in the close, often one-to-one support provided to learners, making it distinctive from a more formal education environment. At the same time, the project moved to becoming subject to the quality assurance as well as funding mechanisms that embrace the rest of the post-16 learning and skills agenda in England. Thus it was monitored by the quality watchdog the Adult Learning Inspectorate (ALI) in the same way that Further Education colleges and other training providers are.

Further, operating in the same public funding environment as other learning and skills providers for Basic Skills and courses up to Level 2, has meant susceptibility to the constraints of funding that might seem contrary to the learning aims of the project. Funding was on the basis of contracted numbers of learners. Any learners taken over and above this contracted figure were not funded but the cost had to be borne by the project, whilst under-recruitment lead to quite immediate claw-back of funding – the project experienced both these circumstances during its duration. This meant a number of peaks and troughs in enrolments during the two years which are representative of funding constraints rather than the supply of people wanting to be enrolled on courses. Enrolments dipped dramatically towards the end of the first year of the project as funding for that first year ran out, but were able to resume in September with the second year of contract funding. Whilst there were plenty of new learners wishing to enrol, the project was not funded to take them and so could not. The project had to be careful not to over-recruit above numbers of funded learners. In the second year, a period of intense recruitment lead to another temporary cessation, because of what the funders described as 'over-performance'. Other constraints were perceived to be the limitations of a two-year funding schedule in itself, placing an emphasis on obtaining numbers of new enrolments so as to maintain funding, but constraining the ability to continuously develop and progress individuals through a series of higher level qualifications because of lack of time and lack of funding for higher qualifications. In addition, during the project University for Industry (UfI) funding dropped, leading to an acknowledgment that learners in the future will need to be charged more than present, and that the centre will have to find other ways of financing its activities.

Thus this partnership is not without its potential conflicts and contradictions here. In addition, although the learning provided by the trade union clearly had a focus on basic skills, the venture risked losing distinctiveness as it became embedded in the public-funded post-16 learning and training sector.

Partnership with the Community

The fourth dimension of partnership here is with elements of the wider community. The notion of community unionism is one that offers further potential as a union renewal strategy and can be defined further (Wills, 2001), but in this case study it has a number of elements, including relationships with other community agencies and bodies, and cognisance of geographical location, socio-economic dimensions, the inclusion of a breadth of learners from different sources, and varied learning outcomes or uses.

Thus, an aim of the project was to service trade union members, families, friends and potential members, with access at times and venues convenient to the learners. Face-to-face support was provided by the centre – with an emphasis on group work with representatives and learners. The centre itself had a convenient town centre location, close to rail and bus stations. Opening hours were 9–5 three days a week, 9–9 two days, and 9–1 on Saturday. In addition, it had an outreach satellite in an urban regeneration project, located in a local ward with a high multiple deprivation index. As an indicator of community access, learners were referred by Learndirect (and self-referrals – the centre was in the Learndirect directory as an accredited centre). There were also relationships with the local Learning Partnership and with voluntary organisations such as 'Relate' who sought to provide their training to counsellors within the centre.

The records of activity have shown that the centre was used at different times of the day by learners, with the largest number of learners attending in the mornings and relatively big proportions attending at lunchtimes and evenings. In duration, the biggest proportion spent 2–3 hours at the centre (one even spending all day). The centre was consistently used on Saturdays by a regular band of learners, many of whom could not get time off work during the week, and who valued small group contact with the tutor.

In terms of geography, there was a large spread of learners by home address. The biggest concentrations were related to the two bus garages, to town itself and, perhaps linked to the involvement of travel-based unions and occupations, around a proximity to the main line railway station. However, the catchment as a whole was diverse, and incorporated rural as well as urban addresses, learners coming from over 40 towns and villages across four counties and London.

A further aim of the project was to engage individuals into learning, increasing learning opportunities for the workforce and critically for groups of employees that may have been previously disadvantaged in accessing learning opportunities. This followed four of the main ULF themes which were Basic Skills / Skills for Life provision; improving access to learning, including through ICT (Information Communication Technology); improving access to learning through high quality information, advice and guidance; and enhancing equality of opportunity and social inclusion. A further related aim was to tackle the growing 'digital divide' through raising awareness and uptake of ICT. Thus, as previously outlined, courses taken have focused on ICT. Somewhat misleadingly, despite its title, 'Skills for Life' was also delivered here in the ICT context, delivering numeracy and literacy largely through computer-based training. The take up of courses, measured by enrolments and learner activity mentioned earlier, is an obvious sign of these strategies in operation. Although evaluation of the learning outcomes beyond such simple measures has not been a feature of the project, anecdotal information suggests not only gains that have enabled learners to do their jobs better, but outcomes which also contributed to broader societal and quality of life benefits such as 'confidence', a sense of 'well being' and 'fulfilment' and practical advantages such as learners being able to help their children with their homework, of the kinds also suggested in chapter seven.

Outcomes have also been linked to the local economic agenda with, as the ULF bid states, the local Learning and Skills Council aiming to encourage a supply of skilled labour that will encourage high value-added sectors into the county to offset the sharp decline in manufacturing jobs. There is a recognition by project staff that this requires Level 3 and 4 qualifications, but that the significant role of the centre was first assisting workers in achieving Level 2. In addition, whilst Level 2 funding is provided by the government via Learndirect, the project could not offer Levels 3 or 4 qualifications without charging – which was likely to inhibit access by some learners.

The equal opportunity and social inclusion dimension was highlighted further in the aim of the project 'to ensure equality of access to learning irrespective of gender, ethnicity, age, disability, religion or social class (and learning difficulty) and to work to overcome all previous barriers to learning'. There were social reasons for this – linked to evidence of deprivation at ward level, despite relative prosperity in the county as a whole.

Gender analysis shows that around 70 per cent of learners were male and 30 per cent female, a bigger proportion of male learners than the national average for these funded projects and a bigger male emphasis than intended in the aims of the project. To some extent the gender imbalance can be attributed to the influence of TGWU-dominated link centres and the largely male bus drivers and technicians. It is therefore of interest to see whether broader non-union use of the centre may have provided the means of addressing the issue of gender imbalance. Around ten per cent of users were non-union members, largely from the 'community', particularly referred by the local Learning Partnership, or walking in off the street. On this score, a greater proportion of male learners were trade union members compared to female learners who were as likely not to be union members as members. Thus potential for including more women learners may come through recruiting learners from different workplaces/unions and/or from non-union/community sources. In recognising this issue, the project did set an aim part-way through operation to more explicitly seek to reach female learners, and to attempt to establish links with womens' groups and single mothers within the community through the local Learning Partnership.

In terms of ethnicity, around 75 per cent of learners were white and around 15 per cent Asian/British Asian, with relatively few other ethnic minorities. This is a smaller proportion of white learners and a larger proportion of Asian learners than the national average for these funded projects. As far as can be ascertained, this effect may again be due to the large proportion of TGWU learners from the bus company. Although by no means limited to one group, this analysis would suggest the project has more work to do to include a more diverse ethnic mix of learners particularly in The Learning Centre itself, a need recognised by the project management as it considered broadening out to offer ESOL (English for Speakers of Other Languages) courses and to investigate a role in offering citizenship courses and certificates.

The ages of learners was across the age range, with the oldest being born in August 1924 and the youngest April 1988. Compared to national figures, the project had a smaller proportion of younger learners (under 25) but a larger proportion aged 55 and above, including a larger proportion of over 65s. The inclusion of the older learners was seen as a positive aspect of the project and it was felt that this may be attributable to the community emphasis of the project. It was recognised that the low proportion of young learners may be a reflection of the workplaces the project draws upon, but nevertheless, before the ending of the project there was an intention to discover more about the learning and advice needs of under 25s.

The project had a higher proportion of learners with disabilities. Overall, the majority of learners in the project came from three major workplace link centres, providing predominantly white middle aged male learners, albeit with a sizeable Asian minority. At the same time, as a multi-union learning centre the project was also 'marketed' to retired members and, in its referrals from community groups, the project attracted a group of learners who tend to be unemployed and who had a higher proportion of disabilities than those in work. Qualitative information suggests that of the approximately 10 per cent of learners who were non-union members, many of these were not non-union employees from the same workplaces but included a wider pool of learners aimed for in the project, from the likes of friends, family and parents, although it was not clear what this meant in terms of the relationship these learners had with unions and union members.

In general, one notable tension was between the aim of the project for broad social and community inclusion on the one hand, and the reliance on computer-based training on the other. Almost all the learning was computer-based, much of it intended to be commenced in the learning centre itself, and then accessed and worked upon independently at home or in another setting. There is evidence of a high quality of interaction between tutors and learners through the internet. Such an approach brings great potential advantages in terms of flexibility of time and place of learning. However, this medium of access to learning requires learners to have access to a computer at home. Initially this was a problem for some, although computer ownership has increased even in the two years of the project and indeed learners could have access in other locations in the community setting (for example, in the public library). Evidence suggests that many learners in the bus companies did not have access to a computer either at work or at home (at work because of the nature of their job – bus driving). This hindered their ability to learn and undertake courses as they were restricted to accessing the materials only in short bursts during breaks at work. Further, what still remains a problem is lack of broadband access for home users. Without broadband it is extremely difficult to complete courses. In light of this, as well as concerns about the limited range of courses available, the project would have needed to further explore a strategy for non computer-based programmes. Towards the end of the project, a 'blended learning' approach was being devised, with a combination of computer-based, book source and workshop activities. As a note for further research, more information is still required to enable commentary on the use of the learning facilities such as these, at a distance and outside of centre opening hours, through tracking of remote log-on data.

In order to illustrate the range of learners involved, and their histories of involvement with the project, the Appendix to this chapter gives case studies of six learners' involvement with the project over time.

Conclusion

The Learning Centre case study demonstrates a complex set of multiple partnerships with a variety of players; namely multi-union partnerships, partnerships between unions and employers, partnerships between unions and other education and training providers, and partnerships with the community. It highlights the great potential that trade union learning initiatives have for broadening the appeal and reach of unions and for the union renewal agenda. Partnership arrangements between trade unions have the potential to enable unions to take ownership of the activities around learning and develop activism across the union movement. As a result, there is some optimism that 'capacity-building' of the multi union partnership has gone some way to being achieved. Partnership arrangements between employer and trade union provide opportunities for unions to inhabit the terrain of learning and training, given the keenness of (some) employers to buy into the prevailing productivity and skills policy agenda. This enables unions to reinforce their role in the social justice context and at the more micro level again to increase membership and activism and hence renewal, both servicing and organising.

Whilst multi-union and employer partnerships are perhaps more obvious manifestations, there are other dynamics here, notably partnerships with education providers and with the wider community. These are emerging as increasingly important. Arrangements with colleges and other education and training providers enable unions to service a broader range of learners and to legitimise their activities in this field through accredited and quality assured education provision. Such relationships are one dimension of the partnership that is developing with community which includes working with recognised community groups and bodies and which enables unions to identify with particular geographical locations, and be inclusive taking into account socio-economic dimensions, a breadth of learners from different sources and varied learning outcomes or uses. Such moves are enabled largely by computerised learning technologies.

However, The Learning Centre case would not be complete without bringing the story up to date. The project described here ran for two years, 2004 to 2006. What happened subsequently was a fundamental change to the nature of The Learning Centre and its work. Essentially The Learning Centre continues but there has been a 'change of ownership' as it is now part of another new ULF project which funds a number of learning centres nationwide, led solely by Amicus. Under this arrangement, the learning project manager and others employed within the project have become Amicus employees; in fact the manager of the original Learning Centre project now has a nationwide learning centre project management role for Amicus, with The Learning Centre itself subsumed within this. The original multi-union ownership structure no longer exists.

The implications of this are still becoming apparent, but what it does mean is that the project now operates according to Amicus' own union learning policy. There would now appear to be increasing emphasis placed on a preference for learning at the workplace, for electronically-based forms of learning and for supporting ULRs' workplace activities and, within this context and that of cost constraint, the future of some learning centres appears to hang in the balance. Points for further discussion here clearly lie partly around cost of running centres, around convenience of access, around the extent to which learning is seen to be mainstream or separate in union activity, and in the independence the off-site centres provide to unions' learning agendas and the anonymity they afford individual learners. The change of ownership also means that, although learners who are members of other unions are tolerated, inclusion of non-union members and engagement with the community is now no longer a feature of the project; to the exclusion even of redundant and retired former union members. Despite this, some vestiges of multi-union cooperation exist, as the existing TGWU satellite centres continue to operate with learning support provided by The Learning Centre. (Indeed a number of additional workplace learning centres are also now supported, and these are also non-Amicus.)

Thus it seems that partnerships such as those established in the original project offer advantages but are also dogged by problems, conflicts and uncertainties. In particular these arise from unions' attempts to colonise a wider range of activities and be seen to have populist appeal to a wide variety of actors. It would seem that the prospects for multi-union partnership are under some tension, as the demands of limited resources, time and loyalties mean that learning representatives and learners have to make difficult decisions about where to undertake their activities; in the multi-union centre, or based around their own union's facilities in their own workplace.

The conflicts inherent in the employer-worker relationship are also evident here, specifically so in the context of partnership arrangements with employers. Analysis of the learning and learners suggests that the project partially met one of its aims to work with employers to improve skills and productivity, however, this was hampered by employers' reluctance to extend the relationship to include bargaining on training, a reluctance that restricted day-to-day learning activities through inability of learners (and learning representatives) to get time off for their activities. In addition, although the project undoubtedly improved the quality of working life for learners by enabling access to those previously disadvantaged, through raising awareness and uptake of ICT, and by seeking to ensure equality of access to learning, at the same time much of the learning taking place may be seen to be work-related and arguably constraining in nature, preparing workers for low paid service jobs.

Projects such as the one described here operate in a meta policy context where there are constraints in the relationships between the three main stakeholders of state, employers and employees. In particular, there is a strong element of market-based competition for scarce and often short-term funding resources. Through these projects, unions are embracing state funding through the ULF and thus work to some advantage with government funding and quality assurance agencies. However, the precarious nature of ULF funding reveals the difficulty for unions' own partnerships, the need to further strengthen partnerships with mainstream education and training providers, and the dangers of defaulting to partnership arrangements that are more heavily influenced by the employers' agenda. The new project is now seeking to develop new income streams from commercial programmes and testing for professional institutes. This begs the question whether it is possible for such projects to continue without public (ULF) money, without becoming more of a commercial business-oriented training organisation and without a dependence on the goodwill of employers to provide the likes of premises and other facilities.

Partnership arrangements with 'the community' appear to offer a potential way forward for unions' renewal. Unlike the examples described by Wills (2001) and Wills and Simms (2004) which have an explicit organising agenda and a wide-range of activities, it may indeed be possible to build community unionism using learning centres as the catalyst. The way in which The Learning Centre had built links with the community was perceived to be a strength of the original project. However, it is clear that the range of ways in which the project engaged with the community was limited and had yet to be developed to its full potential. There are undoubtedly issues for further discussion here, particularly around the appropriateness of using the Union Learning Fund for non-union learning activities and the ways in which unions' offerings of courses may be distinctive from that of other providers. Nevertheless, the opportunities offered both to the learning and skills agenda (offering an anonymous and independent learning environment and one where learners could receive close one-to-one support) and to the union renewal agenda, appear worthy of much further development. More would need to be done to extend the breadth of the activities that were and could have been part of this project – breadth of learning activities themselves, breadth in terms of other supporting infrastructure and breadth of links with other established community organisations – in order that projects like this can be seen as a basis for 'reciprocal community unionism' in terms of sustaining community life as well as fostering trade union growth (Wills and Simms, 2004).

The challenge for trade unions is to find a way forward in exploiting the advantages that partnership and multi-partnership arrangements in learning provision can bring, whilst retaining a distinctiveness in their activities and an independence in action that defines modern trade unionism.

References

Ashton, D. and Felstead, A. (2001), 'From Training to Lifelong Learning: The Birth of the Knowledge Society?', in Storey (ed.).

Bach, S. (ed.) (2005), *Managing Human Resources: Personnel Management in Transition.* (Oxford: Blackwell).

CIPD (2004), *Trade Union Learning Representatives: The Change Agenda.* (London: Chartered Institute of Personnel and Development).

Forrester, K. (2004), 'The Quiet Revolution? Trade Union Learning and Renewal Strategies', *Work, Employment and Society,* 18: 2, 413–420.

Heyes, J. (2000), 'Workplace Industrial Relations and Training', in Rainbird (ed.).

Kersley, B., Alpin, C., Forth, J., Bryson, A., Bewley, H. Dix, G. and Oxenbridge, S. (2005), *Inside the Workplace. First Findings from the 2004 Workplace Employment*

Relations Survey. (London: Economic and Social Research Council/Department for Trade and Industry).

Rainbird, H. (ed.) (2000), *Training in the Workplace. Critical Perspectives on Learning at Work*. (Basingstoke: Macmillan).

Shelley, S. (2005), '"Useful" Outcomes for Workers in Trade Union Learning Activities. The Significance of Attitude and Ownership'. University of Hertfordshire Business School Working Paper Series 2005:5. (Hatfield: University of Hertfordshire).

Storey, J. (ed.) (2001), *Human Resource Management: A Critical Text*. 2nd Edition. (London: Thomson Learning).

Sutherland, J. and Rainbird, H. (2000), 'Unions and Workplace Learning: Conflict or Cooperation with the Employer?', in Rainbird (ed.).

Tailby, S. and Winchester, D. (2005), 'Management and Trade Unions: Partnership at Work?', in Bach (ed.).

TUC (2004), 'Groundbreaking Learning Centre Opens to Boost Local Skills', TUC Press Release, 4th October 2004.

Wills, J. (2001), 'Community Unionism and Trade Union Renewal in the UK: Moving Beyond the Fragments at Last?', *Transactions of the Institute of British Geographers,* 26, 465–483.

Wills, J. and Simms, M. (2004), 'Building Reciprocal Community unionism in the UK', *Capital and Class,* 82, 59–82.

Appendix

Case Studies Of Learners' Activity Over Time

Learner 1.
Over state retirement age, female, lives in a town 10 miles away.
TU: none initially, although an affiliation later recorded to 'Unite'.
Word Skills Check, November 2004 (and twice, in January and April 2005).
Numbers Direct fractions, February 2005 (and 3 times in March).
Numbers Direct decimals, March 2005 (and 3 times in April)
Numbers Direct length, March 2005 (and 3 times in July)
Numbers Direct weight, April 2005 (and 3 times in Sept)
Unidentified course, August 2005
Numbers Direct measure, shape and space, September 2005 (twice)
All completed.

Learner 2.
Over state retirement age, male, lives locally to The Learning Centre.
TU: none.
Switch On September 2004, with four further activities.
IT2 electronic communication November 2004. (2 more in January)
Skills for Life initial assessment May 2005
IT2 electronic communication June 2005
All completed.

Learner 3.
Age 30–40 male, lives in a village 5 miles away.
TU: GPMU.
A ULR
Numbers Direct, November 2004 (and twice in July 2004)
Preparing for Testing Literacy L1, November 2004 (5 times)
Preparing for Testing Numeracy L1, November 2004 (3 times)
Key Skills Primer- Communication Skills, December 2004
Subsequently five other courses, all completed; and has since been actively enrolling learners for the remainder of the project.

Learner 4.
Age 30–40 female, lives locally to The Learning Centre.
TU: TSSA
A ULR

Number Skills Check August 2004 (plus 2 transactions September 2004, and 1 in November 2004).
Spreadsheets, September 2004 (twice)
Preparing for Testing, November 2004
Numbers Direct 1, January 2005 (4 times)
Online National Test in Adult Literacy, February 2005
Numbers Direct 1, February 2005 (twice, plus 3 times in July)
Online National Test in Adult Literacy, February 2005
All completed.
In addition, she enrolled one learner in January 2005 and another 2 in March 2005.

Learner 5.
Age 40–50 female, lives in a town 10 miles away.
TU: RCN
Initial Assessment, April 2005 (twice)
A Way With Words, April 2005 (twice, plus once in May)
Then appears to have dropped out.

Learner 6.
Age 60 plus.
No TU; walked in off the street.
Initial assessment November 2005
Number Skills Check
Word Skills Check
Described a childhood without schooling and a status as illiterate.
Subsequently undertook 'A Way With Words' course.

SECTION IV

DEVELOPING A FUTURE AGENDA

Chapter 12

Globalisation and Trade Union Education

John Stirling

Introduction

The literature on globalisation is extensive and within it there is a significant stream of analysis concerning its impact on labour and the trade union responses (see, for example, Fairbrother and Yates 2003; Frege and Kelly 2004; Harrod and O'Brien 2002; Moody 1997; Munck 2002; Waterman and Wills 2001). This literature demonstrates the active agency of trade unions in the global restructuring of both private and public sectors. This activity is underpinned by the development of trade union education programmes that have built on established training strategies but have also used innovative content and methods. Without this supportive framework of educational activity, trade union responses to globalisation would be severely undermined and yet there is little by way of research and analysis of the most recent developments in trade union education in this global context. In some respects this is not surprising as trade union education is dominated by the demands of rapid response delivery and pragmatic programmes where skills development have taken priority. As Spencer (2002) cogently observes 'most of the labour education courses provided by unions are *tools* courses' (his emphasis). That is, in this context, they seek to provide the knowledge and skills necessary to respond to the immediate impact of globalisation as it occurs through restructuring, job loss, employment change and the challenges this brings to existing collective organisation and bargaining.

The 'tools' to tackle globalisation are not, however, the only issue for the delivery of trade union education programmes, as an effective response also requires trade unionists to work together across national boundaries. Programmes restricted to a national based delivery are challenged not to reinforce the 'divisions of labour' between trade unionists in different countries that globalisation fosters through regime shopping and social dumping. However, generating and delivering programmes across national boundaries raises new questions for pedagogies as classroom based activities encounter cultural differences and language barriers.

Globalisation in the trade union 'classroom' raises issues of new organisational strategies, new areas of knowledge and new skills to be learnt in a context of cross national cultures and with different levels and types of trade union representative. Moreover, while participants may share common, class, values as trade unionists they may be divided by national interests in seeking jobs and investment from private sector employers.

The underlying argument of this chapter is for the centrality of trade union education to the process of union renewal in the context of globalisation. Even where it exists, discussion, debate, analysis and empirical research on trade union education remains at the margins of the furious debates over trade union renewal. Education remains seen as an adjunct of change, not its motor. This is reflected in, for example, the burgeoning British literature on 'new unionism' (see for example Danford *et al.* 2003; Gall 2003 and Kelly and Willman 2004) where there are few references to trade union education programmes and yet it is precisely these programmes that are to deliver change and renewal. As the trade union movement is transforming new unions need new learning in two ways. Firstly, for trade union education to be recognised as at the critical centre of delivering effective change rather than an add-on activity. Secondly, that trade union education itself is knowingly re-politicised and confronts what divides trade unions globally as well as what unites them.

In pursuing that argument it is necessary to briefly locate trade union education in a conceptual and historical framework in order to demonstrate the challenges of globalisation and the responses. The chapter will then go on to examine four key issues that face trade union education programmes in terms of their content, the participants, the methods engaged and the delivery. The chapter draws particularly on programmes for the Commonwealth Trades Union Council, the Trade Union Advisory Committee of the OECD, the European Trade Union College (now part of ETUI – REHS), and UK trade union organisations. The analysis derives from discussion with tutors and participants in the programmes. Its starting point is developments in the UK and to that extent it remains ethnocentric and Eurocentric but the argument draws on work written and delivered beyond the UK and Europe in the United States and West Africa as well as documentation from global union organisations.

Development and Change

There are a number of factors that have driven the process of globalising trade union education in the UK from a starting point where international activity was severely limited. Like trade union movements themselves in the period of post-war economic reconstruction in the Northern economies and the creation of national welfare states, trade union education programmes were largely parochial in character. The need for delivering an international dimension in programmes in the UK was a fringe activity in a massive expansion in the 1970s based in strong workplace organisation and autonomy. Where workers looked beyond their workplace, it was largely to other workplaces in the UK in the same organisation and to the building of ever more complex shop steward structures. Trade union education, especially in the turn towards workplace skills delivery, largely underpinned this process and built an approach based on a particularly British pluralism.

The three key driving forces internationalising education programmes have been rebuilding union organisation, the development of 'Europe' as a key actor in UK employment relations and the simple growth of awareness of globalisation as an issue.

Membership decline and subsequent rebuilding of organising strategies has highlighted the global dimension of the challenge to workers in both public and private sectors. Similar challenges exist in other countries and their responses have filtered into UK education programmes focussed on union organising. The outcome has been both a focus on organising across national boundaries as an important strategy and importing organising strategies and the educational programmes that go with them (Heery 2000; 2003). In the UK, for example, US models of organising have been influential in the TUC's organising Academy and tutors from North America have been used to deliver programmes such as on the union busting strategies typical in the USA.

Organisational and legislative developments in Europe have further encouraged the development of international trade union activity in and beyond the UK. 'Europe' is often discounted in discussions of globalisation but it is, of course, a significant player and awareness of its activities is often the first step that local UK union activists take in building a perception of trade unionism beyond their own boundaries. In particular, the enlargement of the European Union, the implementation of Directives based in the 'Social Charter' and the establishment of European Works Councils have been important. The first has raised questions of organising migrant workers and developing training materials that encourage and support UK trade unionists in building solidarity in the face of potential exclusion and animosity. European Directives have indicated the importance of the European Union as a source of workplace regulation. Finally, European Works Councils have provided forums for perhaps 13,000 – 15,000 European trade unionists to meet and training programmes have grown exponentially due, in part, to continuing European Commission funding (Stirling 2004). In each case, whether directly or indirectly, international issues are raised in the context of globalisation.

Beyond Europe, there is the broader issue of the development of globalisation and the labour movement response. In one respect awareness has grown simply in response to the news media as international conflicts or stories of famine and natural disasters impinge on daily life. Consumer goods demonstrate globalisation daily as supermarket shelves stock out of season produce grown abroad or 'fair trade' products become increasingly visible. In relation to work and employment, jobs in the private sector shift abroad or people become employed by multinational companies and, in the public sector, global strategies on privatisation or deregulation impact in the UK.

The challenge of globalisation for trade union education is felt then through the need to develop an international perspective in core programmes, to establish more specialist courses dealing with the needs of European Works Councillors, for example, and the necessity to work in delivering programmes with trade unions beyond national boundaries. These demands raise significant problems for what we have argued are generally culturally constrained and nationally focussed programmes.

Traditions of trade union education do not derive from a single source and the relationship between the local classroom and the global workplace is contested terrain. This is particularly the case when delivering programmes in an international context where participants bring different understandings of process and varying ideological positions. The global sharing of views about core trade union values derived from movements in the over-developed economies cannot necessarily be assumed as in, for example, the views of former Soviet bloc trade unionists towards privatisation or delegates from developing countries towards global labour standards. Neither is there a necessary unity of purpose or shared political analysis between workplace activists and context constrained trade union officials. A neutralised (or neutered) trade union education programme that seeks to ignore such difficulties by focussing on the delivery of upgraded skills cannot succeed. The acquisition and application of knowledge is equally a 'skill' and a growing awareness of the significance of global capitalism inevitably raises the questions of how it is to be effectively challenged, whether that is at the level of a single local workplace or in the context of wider political struggles.

Building Trade Union Education

Trade union education is a product of the demands of trade unions themselves for trained representatives that are able to maintain the activities of the union as a functioning organisation both internally and externally. As such, it reflects the general ethos of trade unionism as a set of core values rooted in collectivism and the particular strategies of individual unions embedded in national systems of employment relations. This is further reflected in both delivery and content, in that trade union education mirrors the democratic values of unions as organisations and their commitment to broader issues of social justice. Alongside this broad issue of content reflecting values are two further determining characteristics: the need to develop skills and the necessity of working with adults. Skills development has been at the heart of education programmes as unions seek to enable their representatives at different levels to manage the business of the union, act on behalf of members, bargain with employers and influence governments. This has been developed within a framework of adult education that has supported active learning strategies that draw on the knowledge and experience of the participants. These broad generalisations reflect practice in trade unions across national boundaries but they are not without difference in emphasis or divergence in strategies.

Hyman's (2001) analysis of trade unions in Europe can be stretched to suggesting his categories apply globally and that they provide a useful way of differentiating approaches to trade union education that resurface in discussions of globalisation. Hyman suggests a 'geometry' of trade unionism focussing around the three points of class, market and society and argues that different trade union movements in Europe reflect different emphases and orientations. Hyman restricts himself to three countries and defines British trade unionism as 'between market and class' (2001, 66); German as 'between society and market' (115) and Italian as 'between class and society' (143). If trade union education reflects national trade union movements, then we would expect cultural differences in content and approach and, at its broadest level, this would seem to be the case. The strong historical class orientation of trade unions in Italy, for example, is reflected in persistent, ideological divisions in the trade union movement. In terms of trade union education, we can perceive an historical orientation to content that is politically focussed and seeks to differentiate between confederations in relation to their class orientation. In its turn there would be a tendency towards knowledge based education programmes that would necessarily be 'expert-led' rather than student-centred. The historical divisions have been less significant more recently and a renewed focus on workplace organisation would now challenge some of these traditions (Regalia and Regini 1998). The market orientation of British trade unions with its single confederal centre, the TUC, shifts the emphasis towards skills development in general and bargaining skills in particular. This enables a clear student-centred pedagogy as education focuses on developing skills that have practical application. Reviewing the German case with its 'society' emphasis we can see education programmes that focus on the juridical nature of German industrial relations with divided functions between trade union roles and those of the works councillor leading to different educational provision and a more balanced approach between skills and knowledge. While these differences are suggested at the broadest level and subject to change over time we would expect to see trade union education programmes reflecting these different traditions and for these to be reinforced by cultural differences.

Extending the argument globally is beyond the scope of this chapter but it is clear that the core argument will hold. For example, trade unions involved in liberation struggles or making other powerful links with political parties will see this reflected in their education programmes. Equally, they will often need to deal with the legacy of colonialism that has often seen inappropriate industrial relations systems imposed through pre-independence legislation or situations where military interventions in government have severely restricted the activities of independent trade unions. In such circumstances, trade union activity is clearly markedly different from the institutionalised relationships of their counterparts in the Northern economies with employers and governments. Again, the strategies of trade unions in their day-to-day activities are reflected through their education programmes but they may be rooted in a colonial framework. Trade unions from the North have equally 'exported' ways of behaving, as have colonial governments. While this process is strongly challenged today, funding for training from North to South and the education of key activists in the Northern economies remains an influential factor in the delivery of programmes. Conversely, the argument that a growing and active trade union movement in the South has much to teach the established trade unions of the North is gaining weight.

In sum, trade union education programmes that seek to address issues of globalisation are faced with considerable difficulties in terms of the 'cultural' differences between national trade union movements reflecting their own traditions and employment relations systems (or lack of them). Participants in programmes bring those differences with them and this raises the key issue of 'understanding each other' (often across language divides) before discussion or action in relation to globalisation can be developed within programmes.

Globalisation as Content

The content of trade union programmes on globalisation is a contested terrain, as different trade unions will not necessarily share the same analysis or have common interests. Global union organisations are, therefore, faced with the problem of delivering programmes that can cross global boundaries. The materials from global trade union organisations such as the International Confederation of Free Trade Unions (ICFTU) and the Global Union Federations (GUFs) are used as the starting point for analysing content in this chapter. It is clear that there are commonalities in identifying key themes that invariably focus on understanding globalisation; analysing its impact and developing an effective response. This has two dimensions in terms of using existing institutional mechanisms to bring pressure to bear on companies and other organisations and building solidarity with other trade unionists in the same company, sector or more generally. This in a context where globalisation is rarely directly challenged but rather its outcomes for workers are dealt with through ideas of social responsibility, transparency and social dialogue. The ICFTU, for example, reviews the damaging effects of the globalisation process and argues that:

> The international trade union movement is seeking ways to incorporate into the globalisation process the protections which were achieved in many countries at the national level and to enable workers and their unions to participate effectively in the global economy and building a democratic framework for it (2001, 18).

This 'effective participation' is dependent on the key issues identified above and we can see educational materials designed to raise a general awareness of the issues of globalisation. One of the earlier examples of this in the UK was published by the Commonwealth Trades Union Council (CTUC 1995) and focussed on raising awareness of the global economic framework and its impact on the economies of the South followed by analysis of the role of multinational companies. A similar approach was taken by the education pack (IUF 2002) from the Global Union Federation for food workers that has, for example, sections dealing with colonialism, trade and commodities, debt and structural adjustment. In other cases the more general issues of globalisation have focussed on key issues for a sector as in the case of the Global Union Federation for textile workers (ITGLWF 2004) with its analysis of global supply chains.

Issues of impact are analysed at different levels in relation to economic sectors, labour markets, the organisation and the workplace. These impacts are often developed in education materials by using case study examples of countries, companies or workers but there is significant opportunity at this level to draw on the participants' own experience and activities reflect this. Further activities might focus on anticipating impacts through anticipating change as has been central to the project Trade Unions Anticipating Change in Europe (TRACE) sponsored by ETUI – REHS. In one collaborative project Portuguese and Spanish trade union confederations in the textile sector developed a matrix that could be used to enable workplace representatives to analyse the activities of their companies and help to predict change so opening the way to early consultation and negotiation.

Building Solidarity

However, it is the response to change and the building of solidarity that is the key issues for unions and, consequently, the key element in education programmes. Three discreet elements can be identified in terms of establishing the general principles of a response, identifying and using existing laws and institutions and building solidarity between unions at different levels.

In terms of the general principles we are returned to the political questions raised earlier and again in the conclusion. The question of opposing change is carefully dealt with, as restructuring is an ongoing part of the business cycle with beneficiaries as well as losers. A European Metal Workers handbook and accompanying training materials illustrate the general approach of seeking 'socially responsible' restructuring:

> The EMF does not accept that workers are the only ones to pay the price for restructuring. Socially responsible change should create the conditions for growth, development and viability for the company as well as for employment. Accompanying measures should be offered and negotiated (early retirement, retraining …) if redundancies are inevitable (2006, 13)

Alongside variously described ideas of social responsibility run the mechanisms for establishing them, incorporating them into agreements and implementing them. This requires some understanding of the institutions of the international trade union movement on behalf of course participants but it is often difficult to present this in a way that is meaningful and understandable whilst demonstrating its relevance to workplace representatives. In reality such representatives will rarely be actively engaged with these organisations but they nevertheless represent the trade union institutional contact points with global decision makers. They also provide expertise and access to legal levers that might challenge some of the decisions impacting on workplaces. Uni-Europa, for example, developed a guide for trade unionists using the EU co-determination procedure and the EMF has established guidelines for EWCs in using European regulations in the case of mergers and acquisitions (both as part of their TRACE projects). The Trade Union Advisory Committee (TUAC) to the Organisation for Economic Cooperation and Development (OECD) also produced training materials for EWC members in using its guidelines on multinational enterprises. This, again, illustrates some of the difficulties in developing educational materials on global issues, as the regulations can be complex in the first place and the procedures for implementing them more so. There are also questions of how cases are to be pursued and by whom that will certainly raise issues in an educational situation discussing action and implementation in relation to legislation and regulatory codes of practice.

This leaves unions with developing their own procedures through collective bargaining and the most common form of global regulation has been the International Framework Agreement (IFA). The first stage in an educational context is distinguishing them from the plethora of non-negotiated codes of corporate responsibility supported by NGOs or introduced by companies themselves (see, for example, Miller 2004). Once that is established there are now clear principles incorporated in the IFAs that derive from ILO conventions in areas such as the rights of association and collective bargaining as well as issues such as child and forced labour and discrimination and equal opportunities. Much of the international training material on globalisation contains activities centred on these as well as providing model agreements such as that in the ITGLWF package.

Finally, there are strategies in programmes for building solidarity through establishing and maintaining contacts with equivalent trade unionists in other countries. This can range from quite general educational activities related to ideas such as 'twinning' between union branches to building campaigning activities around particular issues. In Europe, EWCs can become a focus for such activity as they draw their membership from trade unionists (and non-members) across national boundaries. However, very few EWCs have converted into world councils so their activities are geographically constrained and there are major difficulties in an EWC concluding any agreements that go beyond those boundaries. Again, an issue that is likely to raise considerable classroom discussion.

Understanding Each Other

An analysis of globalisation and its delivery in a trade union classroom where different national cultures are represented requires a starting point that explores the potential differences and conflicts between participants. In this respect strategies to deal with globalisation through analysing its impact cannot begin other than with the direct experience of the trade unionists in their own countries and the communication of this through the group. Conflicts of national interest can be particularly marked where participants in programmes are from the same multinational company where restructuring may lead to inter-plant competition for investment and jobs. In Europe, it is the burgeoning programme of EWC training that most clearly demonstrates and deals with this difficulty. Materials developed for ETUI-REHS are typical in beginning training for EWC members by working with them in raising awareness of difference. This in its turn raises questions of value that are more difficult to deal with in the sense that national laws or collective agreements may be perceived as better or worse with the implication that some participants need to 'catch up'. This may be dealt with in two ways; through developing ideas of mutual respect about different approaches to employment relations or trade union organisation and by exploring good practice that can be shared and applied across national boundaries.

This challenge of dealing with difference is further illustrated in building alliances between European Works Councillors and trade unionists from the same countries in the United States of America. The transatlantic labour dialogue programme provided stark contrasts of both employment relations systems, cultures and approaches to trade union organising strategies. Across these boundaries it was not simply language that could be a dividing factor but the understanding of the context for terms such as 'collective bargaining' or 'union representative'. These cannot simply be translated as if there is a shared understanding that collective bargaining arrangements, for example, are the same between different countries. Moreover, if we pursue this transatlantic example as illustrative of a common problem, it is clear that there are marked differences in organising strategies. For instance, trade unions in the USA face an often hostile anti-union approach from employers that is lacking in European countries characterised by social dialogue. Following from this, confrontational strategies from US unions seeking to negotiate with multinational employers might be alien for trade unionists in, for example, Germany where collective bargaining agreements, works councils and Board level participation systems are in place that give ready access to senior management.

In the USA these challenges have led to education programmes that are workplace focussed and directly aimed at rebuilding organisation in ways that directly challenge employers and build links with communities (see examples in Burke *et al.* 2002 and Delp *et al.* 2002). The importation of education programmes across trade union movements raises major problems where they are taken out of their employment relations' context. These challenges are magnified on the rarer occasions that education programmes are resourced to bring together trade unions from the global North and South. Issues of transnational investment may highlight problems of regime competition through undercutting labour costs and questions of basic trade union rights are likely to be highlighted. As we have seen, this latter point is a central one in the trade union education materials on globalisation.

The issues surrounding how trade unionists understand each and the different cultures and employment relations framework is not simply a matter for an 'ice breaking' activity at the start of a course drawing new people together. Rather it is a key part of the content of any globalisation education programme as without it solidarity cannot be effectively built where misunderstandings and mistrust exists. Only once that mutual understanding is established can consideration be given to the development of further skills in relation to responding to globalisation.

Developing Skills

As we have indicated, a key focus of trade union education programmes has been on the development of skills but what, precisely, are the skills necessary to deal with the questions raised by globalisation? We are not faced here with the more straightforward objective of supporting a trade unionist in becoming a better negotiator in pay bargaining or a better advocate in representing members. Any effective response to the issues globalisation raises for trade unionists rests on building transnational alliances that are severely pressured by the often divisive nature of restructuring. The key skills in this context are related to building effective cross-national communications and then developing strategies for international action that is inclusive. Developing skills in building networks for the twofold function of exchanging information and driving action is essential but challenges traditional ways of organising, and, with it, the roles of union representatives. Trade union education programmes are therefore faced with a particular dilemma in that such skills development is not 'neutral' in the sense of simply equipping somebody to do something better but they also require individuals to do things differently.

For example, collective bargaining is most commonly organised nationally and within countries on the basis of established traditions. Globalisation forces the recognition that employers decisions about key employment issues such as jobs and labour costs are taken beyond those national boundaries that constrain collective bargaining. This raises a number of issues for delivering skills development in this context. Firstly, there is the need to develop skills in information gathering so that organisational strategies can be analysed and potential decisions anticipated. There are publicly available information sources that are readily accessible but key sources of information are embedded in the knowledge of local trade unionists in particular workplaces which means that information networks need to be built and packages of material have been developed that do this.

In this sense building an information network is a skill that can be demonstrated and learnt in education programmes but it raises to two further issues. Cross-national networks return us to the issues of language and cultures that we have discussed earlier. They also raise questions of union organisation that challenge education programmes in relation to union structures and policies. Networks are commonly developed in response to particular needs by those who have those needs so they may not necessarily fit with existing union structures and may, indeed, clash with them. Informal networks between workplace representatives may challenge established union hierarchies and networks, for example, within transnational companies and may challenge trade union organisation where it is sector or country based. The delivery of skills development in education programmes then challenges its 'neutrality' as the skills themselves lead to the questioning of particular modes of union organisation. Trade union education programmes have inevitably done this in the past but this has been confined to national debates whereas globalisation raises issues where trade union organisation has not matched the rapid changes that it has faced. This organisational response is clearly beyond the scope of this chapter (see, for example, Waterman (1998), for a sustained critique of global union organisation) but it has significant implications for delivering international trade union education programmes. Those programmes, as we argued at the outset, are a reflection of national systems and cultures whereas we have some considerable fluidity in international union organisation policies and strategies as well as European and global trade union organisations that strive to be representative, active and co-ordinated on severely limited resources.

Nevertheless, beyond these wider questions raised by building cross-border networks through skills development in the classroom there remain key questions about particular skills. In terms of communications, the trade unions most immediate problem is the straightforward one of language difference. Language skills can be regarded as an individual responsibility that is not compatible with the collective learning traditions of trade union education and something that might be provided or resourced from State education systems. This neglects the particularities of the language of trade unionism and its particular cultural context and there has been some limited support for language training at the European level. Where that is not available, then running education programmes using interpretation raises further questions both in terms of resources (availability and cost) and the difficulties of managing interactive learning.

Language also raises questions for Internet usage as well as the skills necessary in effectively using that resource. Developing distance learning training packages online is becoming increasingly important (see below) but the skills necessary to access and utilise the Internet, as an information source and a networking facility are essential for building cross-border networks. This requires classroom training, which is not solely a trade union activity as computer literacy can be developed from a range of different resources. However, its use in a trade union context requires specialist training with hands on access in a classroom and skilled trainers in support. The logistics of this and the resources required in the Northern economies are significant but can be close to non-existent for trade unions in developing countries. This is equally true outside the classroom of course and is a further inhibiting factor in generating genuinely global alliances in sectors and companies.

The building of effective education strategies to support trade union challenges to globalisation requires, then, the development of a range of new skills such as languages, communicating across the Internet and building networks. It also requires the application and development of existing skills in new environments that are unfamiliar and also potentially challenging to existing organisational frameworks and hierarchical power structures. The issues of skills development raise critical issues of pedagogy and further questions of the role of the trade union tutor.

'The Method'

It is now a commonplace to record that trade union education methods have their roots in an adult education pedagogy that is embedded in the experience that participants bring to programmes and centred on interactive learning. This coincides with trade union values of collectivity and solidarity as against the individualistic notions of personal achievement that is part of school and post school education. It also assigns the tutor the role of facilitator and leader rather than an expert distributing knowledge. However, dissemination of 'the method' remains patchy if rarely directly challenged and Croucher's (2004) interesting study of programmes in Moldova, Ukraine and Belarus suggests that there remains a need to continue to revisit debates about pedagogic practice. Globalisation provides another opportunity to review pedagogy and the role of the tutor.

Beginning with experience is, in one sense, straightforward for, as workers, consumers and citizens we all experience the effects of globalisation. Education programmes can begin from that experience and progress towards the understanding of the reality and how it might impact differently on course participants. This is the bedrock of programmes where the shared experience in the classroom also derives from a common work experience in terms of a sector or an individual company. However, two further issues then emerge firstly in relation to delivery and secondly in relation to the role of the tutor.

Globalisation is a complex and contested concept and the strategies for challenging it turn on differing political and ideological conceptions. This raises issues for delivering more expert-led inputs into trade union education with the concomitant question of who is the expert and how might they lead? Globalisation education programmes may be delivered with other agencies where trade unions do not have the expertise internally and they will, of course, work with organisations that can and do share their values. In particular, globalisation has challenged unions to work with the Non-Governmental Organisations (NGOs) that deliver development education programmes and work with local communities. Trade unions and NGOs have often been uneasy allies even if sharing broadly common values of social justice. Their organisation remains different in that generally trade unions are membership associations with democratic structures while NGOs have a less direct relationship with their contributors. NGOs are more likely to take campaigning stances, sometimes short-term, that can be highly critical of employers while trade unions are seeking long-term agreements and negotiating rights that may temper criticism in some circumstances. Nevertheless, globalisation has encouraged common action and this has been transmitted into delivering education programmes.

However, globalisation education programmes remain largely delivered by unions themselves and led by experienced tutors which returns us to the second part of the question. Trade union educators have been trained themselves within the now dominant methodology of student-centred learning leaving political ideology and strategy to union policy makers or as part of the discussion in the class. Enjoined to be a 'facilitator' rather than a director the tutor in an international class must deal with their own preconceptions and political position as well as those of the participants, in the context of managing a programme constrained by official policy decisions and practice. As we have suggested, policy in relation to globalisation can be clear at a general level in terms of ideas of 'social responsibility' and 'social dialogue' but implementation in practice and questions of degrees of resistance or accommodation to globalisation raise inevitable political questions. As with the discussion in relation to skills development we return to the issues globalisation raises in relation to an 'apolitical' or 'neutral' delivery. Of course, trade union education is already laden with the more general collective values but an analysis of globalisation and agreement about strategic responses may be less commonly shared. If analysis and policy is to be communicated to union representatives then there are methods for doing so that remain student centred but they will be 'led' by tutors in the sense that the policies and arguments will reflect particular political analyses. It is clear that such a political argument is necessary if the neo-liberal policies of national and supranational state agencies are to be understood but it is less clear what the argument is, who should transmit it and how. We might also ask and to who?

Participating in Programmes

Participation in trade union education has been determined by need, individual initiative and the availability of resources. As globalisation's impact stretches from international decision making to local implications it is arguable that education programmes need to be available to all levels of trade union representative. This is particularly the case if the implications of globalisation for restructuring in different sectors or organisations are to be anticipated and responded to through co-ordinated action. This leads to three particular issues that, again, challenge the traditional organisation of trade union education. An analysis of 'needs' carries with it a division in education programmes that coincides with the hierarchical structure of trade unions. General secretaries have different 'needs' to shop floor representatives in terms of the knowledge they require and the skills they must learn. The involvement of senior union officials in a course for workplace representatives is likely to be in the role of expert in relation to a particular organisation or a particular skill such as negotiating. This is challenged by globalisation where co-ordinated strategies are a necessary part of effective organisation and where workplace representatives need to be aware of global union strategies and senior union officers need to understand the response of local trade unionists. Projects such as the Transatlantic Labour Dialogue and the TRACE programme on restructuring in Europe both worked in delivering education programmes where union full time officials worked in classrooms with workplace representatives as equal participants. In this way a mutual understanding of policy and problems was able to emerge and be understood and all parties became committed to the action that results from the programmes. Without this interaction potential frictions occur that reinforce supposed 'bureaucrat' and 'rank-and-file' divisions.

The second issue in relation to participation is that of cross-national involvement. Programmes on globalisation can be nationally based and awareness raising materials and classes have been developed and used in the UK. However, we have suggested that delivery in a single country has the potential to reinforce national divisions and may encourage patronising attitudes in relation to North/South issues which sees trade unions in developing countries as enfeebled and in need of help. There is no doubt that many trade union movements will need material resources but this neglects their own vibrancy and activities that are often in advance of moribund union strategies in the Northern economies. The key to challenging preconceptions and building global alliances is through education programmes that bring together participants from different countries. There are clear obstacles, including those we have discussed above, but without first hand contact it will be more difficult to generate effective trade union responses to globalisation.

The final issue in this respect is resources and this is a major barrier to developing effective programmes. Trade unions in the European economies, North America and Australia have faced membership losses that have led to severe financial restrictions and often significant cuts in educational provision (Bridgford and Stirling 2000 deal with this in Europe). This also has implications for the funding of global organisations that rely on funding support from affiliated organisations that are cash starved. Alternative funding has often come from the State in the Northern economies but neo-liberal policies and unsympathetic right of centre governments have restricted that avenue. In particular, courses that do not have a 'practical skills base' are less likely to be funded and it is more difficult to argue this case on globalisation programmes. Supra State bodies such as the European Union have been an alternative particularly in relation to cross-national training for European Works Councillors but that is also constrained (Stirling 2004). Trade union movements in the developing countries have even severer constraints on income and resources for education and may rely on funding from unions, NGOs and government agencies beyond their own boundaries.

One response to these constraints has been the development of online learning as a way of increasing participation in programmes. The pedagogical limitations of this are significant given the collective learning orientation of trade union education programmes. Clearly, information and knowledge issues can be dealt with in terms of materials and there is widespread experience of writing distance learning materials that are interactive. The Intern*et al.*so offers other direct communication methods between participants on line and with tutors but the latter is resource intensive. The Transatlantic Labour Dialogue programme offered both classroom based resources and an online facility that works within the experiential learning framework but it is geared to building solidarity through the shared experience of working for the same company. There is little doubt that on line learning can build global networks in a way that would be impossible to resource through classroom contact but it needs to be supported as far as possible by face-to-face activities. Furthermore, while online learning may reduce resource implications in the Northern economies this approach can exclude trade unionists in countries where access to the appropriate hardware, software and reliable power sources can all be highly circumscribed.

Conclusion

Lillie and Martinez Lucio (2004, 174) argue succinctly that:

> The development of a new international dimension of union activity is real and has both formal and informal characteristics. International union action is sometimes strategic and intentional but sometimes unions are forced into international contact through shifting production structures, management strategies, or through the international nature of the problem they are dealing with. Any strategy for union revitalisation must account for this growing international dimension if it is not to be continually undermined by transnational inter-union competition within firms and sectors. The ability to sustain their role by redefining union structures, interests, and power bases along transnational lines is a fundamental challenge for union revitalization in the coming years.

It has been the argument of this chapter that it is precisely these challenges that face trade union education programmes and that they are central to any 'revitalisation' that can or will take place. It has also been argued that trade union education programmes cannot be understood if they are decontextualised from national cultures, employment relations frameworks and trade union traditions. They are dependent on, and transmitters of, union policies and strategies within that context and through pedagogic methods rooted in adult education and experiential learning. In the Northern economies, particularly Europe, where there is an established institutional framework for employee relations that legitimises the role of trade unions there has been a strong focus on the skills necessary to represent and bargain on behalf of union members. In the emerging economies where exploitation is unmediated by institutions and felt in extreme by workers, trade unions have had to confront directly the political issues this class conflict raises. Fischer and Hannah's (2002) discussion of the markedly different approaches to training taken by trade unions in the UK and Brazil exemplify this point. In Brazil, the question of union involvement in vocational training is directly related to issues of citizenship which, in turn, draw on the experience and demands of different social movements and raise directly political questions.

> In contrast to CNM/CUT [the Brazilian trade unions], the G[raphic] P[rint] M[edia workers] U[nion] does not seek (at least publicly) to consciously challenge, or provide alternatives to, the power of capital (2002, 112).

Trade union education programmes that develop cross-nationally will need to confront these differences in approach and engage in the political questions that globalisation raises and which are responded to markedly differently by different union organisations. In doing this in a context of experiential and student-centred learning the issues will be starkly faced, as trade unionists from different countries will have markedly different experiences. One outcome is for trade unions to eschew cross-national training (it is invariably resource expensive) and deliver nationally based programmes on globalisation. This is a necessary process and complex questions of cross-national solidarity can be generally addressed but they do not provide the hard experience of interaction with trade unionists from different countries. Trade union education programmes are geared to generating action beyond the classroom and internationally based classes offer the opportunity to explore real issues in relation to building global solidarities. The development of good practice in this context is in devising action that can deliver and is sustainable. This returns us to our opening argument concerning the need for mutual understanding leading to respect and trust. Educational provision can make that contribution to revitalisation in a way that is difficult to manage or achieve when faced with immediate problems.

Globalisation has provided a different context for trade unions and required new strategies that cross national boundaries.

> Not only may trade unions begin to look at the potential for strengthening localised forms of representation, but increasingly they face the prospect of internationalised forms of negotiation and bargaining (Fairbrother and Rainnie 2006, 5).

The challenges of globalisation for the unions are in the shifting of decision-making. As Fairbrother and Rainnie indicate this can be downward as in, for example, the public sector where neo-liberal policies have led to decentralisation. Upwards shifts have been to levels in organisations or supra-national agencies where unions have limited institutionalised responses and severely constrained power. In both cases demands are made on trade union education programmes that return us to key questions of skills delivery. Downward shifts in bargaining lead to workplace negotiations where national agreements formerly existed and raise issues for training a new swathe of bargainers who must work within continuing national union policy frameworks. The upward shift in decision-making does not necessarily lead to an upward shift in who might be involved in bargaining. Discussions in relation to the articulation of relationships between national, regional (for example, European) and global union organisations are beyond the scope of this chapter but they raise key questions in relation to the locus of power in union organisations that will need to be incorporated into education programmes. Moreover, international bargaining may remain part of the province of workplace representatives. For example, the institutional structure that creates EWCs specifically limits membership to employees of the company. While many agreements allow experts who are normally full time union officials the numbers available to be actively engaged with each EWC is severely limited.

While EWCs are not bargaining agencies in themselves they are often the focus of negotiations in cases of global or European restructuring.

Bargaining outcomes can, of course, lead to conflict and, in turn, campaigning and industrial action strategies being developed by trade unions. This raises further issues for education programmes as organising and campaigning skills now need to be developed in this global context and issues of industrial action and strikes invariably raise issues in terms of different approaches from national union movements. For example, trade unions committed to partnership at the national level may find it difficult to engage with unions more prepared to take militant industrial action. These are not necessarily competing strategies and may be complementary in global disputes but the differences will need to be dealt with in education programmes.

Globalisation is, then, requiring new skills or the application of existing skills in new circumstances. It raises key political questions and provides distinct challenges to the delivery of programmes in an international context. It offers an opportunity for education programmes to be at the centre of the revitalisation of trade unions but there remains a need for major investment at a time when many unions are retrenching and shifting resources out of their training budgets.

References

Amoore, L. (2005), *The Global Resistance Reader.* (London: Routledge).

Bridgford, J. and Stirling. J. (eds.) (2000), *Trade Union Education in Europe.* (Brussels: ETUC).

Bronfenbrenner, K., Friedman, S., Hurd, R. W., Seeber, R. L. and Oswals, R. A. (eds.) (1998), *Organizing to Win: New Research on Union Strategies.* (Ithaca: ILR Press).

Burke, B., Geronimo, J., Martin, D., Thomas, B and Wall, C (eds.) (2002), *Education for Changing Unions.* (Toronto: Between the Lines).

Croucher, R. (2004), 'The Impact of Trade Union Education: A Study of Three Countries in Eastern Europe', *European Journal of Industrial Relations* 10:1, 90-109.

Danford, A., Richardson, M. and Upchurch, M. (2003), *New Unions, New Workplaces.* (London: Routledge).

Debrah, Y. A. and Smith, I. G. (eds.) (2002), *Globalization, Employment and the Workplace.* (London: Routledge).

Delp, L. (2002), *Teaching for Change; Popular Education and the Labor Movement.* (Los Angeles: UCLA Centre for Labor Research & Education).

Eade, D and Leather, A. (2005), *Development NGOs and Labor Unions: Terms of Engagement.* (Bloomfield: Kumarian Press).

European Metalworkers' Federation (2006), *How to Deal with Transnational Company Restructuring.* (Brussels: EMF).

Fairbrother, P. and Rainnie, A. (eds.) (2006), *Globalisation, State and Labour.* (London: Routledge).

Fairbrother, P. and Yates, C. (2003), *Trade Unions in Renewal: A Comparative Study.* (London: Routledge).

Ferner, A. and Hyman, R. (eds.) (1998) *Changing Industrial Relations in Europe.* (Oxford: Blackwell).

Fischer, M. C. B. and Hannah, J. (2002), 'Trade Unions, Globalisation and Training', in Harrod and O'Brien (eds.).

Fitzgerald, I. & Stirling, J. (eds.) (2004), *European Works Councils.* (London: Routledge).

Frege, C. M. and Kelly, J. (eds.) (2004), *Varieties of Unionism: Strategies for Union Revitalisation in a Globalising Economy.* (Oxford: Oxford University Press).

Gall, G. (ed.) (2003) *Union Organizing.* (London: Routledge).

Harrod, J and O'Brien, R. (eds.) (2002), *Global Unions? Theories and Strategies of Organized Labour in the Global Political Economy.* (London: Routledge).

Heery, E., Simms, M., Simpson, D., Delbridge, R and Salmon, J. (2000), 'Organising Unionism Comes to the UK', *Employee Relations*, 22:1, 38–57.

Heery, E., Delbridge, R., Salmon, J., Simms, M. and Simpson, D. (2002), 'Global Labour? The Transfer of the Organizing Model to the United Kingdom', in Debrah and Smith (eds.).

Hyman, R. (2001), *Understanding European Trade Unionism.* (London: Sage).

International Textile Garment and Leather Workers Federation (2004), *Global Companies, Global Unions.* (Brussels: ITGLWF).

International Union of Food and Allied Workers (2002), *Getting to Grips with the Global Food Trade.* (Geneva: IUF).

Kelly, J. and Willman, P. (2004), *Union Organization and Activity.* (London: Routledge).

Lillie, N. and Martinez Lucio, M. (2004), 'International Trade Union Revitalization: The Role of National Union Approaches', in Frege and Kelly (eds.).

Miller, D. (2004), 'Preparing for the Long Haul: Negotiating International Framework Agreements in the Global Textile, Garment and Footwear Sector', *Global Social Policy* 4:2, 215–239.

Moody, K (1997), *Workers in a Lean World.* (London: Verso).

Munck, R. (2002), *Globalisation and Labour: The New Great Transformation.* (London: Zed Books).

Regalia, I. and Regini, M. (1998), 'Italy: The Dual Character of Industrial Relations', in Ferner and Hyman (eds.).

Spencer, B. (2002), *Unions and Learning in a Global Economy.* (Toronto: Thompson Educational Publishing).

Stirling, J. (2004), 'EWC Training for Global Labour Networks', in Fitzgerald and Stirling (eds.).

Stirling, J and Tully, B. (2004), 'Power, Policy and Practice: Communications in European Works Councils', *European Journal of Industrial Relations*, 10:1, 73–89.

Waterman, P. (1998), *Globalization, Social Movements and the New Internationalisms.* (London: Continuum).

Waterman, P. and Wills, J. (eds.) (2001), *Place, Space and the New Labour Internationalisms.* (Oxford: Blackwell).

Chapter 13

New Developments in Union Learning

Liz Rees

TUC Education is our flagship service, the way in which most trade unionists first make real contact with the TUC (John Monks, TUC General Secretary (1992–2003), 2001).

This edited collection comes at an interesting time for trade union education. The twenty-fifth anniversary of the publication of the first Stage 1 Union Representatives course will be marked by a new edition of this influential programme of learning for shop stewards and workplace representatives. Figures prepared for the 2007 Trades Union Congress (TUC) show that participation in trade union education is at an all-time high; higher than in 1976 when the first education packs were prepared and launched and at a time when the trade union movement was more than five million stronger. National union education officers report similar growth and vibrancy in individual union programmes.

Even more significantly, the launch of Unionlearn, the body which provides a strategic framework for union work on learning and skills as well as trade union education, took place in May 2006 at a major conference addressed by former trade union studies tutor, the Rt. Hon. Gordon Brown MP, Chancellor of the Exchequer. The new body will provide a coherent framework for bringing together and maximising union work on learning and skills as well as trade union education and, with a budget of £12m in 2007–8, will be able to help the union movement punch its weight in an area in which it has a long and progressive history.

This chapter aims to describe and explore recent developments in trade union learning from the Unionlearn/TUC Education perspective and to reflect on their significance. Individual unions have their own programmes, some delivered by TUC Education on their behalf and others developed and delivered by them. An account of each union's own programme would make for a much longer piece of work, so, whilst this chapter will make reference to aspects of unions' own programmes, they will not be covered in detail. For those with further interest, some unions have histories of their own education provision, such as Fisher (2005).

Training Union Officers and Representatives

The key to an effective employee voice at the workplace is training union workplace representatives and professionals to a high standard. Since 1976 TUC Education has offered high quality training through a partnership with colleges and universities across the UK. Courses are provided for union representatives, health and safety representatives, learning representatives, pensions trustees, equality representatives and there are courses offered for the emerging role of environment representative. There has always been a strong internationalist dimension to the training and this has increased and is demonstrated in a number of new initiatives. Since 1996, the training has been accredited in partnership with the National Open College Network, and since 2004, the offer has been extended to union professionals (paid officers and staff). Training is also designed and delivered for trade union studies tutors, who are employed by colleges but are recruited with the involvement of the TUC Regional Education Officer (REO) and trained by TUC Education.

TUC Education has gone from strength to strength in recent years, with over 48,000 course enrolments each year. The programmes are organised by eight Regional Education Officers (REOs) and delivered locally through dedicated units in more than seventy colleges of further education across the UK. All course materials are designed, developed and provided by the TUC and tutors are recruited for their expertise in trade unionism and the world of work. Union representatives in recognised workplaces have the right to paid time-off to participate in courses.

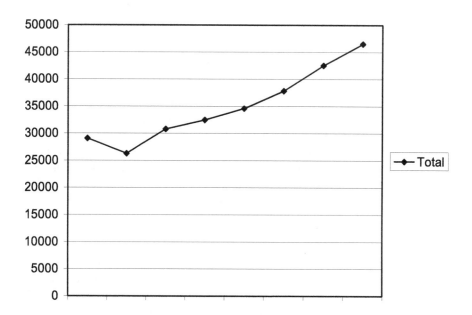

Figure 13.1   TUC Education. Total representatives attending TUC courses 1998–2005

(Source: Unionlearn 2006a, 17).

Quality has to be taken very seriously within TUC Education; ten consecutive Adult Learning Inspectorate reports rated provision as Grade I and characterised as 'outstanding'. This standard has been unmatched by any other curriculum area across adult education, and a reputation for quality and innovation has grown. The internal quality cycle is key and depends on the active involvement of the national team, the REOs (who work closely with their counterparts in unions at regional level as well as managing the work of the TUC units), the Course Co-ordinators (who meet regularly at regional level) and tutor teams within units. The national team works closely with policy departments across the TUC and with national union education officers, who meet three times a year and who actively participate and advise on strategy and course development. The awarding body, the National Open College Network, moderates the programme.

Methods and Values

Day to day activity in trade unions is dependent upon certain shared values and attitudes. These values and attitudes underpin the work of TUC Education and are reflected in our approach to teaching and learning. TUC Education has described them in this way since the 1990s, following a functional analysis of the role of trade union officers and staff.

Justice and Fairness

Demonstrable fair treatment in all aspects of work with open and just procedures for dealing with complaints and grievances from individuals and groups.

Equality and Equity

Equality of opportunity and equity of treatment require the elimination of prejudice and procedures which openly or covertly discriminate against people on the grounds of gender, race, religion, sexual orientation, disability and age.

Democracy

The greatest possible involvement in decision making at work and participation in the activities of the union by members. Advocating and implementing procedures and practices and providing information which encourages such participation

Unity

Maintaining cohesion between members and groups of members in working towards trade union objectives. Having regard to the legitimate needs and aspirations of all members, as well as those of the majority.

The methods are designed to enhance representatives' capacity for working collectively and cooperatively; so that what is studied is re-enforced by the way it is studied. So as well as focusing on the issues raised in the value base above (negotiating skills, equality, communicating with members and managers, etc), the way representatives work together on courses and in workplace activities develop the kind of collective, shared, involving work methods unions value and rely upon. Those who attended the launch of Unionlearn in May 2006 would have been struck by how the Chancellor of the Exchequer was able to field a question on how we develop citizenship by referring to the methods he used in trade union education many years previously. TUC Education has always used active learning methods, long before they became accepted practice in further education. They are integral to our approach, and unions and their representatives expect that their experience and knowledge will be the starting point for the course.

Trade unions have distinct aims and most learners attend courses in a representative capacity. They want to develop their role, knowledge or skills base, often in relation to one particular problem or issue which has prompted them to seek training. In working together, seeking to involve everyone, encouraging discussion of difficult issues, and developing research and planning skills, active learning techniques develop and reinforce the values that are the basis for union activity. By working in pairs, groups and as a course meeting, learners both work on issues and problems, and learn to listen, debate, cooperate, plan and organise with their colleagues.

Most representatives' experience of learning is rooted in schooldays, and they anticipate that all organised learning will be similar. To benefit from the course, representatives need a new attitude to and experience of learning where their active contribution is expected and valued by the tutor and other learners. Talking about problems at their workplace and working with other representatives to determine solutions puts them at the centre rather than on the periphery of classroom activity, and will automatically engage their interest:

> I kept waiting for the day when I came in and would be just sitting there looking blankly and [the tutor] would turn around and say "Wake up, what's that regulation?" ... I've just recently realised that's not going to happen here (Quote from a learner in Capizzi 1999, 19).

Skills development is a vital component of TUC Education, particularly on the core courses. This is because representatives need to be able to do certain things well at the workplace, and in the union. One of the most effective ways of acquiring skills is through experience and learning by doing. Tutors create opportunities for learners to practice the skills they need, through activities in the classroom and workplace assignments and improvement projects.

Most important, representatives on TUC courses are a resource themselves, coming from a wide range of backgrounds and experience, and often with highly developed skills. Whilst they will all have things to learn from the course, they have things to contribute too, and it is the tutor's job to ensure that this knowledge and experience is used in a structured way throughout the course, for the benefit of all learners.

There is a point of view that says that such an emphasis on skills in some way diminishes the representatives' capacity for more political development, and the work done on union and TUC courses is characterised as 'role training' or 'skills training'. This is to misunderstand the way active learning works, particularly with such a committed group of learners as union representatives. The richness of the classroom experience is what is most often commented upon by everyone, from inspectors through to the learners themselves. Using their own experience as the starting point for discussion and activities puts the learner at the heart of the process in a way that no lecture, however interesting, can achieve, and the evidence of personal development as well as workplace development is plentiful. Issues raised and debated in a typical course can range across the political, the social, the economic, the international and the personal spectrum, and the skills of the tutors coupled with the carefully designed curriculum weave these issues into skills development.

An example of this is the work undertaken with the TUC European Union and International Relations Department (EUIRD) on the implementation of a strategic grant agreement with the Department for International Development (DfID). The agreement is designed to raise awareness and build knowledge within the UK trade union movement about international development issues to enhance capacity to take action in this area. The DfID supported the TUC idea of a mini union learning fund to enable unions to bid for resources to develop education initiatives. Amongst the work undertaken is a range of Factfiles developed for tutors and union education officers, designed to help understand the interconnection between the lives of working people across the world. 'Migration and Refugees', for example, includes teaching materials and resources on dispelling myths about migrant workers, 'International Development Education and the Trade Union Role' deals with development and poverty, issues surrounding trade, aid and debt and the union role. All contain advice and support for tutors to mainstream these issues into core classroom courses. Unions and the TUC set out to develop thinking, questioning political representatives, with the confidence to represent their union and their members in a range of settings; with employers, with members, with organisations, in their community and with government.

The Curriculum

The curriculum is extensive and thorough, underpinned by a bank of units of credit called 'Passport to Progress: the TUC Programme'. Materials are continually redrafted and updated, and short courses are added as the union agenda changes and expands. The main programmes are given here, with details correct as of 2007. Full information on courses available is at www.unionlearn.org.uk.

The TUC Core Course Programme

The full curriculum for union representatives (the 'TUC Core Course Programme'), contains the following five courses. Firstly, 'The Union Reps Stage 1 Course' (60–72 hours of guided learning), comprises sessions on the job of the union representative, building union membership, making the union work, using and making agreements, representing members, grievance and discipline, rights and negotiating at work, the representative within the wider union, and looking forward and making plans. The Advanced Course for Union Reps ('Stepping Up'), is 60–72 hours of guided learning through core modules on trade union context; planning, organising and campaigning; plus two other modules on rights at work; collective bargaining; or leading on the collective agenda.

Also part of the core programme, the 'Health and Safety Stage 1 Course', is 60–72 hours of guided learning on the subjects of the role and functions of the trade union health and safety representative; organising for health and safety; preventing accidents and ill health; skills for the safety representative; and planning for the future. As a follow-on from this, the 'Next Steps for Safety Reps – Stage 2 Course' is another 60–72 hours of guided learning on the subjects of building a safe and healthy workplace; building health and safety organisation; keeping up-to-date on health and safety; effecting change in health and safety; and further planning for the future.

The fifth part of the core programme is particularly significant in the context of this book, because it is the training for Union Learning Representatives (ULRs). This takes place over 30–50 hours of guided learning and comprises sessions on getting organised (including the role of the ULR; and statutory rights and facilities for ULRs); working with members (including involving members; skills for life; learning needs surveys; and organising to improve learning opportunities); working with employers (including top tips for a learning workplace; training and learning opportunities; organising to improve learning opportunities); and sessions on skills notes and on building a ULR workplace toolkit.

The TUC Short Course Programme

Short courses are organised as part of regional/national programmes, or on request from affiliates. They can be organised during working time and last between one and five days. A diverse variety of subjects are on offer, with current courses ranging from workplace representation and skills training, to wider campaigning issues. The 'Employment Law Course' includes sessions on family friendly policies; the right to be accompanied; handling grievances and disciplinaries; the Human Rights Act; recognition arrangements; and the Information and Consultation Regulations. The 'Collective Bargaining/Industrial Relations Course' addresses the issues involved in representing members and in partnership at work. The 'Equality Course' includes sessions on women's programmes; tackling racism and discrimination; equal opportunities; lesbian, gay, bisexual and transgender issues; and disability champions at work. The 'Health and Safety Course' addresses risk assessment; dealing with stress in the workplace; preventing bullying in the workplace; dealing with violence in the workplace; accident prevention; control of substances hazardous to health; and discussion of the role of trade unions in international health and safety issues. 'Organising Courses' introduce the subject of organising and organising strategies; whilst 'Skills Courses' are provided on negotiating skills and communication skills; and the 'Information Communication Technology Course' introduces trade unionists to computers and develops abilities at using the internet and using word processing, spreadsheets and databases. There are also 'Induction Courses' for new representatives.

With a wider campaigning remit courses also run on pensions (including sessions that provide an introduction to pensions; pension trustees; and women and pensions); and on 'Trade Unions and the Environment' (including environment terminology and the current debate; the main environmental concerns at each workplace; the main legislation and other information on the environment; reviewing environment management systems; and assessing current trade union policies).

The TUC Access Certificate Course Programme

A third suite of courses provided by TUC Education are three certificate level courses in Occupational Health and Safety, Contemporary Trade Unionism, and Employment Law. The 'TUC Certificate in Occupational Health & Safety' develops understanding of health and safety principle and practice and includes modules on occupational health and safety organisation; occupational health and safety law; occupational health, safety, welfare in the environment; and research, communication, study skills, ICT and working with figures and statistics. This is a Level 3 qualification, accredited through the Institute for Occupational Safety and Health (IOSH) to meet the academic requirement for Safety Technician (Tech IOSH) grade. The two other certificates are also accredited at Level 3.

The 'TUC Certificate in Contemporary Trade Unionism' develops understanding of industrial society and the role of trade unions past and present and includes modules on the development of trade unionism in Britain; trade unions today; the future of trade unions; research, communication and problem solving; and project writing. The 'TUC Certificate in Employment Law' develops understanding of current Employment Law and includes modules on employment relations; sex, race and disability discrimination; work-life balance and protecting workers; representation and union recognition; research, communication and problem solving; and project writing.

Tutors

> Our tutors are the cornerstone of our success in trade union education. Famously described as "monuments to professionalism" in a 1998 evaluation, they are professional, committed and deeply knowledgeable about the trade union movement and its developing needs (Brendan Barber, TUC General Secretary, Unionlearn 2006b).

TUC Education invests heavily in tutor development and without question, this is central to quality provision. Selection of tutors for training is rigorous yet inclusive, involving *Discussion Leader* courses which give Regional Education Officers the opportunity to 'talent spot' amongst active representatives whilst giving representatives the chance to test out whether this role is for them. The introduction of 'Discussion Leader Courses' for women and black trade unionists has given the TUC the opportunity to start addressing the gender and diversity inbalance that exists within the tutor team. The national tutor training (a full week's residential course in London) is a scarce resource, and obtaining a place on the course is conditional on successful completion of the 'Discussion Leader Course' and on the Trade Union Studies Units' needs for tutors. Trained tutors work with a TUC Course Co-ordinator within college units where they are mentored and supported through their first years of teaching. There is an annually published tutor development programme, regular regional updates and briefings and an online community for TUC tutors, (www.tuctutors.org), was launched in 2005. This is well used and exclusive to trade union studies tutors. Tutors use the site to develop professional practice, exchange information and materials, keep up with latest news from Unionlearn/TUC Education, check funding information, participate in consultation on programme rewriting and piloting, etc. A valued feature of the tutor team is their identification with the TUC and its programmes, which gives a national flavour to the work. It is common for tutors to move around and to have a career with several colleges whilst remaining with the TUC programme. Tutors are active in their union (University and College Union) and because of the range of union representatives and workplaces a typical tutor will work with each term, they are exceptionally well informed about the world of the contemporary workplace and union representatives' difficulties and problems. This is fed back to the TUC through the Regional Education Officers (who meet monthly in what is a crucial part of the quality cycle) and it helps maintain the contemporary nature of the programme, the case studies and the workplace activities. A review of TUC Education in 2005, carried out by York Consulting, reported that:

> The structures and mechanisms in place for communication are essential to managing the service and supporting staff. The REO and Tutor Group meetings are essential for the flow of important information to and from the national to the regional components of the service. It also provides the main support mechanisms for staff. The national identity of the service is essential to maintaining the kudos and ethos of trade union education in regional Centres. These two communication mechanisms are pre-eminent in maintaining this focus (York Consulting, 2005, iii).

Tutoring opportunities are rich and varied. As well as teaching on a range of Unionlearn/TUC Education courses and union programmes, tutors have the opportunity to work internationally, either through the ETUI-REHS (the research, education and health and safety institute of the ETUC) or through partner confederations across the world. Some projects which tutors have recently been involved with include work helping establish the new Greek Labour Academy, teaching on courses across the world for the United Nations Staff Association, teaching for the ETUI-REHS and working with PODKREPA, the trades union confederation in Bulgaria.

Online Courses

The first online courses were developed and run on a dedicated learning platform, (www.tuclearnonline.org.uk) developed and maintained by the TUC National Education Centre in Crouch End. This experiment was launched in 1999 with the support of the Health and Safety Executive, who funded some development work on the health and safety programme. During the pilot phase, more than 2,000 representatives undertook some trade union education online and tutors across the country took the innovative 'Learning to Teach Online' (LeTTOL) course offered by The Sheffield College. This course remains the foundation course for online tutor development.

Many lessons were learnt from the pilot phase. Tutors supporting online learning need a wider base of teaching skills than those they use in the classroom. The LeTTOL course, which focuses on pedagogical knowledge built up through personal and collective reflection on practice rather than technical skills, gives the confidence and capacity to get tutors going. Online learning takes more tutor time rather than less. Any thought that this could be a cheap and easy way to roll out classroom-based courses has been long banished. Learners online need human support, mentoring, good facilities for collective work and chat and more individualised support from tutors. Because of this, tutors work with smaller cohorts of learners than the usual 14 to 17 in the classroom. The challenges of working in asynchronous mode are considerable; representatives will log on when it suits them and will expect a reply at once. For a tutor who is used to having all students together in the classroom, this takes an adjustment in thinking and in methodology. Course materials need to be fit for purpose; no-one knows trade union education better than practising tutors, and so rather than buy in a customised package from a major commercial company, TUC Education opted to write online materials in the way they write classroom-based materials, using a small development team consisting of tutors and staff. This involved some hard lessons in what will work on a computer screen, but what was developed was eventually fit for purpose, pedagogically sound and written specifically for representatives in a familiar and accessible way. Finally, the lessons of the pilot led TUC Education to re-evaluate the use of their learning platform which simply was not robust enough to meet the needs and which was riven with technical problems and breakdowns which frustrated tutor and learners alike.

Early evidence is encouraging; a third of all applicants for online courses during the pilot phase worked for small and medium-sized enterprises (SMEs), and a quarter were shiftworkers, both notoriously hard groups of workers to attract to the classroom. A less encouraging piece of evidence is that online applicants are overwhelmingly male, much more so than for classroom-based courses where women representatives make up 32% of all course participants (averaged across all courses).

In 2003, a new 'Online Learning Strategy' was developed by a small team at the TUC (TUC, 2006), and the development process was run as a two year project. This work has transformed the possibilities for trade union learners, both those who have been unable to access classroom based learning and for those who have limited time-off for training. The vision underpinning the strategy is that online courses and learning services provided by TUC Education will be of exemplary quality, highly valued both by learners and unions and focused, like face to face course provision, on maintaining and developing trade union organisation. A deliberate decision to develop a wholly online, rather than blended, approach, was taken at the outset, so as to avoid the assumption that online learning is 'second best', simply for those unable to access classroom provision, and to move to a blended offer as a second step. A phased course development process was established and TUC Education appointed an Online Learning Officer to drive the process. TUC Education has begun the process of transferring its online course materials to a reliable and user-friendly learning environment, 'Moodle'. Courses are now accessible from a dedicated server and website, www.tuclearning.net.

During the past year, TUC Education has made considerable progress in the development of its online programme. An updated and revised version of the Online Learning Strategy was produced to help inform and shape the direction that TUC Education's online offer will take (TUC 2006). Demand for online courses is strong. New courses have been made available and delivered successfully. In the past year (2006), more than 800 representatives completed an online course with TUC Education. It is expected that online course provision will grow rapidly in the coming years with a wide range of new programmes being offered, including 'Why Organise?' and 'Introduction to Pensions Online' and there is real optimism about the prospects for reaching trades unionists and potential trades unionists in the new and emerging economy.

Research is underway to look at the experience of online learners, and a report will be published in January 2008. This will be the first detailed investigation into the experience of trade union online learners, and the report will give the basis for the next phase of development. Research aims are:

- To carry out a detailed evaluation of trade union learners who take advantage of the online option (age, gender, race, sector, etc) throughout the UK: England, Scotland, Northern Ireland and Wales;
- To carry out a qualitative analysis of their experience including highlighting case studies as a response to key questions for on-line learning providers (for example, how best can learners engage in online collaborative working, providing suitable and sufficient tutor support, developing and using supportive course materials, etc);
- To profile a 'typical' trade union learner in terms of their on-line key skills;
- To consider popular knowledge and preconceptions of online learning against the actual reality of learning online;
- To undertake a detailed survey of the tutor's experience of online delivery with a view to developing best practice models for tutors;
- To investigate attitudes and evaluate possible opportunities towards mixed modes of learning including blended learning;
- To evaluate the application process and produce best practice options for TUC Education
- To quantify retention and achievement rates with trade union learners and highlight best practice models; and
- To consider drop-out issues with a view to developing retention frameworks for learners.

So far, this surge in interest has not been at the expense of traditional classroom-based learning and paid release. But this is a concern for unions and Unionlearn/TUC Education, as pressure on paid release continues to grow, and refreshing and extending rights to release, particularly to enable those who choose to learn online to access rights, is a priority.

Accreditation

The impetus to accredit the TUC programme came initially from a government inspector, Bill Owen, who addressed the TUC General Council in 1992. Alan Grant, then Head of the TUC's Trade Union Education Department recalls:

What Bill Owen had to say made a considerable impression on the General Council. He made clear his view that TUC courses were of high quality compared with learning and training provision generally. In the present climate, where adult learning has become increasingly important, the courses are a significant contribution by the TUC to the national learning and training agenda. The training programmes devised by the TUC are tailored to representatives' role in the real world and formal accreditation would reflect this. Moreover, we would be effectively 'shortchanging' our union representatives if we denied them the recognition they deserved and earned through their learning achievements, and which other learners received through less demanding vocational courses (quote to the author 2006).

Other ongoing and linked developments at that time included the first functional analysis of the role of trade union officials, through a standards development project under the auspices of the Employment National Training Organisation (now ENTO), with the intention of developing and offering a National Vocational Qualification (NVQ) for officers. More critically for trade union education, the TUC's capacity to deliver programmes through the Further Education sector was threatened by the government's intention to phase out eligibility for public funding support for unaccredited programmes. These developments combined to initiate a debate about the future of the provision and the direction it should take.

Unions were determined that the capacity to access public funding support for trade union education, one of the few vestiges of social partnership left after so many years of Conservative government, should not be undermined. There were, however, a number of political and pedagogical issues to consider. One important political point was the importance of avoiding the opportunity for a hostile government to legislate or regulate around 'qualified representatives' as opposed to democratically elected representatives. After years of anti-union legislation, union democracy remained vital, and opening up the opportunity for employers to refuse to work with an 'unqualified' representative by the TUC initiating its own qualifications would have been foolish. Another concern was that accreditation would 'individualise' the work undertaken in the classroom and undermine the collective approach necessary to build the work of the union. Tutors were concerned at the increased workload, the possibility of this new responsibility interfering with relationships in the classroom and the dangers of representatives taking their eyes off the ball and becoming more interested in personal than in union development. Others felt that representatives would reject the option to achieve formal recognition; the existing TUC Certificate of Attendance was valued and had a currency of its own.

All these points were debated across the TUC, in General Council meetings as well as national Union Education Officer (UEO) meetings whilst options for accrediting the programme were being considered. Ten years on, these fears have not been realised. Working with the National Open College Network (NOCN), an awarding body whose aims and methods are sympathetic to those of trade union education, the offer to representatives has been transformed, and representatives have voted with their feet. More than 85 per cent (in some parts of the country 94 per cent) of representatives opt for credits, despite the assurance from unions and TUC Education that they are under no compulsion to do so. NOCN has enabled an approach to accreditation which suits the ways representatives learn and the fact that one size will never fit all. Representatives are from all parts of the economy and at all stages of learning and development. *Learning that Works,* an influential piece of research into accrediting the programme, carried out by Capizzi (1999), noted that 21 per cent of course participants had no qualifications whatsoever while 7 per cent had Level 4 qualifications or above. She noted that:

> for the fifth of participants with no qualifications, the achievement of NOCN credits on these courses will be their first nationally recognised certificate in education or training; for the majority of representatives, this is a return to formal learning. On any course, however, the mixture of occupations and educational experience is marked – which adds another dimension to the on-course experience and the significance that accreditation will have for participants (Capizzi 1999, 13).

A key priority at the outset was to avoid any distortion of the purposes of trade union education courses, and Capizzi (1999) also noted that representatives consistently stated that accreditation did not constitute a reason for doing the course. One representative said:

> It's an added bonus – not a reason; the reason for doing it is to become a better rep (Capizzi 1999, 22).

This remains a priority today, and ten years on and with over a million trade union credits awarded, the courses remain dedicated to collective approaches to building workplace organisation.

Training for Union Professionals

Since 1984, the TUC maintained a dedicated National Education Centre (NEC) at Crouch End, north London, where much of the training of full-time officials took place during the nineteen eighties and nineties. At one time a creative powerhouse for trade union education, the NEC concentrated latterly on officer training, but it became difficult to attract enough officers to week long residential courses during the late nineties onward, and in 2004, the General Council decided that the NEC should be closed. Officer training was to be developed as a function of TUC Education and delivered as far as possible at regional level. TUC Education was charged by the General Council with opening up pathways for union officers into a range of learning opportunities as well as giving officers the tools to do their job.

It became apparent that the first task in the development of the new programme should be to establish the nature of the target group, given the changes in the trade union movement since the functional analyses of the nineties. The difficulties with take-up had meant that the NVQ at Level 4, which had been developed from that process, had not taken off, and whilst it could be inferred that there must be an outstanding training need given the demanding and difficult job officers undertake on behalf of their unions, there was uncertainty about both the curriculum and the modes of delivery which would suit officers. A needs analysis was undertaken by the Open Learning Partnership on behalf of the TUC (TUC 2005) and discussion took place with almost five hundred officers about their job roles and their experience of and preference for support through training. The results proved very interesting. There is now probably a greater variety in the roles of union professional officers and staff than at any previous time. There are also new entry routes to traditional union officer posts, including academy trainees, project workers, organisers and administrative staff. Many unions now recognise the value of a team-working or whole union approach to union core activities and campaigns.

A strong case was made for the TUC officer training programme to be extended to cover these wider groups. Target groups for particular courses within the programme would then be defined by union function rather than formal status. To give an example, courses on casework and advocacy would be designed to meet the needs of new or prospective officers, dedicated casework officers, and union staff extending their duties to include casework support. In response to these findings, TUC Education launched the 'Union Professional Development Programme' and during its first year (2005) 352 'union professionals' attended training programmes. An annual 'Women Officers' Summer School' was established and additional online support will be launched in 2007 through an interactive website enabling 'union professionals' to access a range of continuing professional development opportunities, online training programmes and to share support, information and best practice. A further research snapshot of the work of union professionals is being undertaken to continue to inform developments, and this will be published in September 2007.

Unionlearn

Unions have always been involved in campaigning and bargaining for education and training. It began with the colleges established for the education of working people, which were set up in the late nineteenth century, closely followed by the founding of the Workers' Educational Association. (For a more full historical account, see Chapter 2 of this volume.) The opening of the TUC Training College after the second world war gave a big boost to the training of trade union representatives. This increased with the huge growth in demand for union representative training as a result of employment and health and safety legislation in the 1970s.

Even in the politically cold climate of the early 1990s, TUC regions formed partnerships with Training and Enterprise Councils. These Bargaining for Skills projects promoted union involvement in training at the workplace. The evidence was clear that unions had a unique role in encouraging members to seek training and in supporting them in finding their way to the right courses. Learning was becoming firmly linked to the organising agenda for unions, and thus core business, part of recruiting and retaining members.

The Bargaining for Skills projects developed into TUC Learning Services under the 'new' Labour Government, extending such activity into areas such as Skills for Life, Information, Advice and Guidance and the training of union learning representatives (ULRs). An important landmark was the setting up of the Union Learning Fund in 1998, which has supported union-led projects on learning with more than £81.5m to date. The explicit purpose of the ULF is to use union expertise and workplace contacts to help create a learning society, to promote employability and social inclusion for workers and to support productivity and competitiveness in the global economy. Many of the union-led projects involved recruiting ULRs and establishing workplace learning centres. This activity was greatly enhanced through the statutory recognition of ULRs in 2003 and the establishment of the Trade Union Hub, which supports learndirect centres. Since 1998, nine rounds of funding have been announced; nearly 500 projects have been developed; more than 15,000 ULRs have been trained and over 100,000 workers have been encouraged into learning.

Unions understood that learning strategies are not just about increasing opportunities for individual members; they are about renewing union activism and strengthening the union voice, which in turn sustains and develops further learning activities. Brendan Barber, the TUC General Secretary, recognised the potential of this idea and responded, as part of Labour's 'Big Conversation' in November 2003, with a proposal which led to the setting up of Unionlearn.

Unionlearn was launched in May 2006 and aims to provide a strategic framework for unions to develop learning opportunities for their members and to assist unions in punching above their weight in the world of learning and skills. Importantly, it brings together TUC Education and TUC Learning Services into one structure that is run by unions. Full details about Unionlearn, its aims, structure and financial plan, are available at www.unionlearn.org.uk, in particular in Unionlearn's Strategic Plan for 2006 to 2009. Therefore, it is not the intention to duplicate all of this information here, merely to draw attention to the key features.

The main functions of Unionlearn are threefold. Firstly, to help unions to become effective learning organisations, by running programmes for union representatives; delivering programmes for regional officers; providing strategic support for national officers; promoting integrated learning and organizing strategies; supporting Union Learning Fund and regional projects; and offering a consultancy service on funding, management, standards, etc. Secondly, Unionlearn is to help unions to broker learning opportunities for their members, through providing support for unions and their union learning reps; supporting learning centres (including learndirect provision); promoting learning agreements and committees at the workplace; establishing websites to advise learners and their union representatives; providing a support service to secure quality provision; and by 'quality marking' provision. Thirdly, Unionlearn is to help unions have an impact on learning and skills policy. It seeks to do this by researching union priorities in learning and skills; identifying and disseminating good practice; helping evaluate unionlearn projects; supporting union members on learning and skills bodies; helping to shape and deliver sector skills agreements.

Though Unionlearn remains a department of the TUC, it has its own Board made up of General Council members and chaired by Billy Hayes, General Secretary of the Communication Workers' Union (CWU); and its income and expenditure goes through a distinct Unionlearn fund and appears separately in the TUC's accounts. With the exception of its initial year 2006–2007 which has a lower amount, income for each of the years 2007–2008 and 2008–2009 is over £22m per annum. Of this, the largest proportion (£14m) is from the Learning and Skills Council mainly in the form of Union Learning Fund monies. £4.9m is from the government Department for Education and Skills (DfES), with the TUC itself making a contribution of just over £1m. In the first year of operation, an additional project funded by EQUAL, a European Social Fund initiative, enabled the TUC to establish Unionlearn as a separate department.

A year on, Unionlearn has some solid achievements to its name. The Unionlearn brand has been successfully launched, with high recognition in the world of learning and skills as well as amongst trade unionists. The perception of unions as key players is growing and external support has been strengthened. The volume and range of trade union education work continues to grow, and participation in major projects such as the piloting of the Qualification Credit Framework (QCF) with the Qualification and Curriculum Authority (QCA) testifies to the regard in which the work is held. The new Unionlearn website attracts a massive 1,200,000 hits each month and new initiatives are launched regularly, as Unionlearn works towards a target of 22,000 ULRs by 2010.

Research findings contribute to the positive atmosphere around Unionlearn. In the Research Paper 'Organising to Learn and Learning to Organise' (Thompson, *et al.* 2007), the conclusions are that:

> On the whole, not only does union-led workplace learning have clear, positive and recognised effects for union and potential union members, learning also has clear, positive and increasingly recognised effects on union organisation. The key point is that trade unions are not lessened by participating in learning but enhanced by it. The findings suggest the argument that union-led workplace learning is narrow because it promotes employability and marginalises trade unions is too simplistic; instead, the case studies indicate that union-led workplace learning can offer renewal to trade unions (Thompson *et al.* 2007, 26).

Further support for this argument comes from Mark Stuart and Andrew Robinson at the Centre for Employment Relations, Innovation and Change at Leeds University, in a report drawn from the most recent WERS survey (2004) (Stuart and Robinson 2007). This report indicates that where ULRs are present, higher levels of negotiation and consultation on training takes place than in unionised establishments without ULRs:

> ULRs are associated with higher levels of training. Where there is a ULR present in a recognised workplace, employees are 8 per cent more likely to report having received 2 to 5 days training. Where there are ULRs, recognition and a representative structure that includes employee representatives, employees are 14.9 per cent more likely to report receiving 10 or more days training (Stuart and Robinson 2007).

In conclusion, Unionlearn is a significant development in the UK trade union movement, bringing together both education and *learning* in one structure. Although undoubtedly facing challenges, Unionlearn is at the heart of the challenge to create a twenty-first century trade union agenda which addresses skills issues in a rapidly changing global economy, grounded in the workplace under the leadership of well trained and supported union representatives.

References

Capizzi, E. (1999), *Learning that Works. Accrediting the TUC Programme.* (London: National Institute of Adult Continuing Education – NIACE).

Fisher, J. (2005), *Bread on the Waters. A History of TGWU Education.* (London: Lawrence and Wishart).

Monks, J. (2001), Taken from the 'Tackling Racism' speech given by John Monks, then General Secretary of the TUC, at Congress House, London, 1st March 2001.

Stuart, M. and Robinson, A. (2007), *Training, Union Recognition and Collective Bargaining. Findings from the 2004 Workplace Employment Relations Survey.* Unionlearn Research Paper 4. (London: Unionlearn).

Thompson, P., Warhurst, C. and Findlay, P. (2007), *Organising to Learn and Learning to Organise.* Unionlearn Research Paper 2. (London: Unionlearn).

TUC (2005), *Union Officer Training Review.* (London: TUC)

——, (2006), TUC Education Online Learning Strategy October 2003. (revised 2006) (London: TUC).

Unionlearn (2006a), *Changing Lives Through Learning. A Guide to Unionlearn.* (London: Unionlearn).

——, (2006b), *Union Representatives Stage 1 – A TUC Training Course for New Tutors.* (London: Unionlearn).

York Consulting (2005), *Review of the TUC Education Service.* (London: TUC).

Chapter 14

Towards a Future Agenda in Union Learning: Developing a Sustainable Distinctiveness

Steve Shelley and Moira Calveley

Introduction

It is clear from the variety of chapters in this book that the field of trade union learning is diverse and rich in its contribution to a number of agendas in the study and practice of education, work and employment relations. This concluding chapter brings together analysis of the various agendas and outcomes of the learning, recognising a likely symbiotic relationship between outcomes for individual learners in a 'learning society' and outcomes for the union movement as a whole. Important discussion has taken place about the ways in which union learning and education is influenced by union organisation and bargaining strategies and, in turn, the ways in which union organisation and bargaining strategies are influenced by union learning and education. This has relevance not only to the union movement and individual learners within it, but also to government and other players, such as educationalists and trainers, with an interest in skill, economic and social policy. This chapter provides both a critique and a review of success of union learning and related union renewal, drawing upon the previous analyses across the union education, training and learning spectrum, and it concludes with pointers for future developments in practice and research for those involved with this agenda.

Consideration here turns firstly to the contribution of union learning to individual, social and economic outcomes, in terms of emancipation, overcoming disadvantage and equalising opportunity, and broader 'life chances'. This analysis is inter-twined with the contribution to the national learning and skills agenda and thus to national economy and society. Further discussion of these contributions is required here, before moving on to consider issues for the trade union movement.

Union Learning

The Leitch Review of Skills (Leitch 2006) provides the latest evidence of skill deficits in the UK. As Lloyd and Payne established in Chapter 4, the causes of this are rooted in the distinctive political economy and wider institutional structures of the UK, with a prevalence of low skilled work outweighing employer demand for high skills. The mainstream policy resolution for skill problems has been focused on increasing the supply of trained and qualified labour, rather than on employers' demand creating a greater proportion of high skilled jobs. From a traditional employment relations perspective, this throws into sharp perspective the different interests of capital and labour, as employers seek to control labour and limit costs through restrictions on the acquisition and use of skill in the labour process, in the context of their broader product and service market strategies. Trade union education has therefore aimed to enable individuals to progress economically by obtaining a greater share of the profits of capitalism; to transform the individual, which may lead to evolutionary, incremental societal change; and to provide a radical education, with an explicit agenda of societal transformation.

Education of workers and training of members as activists and representatives has been ongoing for a century or more of union activity but, as the historical review in Chapter 2 shows, a tension between oppositional conflict and accommodative compromise has often been a visible undercurrent. Union education and training continues, as Rees explains in Chapter 13, and probably contains elements of individual and societal transformation as well as economic progress for individuals through the ability to support members' employment rights and claims. In addition, an examination of the unions' recent heightened role in UK government learning and skills policy, through the Union Learning Fund (ULF), Union Learning Representatives (ULRs) and Unionlearn, and also other tripartite bodies such as the Learning and Skills Council (LSC), indicates both a continuation of the traditional union agendas in education, and a continuation of the accommodative-oppositional tensions, albeit with some new operational activities. As seen in Chapter 3, in many respects the UK leads the way in terms of trade union involvement in a 'learning' agenda that embraces a wide spectrum of liberal humanist, vocational and basic skills training for adult and youth workers, setting an example of union involvement in this field, both the learning and skills at individual and policy levels, and for the potential for these to contribute to union renewal agendas.

Undoubtedly, this recent learning agenda provides opportunities for unions to obtain funding and to gain a legitimacy through accreditation of learning that comes from being part of government-initiated qualification and assessment structures. There is potential for union learning initiatives to play a part in regeneration activities at individual, regional and national levels.

As evangelists for skills at workplace level, unions have had notable successes in widening and developing individuals' access to learning opportunities that enable people to change their lives. In turn, these efforts aim to contribute to the development of a high skills economy in the UK. Various chapters in this volume have illustrated advantageous outcomes for learners, including enhanced access to learning opportunities, concomitant equality advantages, and an emphasis on improving basic skills. Low grade and low or unqualified staff have often been a focus of union learning activity, as McBride and Mustchin, amongst others, illustrate. Arguably, no chapter shows the enormous benefits better than Wray's case studies of union learning initiatives for 'hard to reach' learners, illustrating positive outcomes in terms of practical abilities, confidence and social contact. The affective outcomes of increased confidence and empowerment of learners are very strong recurring themes as illustrated by Shelley's Chapter 7, and those by Forrester and Kirton. At the same time, skill acquisition also extends beyond current roles to include assistance in career progression and for higher qualified workers. Whilst all these efforts undoubtedly continue the traditional agenda of enabling enhanced economic outcomes for members and other individuals, there are also illustrations, in Wray's chapter and in Shelley's chapters particularly, of an extension of motive from an economic to a broader family, community and social agenda, in line with government rhetoric, re-expressed most recently in the Leitch Review, to tackle deprivation and poverty and make other social improvements towards inclusivity and egalitarianism.

Traditionally, trade union education and training has been characterised by a distinctiveness derived from a pedagogy of collective learning and of active learning methods that enable learners to set their own agenda within a broad curriculum. As Forrester identifies, there is potential for union learning to follow a similar pedagogical line. From Shelley's chapter on learning and Kirton's on women-only education, there is some evidence that the distinctiveness of union education is being retained and extended into the learning field, with potential to enable an incremental role of agency in social change. Further, there is potential, as Lloyd and Payne posit, for unions to develop an independent learning agenda at policy and workplace levels, one which will influence skill levels independent of employers' strategies and possibly also influence employer demand for higher skills. The impact at regional levels is shown in Wray's chapter about projects in the north east of England and in Shelley's Chapter 11 where a learning project from the supposedly affluent south-east of England, illustrates potential to unlock funding for causes based, for example, on relative deprivation.

However, evidence of the impact of union learning is currently limited. This is especially so when seeking to establish the impact on employers' skill strategies. Here, the majority of analysis, for example in Shelley's Chapter 7, and in the chapters by Lloyd and Payne and by Forrester, suggests that policy, practice and research in union learning has tended to default to one of an assumed unitarist neo-liberal and human capital paradigm, within a current voluntarist and market-based training and skills environment. In becoming supporters of the government's skills strategy and making a contribution within this framework, unions are currently struggling to avoid dependence upon state funding, qualification, curriculum and quality assurance structures, so threatening their ability to have an independent and critical voice within skills policy. As a result, a number of contributions here (Shelley, McBride and Mustchin, Forrester), have suggested that current union learning has a relatively narrow focus, on increasing supply of qualifications rather than skill demand, and on low level qualifications with little value added. With the Leitch Review recommending public funding only for training that is 'economically valuable' and delivered within government and employer institutional structures of Learning and Skills Council, Sector Skills Councils and through approved, quality-assured government programmes such as Learner Accounts (Leitch 2006), further warning signals should be sounding for those interested in developing a broader and more fundamental impact for union learning.

Although it may sound heretical, challenging the assumption that all learning is necessarily 'good' does have mileage in this analysis of union learning. Holmes (2004) asserts that the current cult of learnerism is oppressive in its conformance to normative behaviours and reproduction of identities and social practices. For Freire and Althusser (Taylor 1993), from a Marxist perspective, the state is part of the capitalist structure in which education is about maintaining the conditions for production, through 'know-how' education and submission to rules. The consumerist and market based context of mainstream learning and skills policy within which union learning is embedded, places an emphasis on consumption of individualised qualification attainment which can be, as Freire (1972) posits, characterised by the need to have rather than to be, and by being materialistic, with qualification-based conformance in a job, salary and promotion structure, the measure of this. Such individualised performativity is replicated by employers in their work organsations; Forrester's chapter suggests that unions are involved now in union learning because of a recognition by some organisations and human resource management practitioners of the commercial benefits of harnessing workers' knowledge.

By contrast, greater independence and power can enable union involvement in a wider range of learning that may be deemed 'useful' in the extent to which it brings about changes to low pay and low skill labour market structures, and enables learners to change their positions in society. However, such union influence is limited by the extent of legislation and by organising capacities. A key issue is, therefore, the extent to which unions perpetuate and conform with the *status quo*, as oppressors themselves complicit in mainstream learning agendas, and the extent to which they enable worker freedom.

In considering their power to effect change in learning and education, in the UK trade unions' influence on delivery through their new institutional position can be seen as relatively limited, falling short of social partnership models that exist in some other European countries. This is partly due to the limited extent of trade union recognition agreements due to the continued absence of this in government legislation, although the demand for a legal right to bargain on training has been central to the policy of the Trades Union Congress (TUC) for many years (TUC 2005). In this respect, as Chapter 3 identified, the UK has much to learn from other countries which have more deeply enshrined corporatist approaches to union involvement in workplace training bargaining.

Statutory bargaining rights or not, there is also a question about whether unions would be strong enough to push employers to make meaningful improvements in training. By illustration, McBride and Mustchin's example of the UK health service is one where unions are working from a position of strength relative to other sectors of employment, where membership is relatively high, where there has been a history of involvement in collective bargaining and where training spend has been a strength. It is suggested that these factors are important in creating sufficient capacity and infrastructure for unions to influence learning provision. Even here, however, unions' roles are limited and compromised. On the one hand, unions have been able to use their traditional bargaining role to extend firstly to involvement in career and pay progression schemes, and thus to a learning agenda that includes both current role and future career development. In addition, arguably such partnership approaches to involvement are not without cost to trade union independence, as McBride and Mustchin illustrate, unions having 'bought in' to the managerial agenda of labour cost control, performance management and labour substitution, provision of narrow vocational skills on the employer's agenda and skills development that is predominantly limited to workers' current roles.

A further illustration of the lack of trade union power is seen in Wray's example of the failed English for Speakers of Other Languages (ESOL) programme, showing all too starkly the dependence on employers' willingness to be involved as a stakeholder in learning projects, and how employer prioritisation of production needs over learning and the constraints of low pay work environments jeopardise the success of projects.

An awareness of these limitations and problems is key if union learning is to deliver a new and distinctive set of outcomes. A major challenge for unions concerns their ability to engage government and employers in measures aimed at raising the demand for, and utilisation of, skill in the workplace. Of great interest here are the examples cited by Lloyd and Payne, from Finland and Australia, together with initiatives such as the NHS's 'skills escalator', discussed more fully by McBride and Mustchin, that combine work design with learning and training issues.

Nevertheless, questions remain about unions' ability to leverage a distinctive learning contribution. Some of the answers could come from drawing on the strengths of traditional practices in union education and training, and extending those more explicitly to the union learning agenda. The equality and diversity agendas are a strong strand through union campaigning generally, and through union education particularly. Kirton's chapter has highlighted the importance of embedding equality issues in union education for increasing union activism. Another strength has been the skilling of workers regardless of employer or culture; union involvement in the English language training for migrant workers is a good example of this. Wray and Stirling both indicate the way in which ESOL provision can enhance the ability of unions to organise internationally.

Curriculum and pedagogy have also been strengths in ensuring distinctiveness of union education. Rather than focus on individual qualification and accreditation, and on individual economic gains, as Rees points out in Chapter 13, 'traditional' trade union 'education' has been made distinctive through delivery by adherence to a collective union-based approach, resulting in a rich experience of discussion that sets topics within the real experiences of workers and within political, social and economic spectrums. Furthermore, Stirling shows how pedagogies between tutor and trainee that are two-way not only enable representatives and activists to deliver union policy consistently, but also enable the kinds of discussions that lead to emergence of new directions for union activity. Developing an understanding of how this aspect of distinctiveness in delivery can be reinforced in the 'learning' as well as the 'education' activities would be necessary. However, strengthening delivery through a pedagogy of student and tutor-led discussion, enabling as Elsey (1986) suggests the incorporation of critical analysis as well as continuing to build self confidence and commitment to action, operating in physical environments that are controlled by union and workers, and emphasising broader educational provision in learning aims, may all be important elements.

There are also questions over the financial sustainability of union 'learning' activities. Various chapters here have illustrated problems associated with funding constraint, uncertainty and short-term or time limited funding patterns. These may be compounded in the future should there be a change of government or key ministers. Figures available from the Unionlearn website reveal the extent of funding dependency on government and quasi-government sources. In contrast to union learning, funding for union education is largely derived internally within the union movement, ultimately through membership subscription and other donations. This may not be the answer for the full range of union learning because, as Stirling's chapter acknowledges, this source is under pressure due to falling membership. Nevertheless, it does provide an alternative consideration in the context of what seems to be an urgent need for the union movement to develop alternative funding streams that may, in some way, be called 'their own', to gain if not independence then at least diversification of funding. There is potential for these to come from members and from charitable trusts and other sources. Further, as Wray illustrates, there is a need to find creative ways to circumvent employer vetos to learning projects and to create alternative stakeholder 'organisations' so as to access funding.

So, a key agenda for unions will be to diversify funding sources away from limited qualification-based public funding and from employer-subsidised learning centres and to develop community-based work with other local learning forum, community agencies and voluntary organisations. In this respect, the chapters by Wray and by Shelley (Chapter 11) illustrate the ability of unions to shape learning projects outside of the workplace and the potential to gain alternative funding from such ventures.

Thus, a recurring theme here is a questioning of the extent to which unions are able to further develop a significant, independent, distinctive and sustainable set of learning and education practices. What has been presented so far, suggests that part of the way forward is to build on practices from the more traditional and long-lived education and training sector of union activity. However, such solutions are largely focused on learning delivery and on the supply side of the skills equation. If unions are to make a different and significant contribution, this should also be judged on the extent to which employers' working practices and business strategies are amended and the extent to which government policy can be influenced in this respect. The ability of unions to influence the learning agenda in these more fundamental ways will be dependent on their power, relative to employers and government. It is here that the synergy between union learning and union organising must be apparent. Arguably, if unions are to gain strength in order to influence the uses of learning and learning policy, development of membership and organisation is key.

It is apparent here that the whole issue of the nature of union learning provision and its subjects, pedagogies and utilisation, needs further research and assessment in terms of its appeal to memberships. Evidence so far does show some growth in the number of activists. The question is whether the potential for greater appeal may also be found in learning and education that has more direct impact on collective bargaining outcomes of a more traditional distributive nature, notably those concerning pay, terms and conditions. Kelly's (1998) mobilisation theory suggests that such immediate and more tangible actions may have a strong appeal to memberships. Therefore, union learning that is independent, distinctive and sustainable and which is seen to have a significant and direct impact on working conditions may be more attractive to new members and activists. The argument is rather circular, but nevertheless important. Learning that is independent and that makes an impact for memberships should be provided. This will improve unions' organisation and power. In turn unions can exert greater leverage on bargaining over learning provision, skill levels and on working conditions at workplace and national levels. In this context, it is likely that current union organisation and bargaining strategies across the range of activities will set the context for union learning activities and influence the appeal of learning. It is, therefore, to the issue of union organisation that this conclusion now turns.

Union Organisation

The current approach of the union movement towards learning must be understood in the context of the role and strategies of trade unions in contemporary employment relations. Despite the more conciliatory approach of the Labour government since 1997, trade union influence in the UK remains limited by its relatively weak institutional place, within the current neo-liberalist government approach.

From the international perspective, Calveley has shown in Chapter 3 commonalities in the contexts for trade unionism of declining membership, and some weakening of trade union power within employment relations structures, even where union roles are enshrined in over-arching tripartite structures. Nevertheless, trade union strength differs from country to country, and is still relatively strong where institutional structures have historically involved trade unions in decision-making. On the training issue specifically, the incorporation of training in workplace or sector bargaining in some countries provides an important organising vehicle for unions, albeit the reality of unions' abilities to organise varies considerably according to such factors as sector of employment and size of firm.

Within this context, much debate continues about the approaches unions should take towards organising through the learning agenda. Approaches include servicing their members by providing a training and qualification service to members who are consumers; organising by providing education and training for activists and re-emphasising the importance of activism and organising of a more oppositional or militant nature in order to win concessions from employers; and more passive, reactive and accommodating' strategies, within which partnership approaches typify contemporary policy. The latter are exemplified at policy level by inclusion in public funding schemes (the Union Learning Fund) and by involvement in institutions such as the Learning and Skills Council. Indeed, it would seem that there are potential gains from what may be called 'buy in' to the mainstream learning and skills delivery, including awareness of union existence, contribution and leverage (of funds, facilities), economic and social gains; which in turn may recruit more members and activists.

Such stances for unions to take more benign or servicing approaches can, it is argued, expand the union role into what may be seen as the less adversarial learning agenda, one that enables possibility of unions cooperating with management around learning, and one which is less threatening and confrontational and that will therefore appeal to new members and activists other than traditional shop stewards (Healey and Engel 2003). Evidence on this score is mixed and not conclusive. A survey by the Working Lives Research Institute found that 78 per cent of ULRs had previously been active in the union movement and that few ULRs were new union members (Moore and Wood 2005). However, it also found that women, younger activists and those from black ethnic minorities were more likely to be amongst the small proportion of ULRs who were new activists. It also supported earlier research (TUC 2004), suggesting that the learning agenda has a positive increase on union membership generally. But despite these figures, in their chapter in this book, Stuart and Wallis find no real indication that, in generating new membership enthusiasm, this had impacted significantly on the strengthening of branch organisation. At best, this may be a very long-term endeavour for trade unions.

An explanation for this, rehearsed in Stuart and Wallis's chapter, is the role of workplace learning bargaining arrangements as a single issue, often dealt with informally through an 'integrative' mutual interest employment relations structure, as an issue of 'partnership', and separate from the more traditional distributive bargaining structures for pay, terms and conditions. Whilst, arguably, this may aid the recruit of new activists who prefer to avoid confrontation, as has been noted in numerous contributions here, this is at risk of losing trade union independence and of delivering employers' training for them which could also turn members and activists off. The question is, what appeals to potential members, current members and activists? Further research is required to determine the appeal of union learning stances towards each of these groups of members, and the extent to which a common appeal may apply to all.

In addition, the separateness of the learning agenda has meant that learning issues are taken less seriously by other shop stewards and members in local union branches, and that those working in the learning field may be sidelined and isolated from the wider union activity and support. This may be explained by views from some trade unionists who believe a more traditional conflict approach brings influence and credibility and who may prefer not to see their hard distributive bargaining machinery diluted by softer integrative arrangements on learning. In addition, in going for a predominantly partnership approach on the learning agenda, there is a risk that the very subject of learning itself is marginalised, and a risk that the value of unions' involvement in the activity is negated. By contrast, Kirton's chapter demonstrates the power of union education to strengthen activist roles within trade unions, an important aspect of union organisation and renewal that is derived from a central role in mainstream union activity, preparation for and location in a traditional distributive bargaining purpose.

Thus, a critique would suggest that partnership approaches to learning may jeopardise development of a distinctive approach to trade union learning (Sutherland and Rainbird 2000); and that there is merit in seeking further gains in the learning and organising agendas through more confrontational approaches. It is, therefore, clear that there are key considerations for union policy in terms of the benefits or otherwise of integrating learning into the traditional distributive adversarial machinery.

This is undoubtedly a difficult and complex balancing act because even if learning and distributive bargaining arrangements are ostensibly separate, they will influence each other, as Stuart and Wallis cite in their example of a recent strike on the traditional area of pay which was thought to have strengthened the union's ability to be able to bargain on learning. Further, it is false to think that learning is benign and uncontested. Taylor (1993) asserts that there is no such thing as a neutral education process, and this is indeed recognised in various chapters here, including those of Shelley, Forrester and Rees. The situated contextual nature of learning in collective organisations and communities of practice, in which there is social participation and development of knowledge of the self about and with others, and an understanding of workplace and union learning within wider societal relationships, arguably contributes to a differentiated nature of union learning, albeit as considered earlier, one that may need to open up greater opportunity for learners to develop critical awareness, reflection and action. As Wray has illustrated, key individual union learning activists, with skill, enthusiasm, imagination, inventiveness and drive, can be extremely powerful. Acknowledgment of social realism, worker agency, and activity theory, discussed by Wray and in Shelley's Chapter 7 and by Forrester, together with Kirton's recognition of learning contributing to collective strategies for social change, leads to a more positive assessment of the potential for union learning to enable learner and societal transformation.

Conclusion: Challenges and Opportunities

There is no doubt that the opportunities arising from such involvement are immense and may enable contribution, not only to individuals' development and to union renewal and organisation, but also to economic and social outcomes through the national learning and skills policy arena, including reassessment of the role of workplaces and work organisations in that context. Referring back to the historical context in Chapter 2, there is potential for contemporary union learning to embody the spirit of the union movement and of union learning, education and training over the last hundred years or more, but also make new contributions in the current context.

The overall summary tone of this volume suggests that there is indeed much to welcome, echoing recent reports published by Unionlearn (Moore and Wood 2007; Thompson *et al.* 2007). However, there is also a broad and strong note of caution here, caution about the value that union learning is adding to the national skills scene, and caution about what it contributes to the strength, influence and credibility of the trade union movement. In addition, there are clearly many challenges facing those working as practitioners and researchers in the field. Indeed, much of the analysis here goes to the very heart of what unions are about, particularly in recognising the contradictions inherent in unionism about promoting workers' interests both within but whilst opposing capitalism, a paradox highlighted by Demaine's (1981, 2) statement that:

satisfactory education for the working people is not possible in bourgeois capitalist society. On the other hand, education is considered to be of considerable importance in the transition to socialism.

Thus, this volume highlights advantages, but also questions and issues about the direction and nature of union learning and where it fits with the political and ideological agendas of the union movement. It is argued here that education is at the heart of resolving these issues so that, in moving towards an agenda for future work, it will be necessary for those involved to be active and critical learners themselves, in order to challenge norms and make changes. The voice from such learning will need to be exercised through the democratic processes of the union movement, in order to define the union role of learning and, in particular, its distinctiveness and sustainability.

The necessity to reinforce good practices derived from union education into the way in which union learning is delivered, has been made throughout this volume, in terms of building on the collective nature and social settings of the pedagogies. In turn, it should also be possible to build on the advantages of union learning initiatives that new funding streams have enabled, particularly access to increased numbers of learners.

In addition, as highlighted by Stirling's chapter, a challenge for the trade union movement is to realise the potential for trade union education to be a central means by which members shape union responses and directions. This can be both nationally and through internationalised education forum in order to confront challenges of global capitalism. Stirling has argued that trade union education should be at the critical centre of effective change and should enable debate about directions and unity across the movement. Extending this further, it can be argued that trade union learning itself should be the subject of debate within trade union education programmes. This could act as a means of bringing learning centre stage, rather than union learning operating as a separate structure. Courses that enable representatives and members to understand and debate the advantages, disadvantages and strategies towards union involvement in 'learning' activities would enable development of distinctiveness of content and delivery, and of practical methods for ensuring sustainability of this distinctiveness. The merger, in the UK union movement, of both union education and union learning into the one Unionlearn structure, would seem to provide this opportunity in practice.

Within these structures should be opportunities for debate about what an involvement in learning means for trade unions' power, in terms of asserting workers' rights, enabling independence of unions' agendas and of considering the extent to which accommodative compromise with employers should be acceptable. It will be important to inform these debates by consideration of the extent to which unions' learning activities are integrated with other bargaining and representational activities, or are separate from these. High levels of integration strengthen unions' influence on the range of distributive bargaining and learning activities both at state level and at workplace level. Further discussion is also necessary about the opportunities for new forms of cause and organisation, such as community unionism, and multi-union partnerships, as illustrated by Wray and Shelley, and the potential that new forms of technology have to enable this.

For those researching in the field, all chapters here have suggested a variety of further challenges and potentials. Clearly, there are methodological challenges. Qualitative research is required alongside quantitative. There is also a need for longitudinal rather than snapshot research; the distinct lack of longitudinal work in all fields of union learning research is apparent, although Kirton's chapter provides an example of how this may be done and is important as one of the very few studies of post-course learning. Research approaches such as these are required in order to get behind the façade of more mainstream and somewhat unproblematic reports of topics and frequencies of learning activities and in doing so to better understand the nature of union learning, much of which does have multiple interpretations. This means engaging with learners and other actors involved in the delivery of union learning on the ground, better analysing what learners gain from learning situations, and recognising, as Kirton suggests, learning in context through an awareness of the 'life-worlds' of learners, the limitations and opportunities that enable them to develop from the learning they have participated in. A specific example would be further understanding of what confidence and other outcomes such as positive attitudes, commitments to learn and to take action, mean, are evidenced and are utilised. In addition, it is clear that there is a need to better understand the links between union learning and education, and union bargaining and organising strategies and to union renewal. For example, advantages and opportunities for individual members' learning and for national learning and skills policy, need to be weighed up against outcomes in terms of union independence, membership, activism and organisation.

In conclusion, the combined outcomes of the contributions to this book are calling for ways in which union learning, in all its broad senses, can be better understood and better made more distinctive in its contribution. Such a distinctiveness can be attained from the dynamics involved in pedagogy, the purpose, the learners and the social context of worker-based learning delivery. Union learning can be independent of other learning and training activities in the education and training arena, financially and in terms of determination of curriculum and of learning attainments, and in terms of its link to union renewal, organisation and appealing to union members. It can therefore be sustainable in a way that makes a distinctive contribution out-with short-term political agendas of party politics and employer business strategies. In this way, union learning has potential to make a significant contribution to individuals, trade unions, employment and society, bringing new benefits to individuals and enabling fresh economic and societal advances at national level.

References

Demaine, J. (1981), *Contemporary Theories in the Sociology of Education.* (London: Macmillan).

Elsey, B. (1986), *Social Theory Perspectives on Adult Education.* Nottingham Studies in the Theory and Practice of the Education of Adults. (Nottingham: Department of Adult Education, University of Nottingham).

Freire, P. (1972), *Pedagogy of the Oppressed.* (Harmondsworth: Penguin).

Healey, J. and Engel, N. (2003), *Learning to Organise.* (London, Congress House: TUC).

Holmes, L. (2004), 'Challenging the Learning Turn in Education and Training', *Journal of European Industrial Training* 28: 8/9, 625–638.

Kelly, J. (1998), *Rethinking Industrial Relations: Mobilization, Collectivism and Long Waves*. (London: Routledge).

Leitch (2006), *Prosperity for All in the Global Economy – World Class Skills. The Leitch Review of Skills*. (London: TSO).

Moore, S. and Wood, H. (2005), *The Union Learning Experience: National Surveys of Union Officers and ULRs*. (London: Working Lives Research Institute).

——, (2007), *Union Learning, Union Recruitment and Organising*. Unionlearn Research Paper 1. (London: Unionlearn).

Rainbird, H. (ed.) (2000), *Training in the Workplace*. (Basingstoke: Macmillan).

Sutherland, J. and Rainbird, H. (2000), 'Unions and Workplace Learning: Conflict or Co-operation with the Employer?', in Rainbird, H. (ed.).

Taylor, P. (1993), *The Texts of Paulo Freire*. (Buckingham: Open University Press).

Thompson, P., Warhurst, C. and Findlay, P. (2007), *Organising to Learn and Learning to Organise. Three Case Studies on the Effects of Union-led Workplace Learning*, Unionlearn Research Paper 2. (London:Unionlearn).

TUC (2004), *New Faces*. (London: TUC).

TUC (2005), *Skills White Paper: TUC response to Skills White Paper*. (London: TUC).

Index

For Product Safety Concerns and Information please contact our EU representative GPSR@taylorandfrancis.com Taylor & Francis Verlag GmbH, Kaufingerstraße 24, 80331 München, Germany

For Product Safety Concerns and Information please contact our
EU representative GPSR@taylorandfrancis.com Taylor & Francis
Verlag GmbH, Kaufingerstraße 24, 80331 München, Germany